Efforts at Truth

*Available from Dalkey Archive Press

NICHOLAS MOSLEY

Efforts at Truth

Dalkey Archive Press

First American Edition, 1995

First published by Secker & Warburg, 1994. © 1994 by Nicholas Mosley.

Library of Congress Cataloging-in-Publication Data

Mosley, Nicholas, 1923-
     Efforts at truth / Nicholas Mosley . — 1st U.S. ed.
     Originally published: London : Secker & Warburg, 1994.
     Includes index.
     1. Mosley, Nicholas, 1923-   —Biography. 2. Authors, English—20th cen-
tury—Biography. 3. Biographers—Great Britain—Biography. 4. Editors—Great
Britain—Biography. I. Title.
PR6063.O82Z465   1995   823'.914—dc20   94-37597
ISBN 1-56478-075-9

Partially funded by grants from the National Endowment for the Arts and the
Illinois Arts Council.

NATIONAL
ENDOWMENT
FOR ♥ THE
ARTS

Dalkey Archive Press
Campus Box 4241
Normal, IL 61790-4241

Printed on permanent/durable acid-free paper and bound in the United States of America.

Foreword

There is debate from time to time about which form of writing can tell more of 'truth' – biography/autobiography or fiction. The argument goes – in biography/autobiography no one ever does quite tell the truth; either about themselves, out of embarrassment and shame, or about others, because here too some awkwardnesses inevitably remain hidden. So novelists, with their freedom to say what they like, might seem to have an advantage: but in what sense can it be said that fiction tells the truth? Fiction makes things up – including, to be sure, things shameful and embarrassing: but might not this be an indulgence, rather than an effort at truth? In much modern fiction there is indeed an overwhelming emphasis on human inadequacy and shame: but it is as if like this novelists are over-compensating for what cannot be told directly about their own lives and those of others.

The situation has thus arisen in which there is an almost complete split between the attitudes of biography/autobiography and those of fiction. On the one hand there are the stories of worldly achievement and self-justification (or, if a biography is hostile, of error that is reprehensible); on the other hand there are the stories of human helplessness and despair, in which it is suggestions of responsibility that seem taboo. In neither case is there much effort to bring these attitudes together, to form what might be closer to truth.

It is this split that makes much of modern literature seem superficial. Human experience in fact – as everyone knows who pauses to reflect upon his or her life – consists of an interplay between shame and justification, achievement and helplessness, darkness and light. A vision of liveliness depends on seeing a pattern between and around opposites; not within the vacuum of a split. Without such a vision life cannot be understood and thus can hardly be dealt with: what indeed can flourish except vainglory and despair?

The loss of such understanding is perhaps due to the loss of a sense of a framework within which human dramas are played out. It was in religion that there was once a recognition of a larger world in relation to which human affairs formed patterns; a belief that human shame and degradation, if acknowledged, could still be put to good effect. And indeed it was felt that there could be little valid human achievement unless it was interwoven with a sense of human inadequacy. But religious attitudes have largely disappeared from the Western world – as indeed have concepts of truth worked out in the form of stories.

For much of my working life I have been a novelist: I have also written biographies. My novels have sometimes seemed unfashionable in that they have suggested patterns, however ungraspable, beyond helplessness and despair; my biographies have been criticised for saying things which, however accurate, it was felt should not be said. I wondered if there was a way in which the attitudes of novel-writing and autobiography might be brought together: a way of saying – Look, this is a story about myself; I at least have come to hope that there are patterns beyond self-justification and shame.

I had the idea that by looking back at my past novels I might have a chance of writing autobiography that was not just to do with special pleading. Most of my early novels were, however obliquely, to do with myself; and indeed, they were in part to do with helplessness and shame. But then, in the light of these manifestations, could not my life be looked at? And in so far as my novels were increasingly to do with the recognition of overriding patterns, could not the validity of these be looked at too? There might indeed be some self-justification here! But at least, in the form of a story, readers might judge this for themselves.

There is a modern literary theory that the interpretation a critic gives to an author's work may be more authentic than the author's own: a critic has a chance to see an author's hidden presuppositions. But it seemed to me that in looking back at my novels I might have a chance of seeing my own presuppositions – and at the same time indeed be helped to look at the life they arose from. And by recognising the interplay between the novels and the life, each might be illumined.

There is a sense in which novels are smokescreens put up to try to deal with the near-desperate pains of reality: there is a sense in which they are not-quite-so-desperate efforts to break through the smokescreens that seem to be put up by reality itself. In either case a novel seems 'true' if a to-and-fro has occurred between looking at experience and looking at the means of expressing this: also if some learning seems to have resulted from the efforts between and within each.

I have called this volume *Efforts at Truth* because, it seems to me, truth is a matter not of certainty but of endeavour – to see the partnership between learning and life, between experience and what is made of life, to see that one never gets to the end of unveiling smokescreens and presuppositions but it is in this attempt that there is a validity in being human. And literature is not only a to-and-fro between experience and expression, it is a to-and-fro between writers and readers who either will or will not have their own recognitions. In the matter of truth and smokescreens we are all in a fog; messages come to us like hooting over waves. In the end we are either on the rocks or we are not – the result of both nothing and everything to do with our own efforts.

PART I

I

In the two books of biography/autobiography that I wrote about my father, Oswald Mosley, and my early life in relation to my father – *Rules of the Game* and *Beyond the Pale* – the story ended in 1947 when my father went back into politics and I, aged twenty-four, married and set off for a new life. Up to this time I had been a member of my family, of schools, of the war-time army; I had been at a university briefly and then had needed to get away. At Oxford I had met my future wife Rosemary, who was just eighteen: she too had wanted to get away. (I have told something of Rosemary's family background in my biography *Julian Grenfell*.)

Regarding my own family – my father had been leader of the British Union of Fascists in the 1930s and had been imprisoned as a security risk during the war. After his release, and my return from the fighting in Italy, I had been close to him for two years. Both Rosemary and myself had felt ourselves under the shadows of powerful families. But now we were free.

I wanted to be a writer: she, a painter. We married: then caught a plane to the West Indies. There for a time at least we would have the chance and the space to do as we liked. We did not have to worry too much about money. I had an income from a trust made by the family of my mother, who had died when I was nine.

For a honeymoon we stayed in Jamaica. Then we plane-hopped down the Caribbean and found a tiny island called Pigeon Island just off the coast of St Lucia. Here there was an English lady called

Mrs Snowball who lived in a house made of bamboo; she was the only resident on the island because local people thought the place was haunted and would not stay there at night. Mrs Snowball used to say that she did in fact hold conversations with the ghost of Admiral Romney who in the eighteenth century had built a fort on top of the hill. She let Rosemary and me stay in a bamboo hut down by the beach. From here Rosemary went out to paint each day and I embarked on my first novel. I had bought a typewriter in Jamaica and it seemed proper that I should teach myself to type at the same time as learning how to write a novel. Two tiny frogs came to watch me each day from the rim of my washbasin. Rosemary went up to the ruined fort on top of the hill beneath which, on the ocean side, the dark sea heaved and blew like a whale.

In the evenings the fishermen would sometimes linger and there would be drumming and dancing on Mrs Snowball's verandah. Then in the mornings there would be the white coral sand and multi-coloured fishes beneath our window in the lagoon. Rosemary was like a mermaid with her long fair hair as if spun from water and light. It was as if we were in some Garden of Eden.

So what was it that I was writing?

Sometimes at night we would listen to Mrs Snowball's cracked radio and would hear news of the renewal of enmity between America and Russia; of the threat of a new world war. And now there was the Bomb!

I knew of the madness of the outside world: had I not been in the war?

My first novel was called *Spaces of the Dark*. This is its story:

A young man, Paul, comes home from the war. He appears to carry with him some great guilt. He goes to visit the family of his greatest friend who had been with him in the war and had been killed. At the home of this friend Paul meets for the first time his friend's sister. They fall in love. But there is a barrier between them to do with Paul's guilt.

There is another woman whom Paul feels he must go and see, who is someone with whom his great friend, John, had fallen in love just before he had gone off to war. Paul now seems to fall in love with this woman, Sarah, too – or is it just that he is obsessed with anyone to do with his friend? To Sarah at least he tells his secret – which was that it was he himself who had killed his friend John: and this was not by one of the accidents that sometimes happen in war, it was as it were deliberately because John had lost his nerve and was planning to give orders to retreat in a situation in which to do this would not only have been disobeying orders but would have been endangering the lives of men for whom they were responsible. (Both Paul and John were junior officers.) And so Paul, as the only means of stopping John, had shot him. The particular situation was thus in a sense saved; and as far as anyone else knew it could have been one of the enemy who had shot John. But Paul is left with his great and secret guilt: and how can he now tell this secret to, or indeed honourably love, this sister whose brother he has killed and who now loves him?

But he tells Sarah, and she tries to give him some sort of comfort or absolution: she even protects him with some violence against a friend who might betray his secret. But if Sarah and Paul are to love – would this not be at the cost of the sacrifice of not only the brother, but now of the sister too who loves Paul?

Paul feels himself in a situation (I had placed him in this situation) in which there seems to be no way out except by his own sacrifice – even his own death. How can one live in a world in which it seems to have been both correct and yet unendurable to have killed one's great friend? And then to love and not to be able to love both this friend's sister and his loved-one. At the end of the story Paul and the sister are out riding in a fog; they come to a road and the sister's horse shies; she falls with the horse on top of her and she breaks her leg. Paul, to prevent the traffic running over her, goes up the road and holds his arms out in the fog and a lorry runs over him and kills him. The sister survives – together with the impression that both her brother and Paul have been heroes. Sarah is left alone with the secret.

This is what I wrote in my Garden of Eden in the West Indies with my beautiful wife; watching the hummingbirds hovering in front of flowers, the dark sea spouting, the rumours of the renewal of wars.

It is just conceivable that an incident such as this shooting of one's best friend might happen in the turmoil of war, though it is unlikely that this would be the outcome of a conscious moral decision. But nothing remotely like this had happened to me in the war, though I had in fact been in a battle like the one into which I had put John and Paul in my book. In the real-life situation my great friend of the time had been very brave; and in fact the officers concerned in the incident had been decorated. So what was I doing writing such a story of despair?

I did not ask myself this at the time. It seemed a necessary and accepted presupposition that all true novels of war should be ones of despair.

This was a smokescreen? an effort to break through?

But through to what?

Most front-line soldiers in war feel little personal hostility to front-line soldiers on the other side; hostility is directed towards politicians and soldiers at the base. So perhaps the killing of a front-line enemy might be like the killing of a friend. And so there is guilt; but also the impression that such action has been necessary. And so in just this confusion there is likely to be despair.

I myself, as an infantry platoon commander in Italy, had not been aware directly of killing an enemy: but I had shot at people, had wounded people; certainly one or two might have died. Amongst my own men for whom I was responsible I had not, again, been aware of any actual deaths: but so many wounded! so many carried away on stretchers! Could there be anything, even in the business of what might be heroics, beyond despair?

In my own case there had also been the particular predicament that I had been in two minds anyway about the justification for this war. My father had been imprisoned for advocating that Britain should stay out of the Second World War: he had said – Let Germany and Russia fight each other and let the British Empire remain intact. (This was what Hitler indeed sometimes seemed to advocate.) In theory I had been half in agreement with my father: in practice – what? I had joined the army partly because this was what society had required of me; but also I had had a gut-level feeling about the propriety of this war. Certainly, however, there was confusion here! The requirement to kill an enemy, so like a friend, might even in such circumstances be like a requirement to kill a part of oneself.

I had had another great friend (not the one who was with me in battle) with whom I had travelled in a troopship out to Africa and then to Italy: this friend and I had been very cynical about people who went blithely off to war: our attitudes had been like those of the early stages of the relationship between Paul and John that I had described in my book. Paul and John had talked of 'going through the motions of war'; of 'watching it with our hands in our pockets as we did the last year at school'. My friend and I thought we might remain somewhat aloof from, if not quite turn away from, what Paul called 'this weary blunder of a world gone mad': we might make jokes about war in the intervals from it: like this we might stay sane. We imagined we knew all about the projections and masochism of soldiers – the need for ordeal, for a cause to be ready to die for, to make up for the insufficiencies of ordinary lives. And then in fact my friend was comparatively harmlessly injured when his sergeant trod on one of their own mines (and from hospital wrote me a poem which contained the memorable lines, 'What else more fitting can the masochist give/Than have his buttocks punctured like a sieve?'). And I harboured the idea that the best thing to happen to me might be to get myself taken prisoner; and then in prison camp I might get on with the sane business of planning my first novel.

Then in the event this came close to being precisely my experience of war! On a frozen mountain-top in central Italy, in the winter of 1943–4, I myself, and the men I had only a day or two before been put in charge of, were in fact taken prisoner in an unexpected German raid (I have described this incident in *Beyond the Pale*). But I knew overwhelmingly that I had immediately to try to get away: what were my cynical schoolboy ideas in the face of such a gut-level feeling of rage? And I did manage to get away – with the help of the man coming after me to shoot me himself being shot by my battle-companion friend – an amazing shot, some two hundred yards – but I had at least made the move to get away. So perhaps what I was trying to say in *Spaces of the Dark* was – To stay sane in war you have to learn to pay it the most desperate respects; but there is still the matter of luck; and it may still be that part of you has to die. And this may involve some sort of despair.

Here is how my hero Paul in *Spaces of the Dark* described how his attitude to war had had to change:

> War is too big a thing to think about from the outside when you are in it – you have got to accept it on its own terms, like the world, and not attempt to value it by some personal idea. To us it was a killing dying silliness but then the world was silly too, and we were part of it, the silly world, the dying people of Europe killing themselves and us killing them too – and we accepted it, the whole of it, and what thereby it entailed – you've got to fight so you might as well fight prettily, you've got to die so you might as well die prettily, you've only got yourselves to think about because the big thing beyond you is entirely unthinkable so you might as well think yourselves pretty – that was all it was – and pride of course too; pride of the right kind, pride in pity, pride in pretty things.

Sitting above my beach of white coral sand I struggled to come to terms with such memories and ideas: what on earth was this life in which one is required to love and to be ready to kill; in which it might be parts of oneself, as well as friends or enemies, that had to die? Stretched between the demands of duty, of conscience, and of self-preservation, are not humans on some rack? Is it surprising that they sing sad songs in their predicament?

Perhaps all heartfelt 'fiction' is an effort to deal with contradictions that otherwise seem unmanageable – the demands of societies at loggerheads with each other and within themselves, the struggles with and against such demands by individuals who are yet dependent on society. Traditionally fiction has dealt with these matters through tragedy or farce: there is resolution through the destruction of an individual, or in the laughter occasioned by his floundering to stay alive. *Spaces of the Dark* has moments of banal and lugubrious farce – the writing lapsing occasionally into the humour of an English public school. But perhaps inevitably my first novel tended mainly to an operatic style of tragedy – this was what had been considered 'literary' by my English public school. This is what I had been provided with by a classical education – stories of the sacrifice of heroes, the killing of enemies and friends. And was it not indeed by such a style of rhetoric that I had seen my father lifting audiences to their feet – 'We shall win, or we shall return upon our shields!'? What chance had I of standing out from such love-and-death romanticising; of escaping from the literary style under the aura of which young men had traditionally gone off to war.

One of my most passionately loved novels at this time was Henry Williamson's *The Pathway* in which the hero is a rebellious young man who returns home from the First World War; by the end he, like my hero, has managed somewhat arbitrarily to get himself killed. It seemed that even those so contemptuous of society were unable to hold out against the sacrifices and guilts that were demanded by society: but how inevitable was this despair? There is no doubt in *Spaces of the Dark* of Paul's scorn of conventional society:

> . . . a world like a gamble in a second-rate casino with the hard, formal face of the man who fears the risk, the high, bright laugh of the woman who loses, the death-mask of the croupier the only man who wins . . . And that is all they are, he thought, blank shapes in a smoke-filled room – these charming chattering social people, living on nerves, dying on charity, bankrupt before they were born.

But the difficulty of course – as my hero Paul never really knew, as I myself did not yet know – is not to see what is wrong with society, but to learn what might be wrong with oneself.

For Rosemary and I in our island Garden, listening occasionally to rumours of new wars and the threat of the Bomb, of course it was easy to see what was wrong with society; what means had we of seeing what was wrong with ourselves?

There is a nihilism at the centre of *Spaces of the Dark* that is epitomised by the operatic story: there are attempts to counteract this by the passion of a voice shouting against a storm. Paul and Sarah imagine a life together (the figure of Sarah was taken from Rosemary); but they see life at best as a matter of moments of illumination, the world does not seem to them to be a place where or upon which they can build. To them the world is 'inevitably a place of killing one's friends, of worshipping a god that sanctifies such murder, of defiling and destroying the beauty that might be loved'. Paul sees that sanity might lie in 'the avoidance of all loyalties, the denial of ideals, the rejection of all dogma, the development and initiation of the individual soul in defiance of the communal madness'. But in attempting this he sees that he has also 'almost rejected life itself'. He has a shot at carrying the nihilism; but after a time this fails.

Rosemary and I had intended, hoped, to have no secrets, no guilt, in our life together; we were to have a shot at being always able to look at truth – for which task we thought we could be sufficient to ourselves. And we had found some Garden. But how in a Garden does one learn?

Perhaps we both had some inkling that we had to be rescued from the enchantments and mists and limitations of more than the social aspects of our backgrounds.

Here is a letter that Rosemary had written to me from her mother's house shortly before we married:

> Just before dark there was a tremendous storm and the sea and wind were very high. I crawled out in the dark along the bottom of a breakwater and climbed up on to a catwalk that runs right out into the sea with a hurricane lamp at the end to keep things off the rocks. The sea was beautiful, merciless and infinite, till one thought one was part of it having known its creation. In the lulls I felt like Dido standing on the wild sea bank, wafting her love to come again to Carthage.
>
> But tonight everything is still, and mad in a different way – knowing no impulse, but with a steady evil inborn madness which must be more dangerous.
>
> Now I'm calm, and the early part of this letter sounds like the *Boy's Own Paper*. But still I shall send it. I probably am the *Boy's Own Paper*. All the dogs have been sick today.
>
> This stillness is awful. I can just hear an owl sounding very very far away like something in a dream.
>
> My love, darling, do come again to Carthage.

2

In the summer of 1948 Rosemary and I returned from the West
Indies. We had thought of staying on to avoid any third world war;
but how can one avoid a Bomb? We still intended, however, to
settle at some distance from our families; from what we saw as our
pasts.

In the meantime we planned to go on a Grand Tour of the art-
works of Europe – to try to see, before they might finally be
destroyed, those manifestations of the European imagination that
seemed to have been attempts to exalt the propensity of humans
for self-destruction and self-immolation.

The odd circumstances of my life (my mother had died when I
was nine and my father had got himself locked up as one of the
most unpopular men in Britain by the time I was sixteen) had made
it difficult for me, I suppose, to cling to ordinary family and social
ties: both my sister and I had taken refuge in what had seemed to
us a magical circle of friends. In my case, these friends were from
my schooldays and from those who had gone with me into the
army; these were now joined by some of Rosemary's friends. It was
with such a group – seven or eight of us – that we planned to go
on our Grand Tour. I had been extraordinarily lucky in the places
I had been able to visit when I had been in Italy in the war – Naples,
Rome, Florence, Venice – but from the galleries and museums in
these places most works of art had been removed and those that
remained had been boarded up. I remember bribing my way into a

basement in Florence and gazing at a crate that was said to contain Donatello's *David*. My generation had grown up starved of works of art; we felt a need to remedy this.

We were to travel, four boys and four girls (should I not call us 'boys' and 'girls'? we often behaved as such) in two cars and a motor caravan converted from an old ambulance. This latter broke down irreparably just south of Dieppe: one of the girls withdrew from the group when the rest of us got drunk in Paris. We continued in the two cars, with an allowance of just one blanket each and a depleted stock of food. This was a time when food in Europe was scarce or expensive and the foreign travel allowance was only £35 per person, and we were to be away for two months. But we planned to travel rough; this would be part of the voyage of discovery.

We travelled to Chartres, Bourges, Vézelay, Avignon; we went on to the galleries and churches and palaces of northern Italy. We gazed at the enormous cathedrals that seemed to lie weightless on the earth; we stood in front of annunciations, nativities, crucifixions, resurrections. All these seemed to be saying something about the nature of human predicaments – of life and birth and death; but with an eye to something beyond them. We stayed for a time in Venice where on the walls in the Accademia Gallery men in bright striped trousers rested elegantly on the oars of gondolas; where the city seemed to be both settling into the sea and rising out of it, like the sun. In Ravenna, Florence, Sienna, there were the representations of saints both tortured and composed: messages seemed to be contained in their concerned, adoring faces. What was it that they had seen – as if around some corner? We went on to Spain where martyred bodies were even more ecstatically torn and bleeding; where in cathedrals reliquaries like tiny charnel houses glorified skin and bones. We went to bullfights and were both appalled and awestruck: well, ordinary humans too might have to become accustomed to looking at death, might they not? We did not go to the religious services in the cathedrals: one of the pecularities of the European aesthetic imagination is that it can be entranced by the kind of beauty that is on offer to it, yet not interested in the springs from which this comes.

I myself at this time was hostile to Christianity. I had felt some

16

religious emotion when I had been confirmed at school, but after this had come to accept Swinburne's picture of Christ as the 'pale Galilean' and Nietzsche's view of Christianity as a priest-induced 'slave morality'. I cannot remember if I tried to make connections between these attitudes and what I felt about the works of art I found so beautiful. I was awestruck by tragedy: and the power of tragedy depends perhaps on not too many sensible connections being made.

With regard to our group of friends – after a time it became apparent that things were not going well. During the war we had been held together by a sense of 'us' versus 'them' ('them' being people who felt righteous in the war: 'us' being those who accepted its terms but still felt strangers to it). But now there was only 'us': from 'them' we were free! And so, as is common when outside pressures are removed, our group began to break up before we got to Spain. This was not, for Rosemary and me, a matter of great concern. We had distanced ourselves from our families; might we not have to accept a distancing from our friends? We had our marriage, ourselves; was not this enough?

But for those quiet, adoring faces on the walls of galleries and churches – this sort of thing had not been enough?

After our Grand Tour we went to live, Rosemary and I, on a small hill farm in North Wales. This I bought for £5,000 which I had saved from the income from my mother's family trust while I had been in the army (I could not touch the capital of this trust). On this farm Rosemary and I planned to continue to paint and to write: we were also to grow corn and root-crops and to tend sheep and cows and chickens. Thus this was to be a continuation of some sort of Garden – but one outside Eden, as it were, where one had to work to put down roots.

My first novel *Spaces of the Dark* was now finished and was on an erratic course round publishers. After two or three rejections it was taken by Rupert Hart-Davis on the recommendation of David Garnett. I was given lunch by the latter at the Reform Club, and he asked me, 'Do you intend to publish under your own name?' I said, 'I never had much trouble with "Mosley" when I was in the army.' He said, 'The literary world is not like your nice soldiers.'

I had by this time embarked on my second novel, which was once more (surprise!) in some ways obviously to do with myself. It was also again to do with things of which I was not wholly conscious.

This second novel, which was called *A Garden of Trees*, was never published. Its story is as follows:

A young man has been travelling on his own in the West Indies; he has been trying to be a writer; he returns to London where he comes across a small but what seems to him a magical circle of friends. This consists of a brother and sister called Peter and Annabelle, aged twenty and nineteen, who are living in a flat in Grosvenor Square while their parents are away; also a slightly older man called Marius who comes from a family of sugar-planters in the West Indies. The magic of these three seems to consist in their ability to create a fantasy out of almost anything or nothing. My nameless hero, who is also the narrator, first comes across Marius at a political meeting in London's East End, where there is a clash between Fascists and Communists; Marius seems to be observing the scene respectfully, but to be seeing it as absurd. My hero has hitherto felt out of place in the world; he now falls in love with, feels at home in, this somewhat fantastical circle of friends.

But it appears that Marius has a wife who is ill in hospital; she has been paralysed by some accident. The awareness of this breaks in on the circle of friends. My hero is taken by Marius to see his wife; he and she talk alone. She tells him that her 'accident' was that she shot herself. She did this in some madness and terror at the emptiness she felt at the heart of her life with Marius – and this was in spite of (as well as because of?) the idealistic nature of their love. My hero sees that there may be some emptiness, some terror even, at the heart of the circle of friends.

He confronts them with the idea that their 'magic' is at the cost of the reality of the immolation of Marius's wife; he bursts the bubble of the circle of friends. The wife dies; but before this she has said to my hero – I want you to see that Marius will be all right. He imagines from this that she means she would like Marius to marry Annabelle. So my hero abandons Annabelle, with whom he is himself in love. He performs his own act of immolation, out of regard for what he feels has been the wife's.

But Marius and Annabelle do not marry; and when my hero returns from another period of solitude abroad he finds Peter drunk and depressed, and Marius and Annabelle in what seems to be the clutches of priests. Annabelle is having a child by Marius, but still they do not marry; and this seems to be a matter of little concern to the priests. The second half of the book is to do with the efforts of my hero to understand what is happening. He confesses to Annabelle – I was wrong: I should have grabbed you when I had a chance! She says – No, one does only what one can; one cannot tell how things will work out. In the end Annabelle miscarries, and Marius goes back to the West Indies where he is killed in a political riot. My hero does eventually marry Annabelle and even seems to have accepted the influence of priests; but there is no active hope in the way things have worked out. At the end my hero and Annabelle go rowing in a small boat: the last line of the book is: 'The sea was no good for them and they crawled to eternity.'

Now what was happening in my life at this time?

Rosemary and I were living in our lovely low-built grey stone farmhouse like something crouched in the long grass of the hills of North Wales. We kept cows which produced just enough milk to pay for their feed, hens which were apt to drop their eggs from the branches of trees, sheep which got water on the brain and their heads stuck in fences. We had two geese, one of which we killed and ate and the other would come and honk outside the window of the room in which I worked, imagining that it saw its lost mate in the glass. We had a pig whose throat was cut by the local slaughterer and which died, grunting reproachfully, in my arms. We were helped by a couple called Mr and Mrs Davies who lived in a cottage on the farm; I was taken under the wing of a kindly neighbour who taught me that I should wear a cap and carry a stick at livestock sales. We balanced our books through the mercies of something called the Hill Farm Act, which gave subsidies to farmers for doing almost anything on such stony land. In the early mornings and evenings I wrote my novel. I had a black cat that used to lie in the

19

coal scuttle, the contents of which occasionally, absent-mindedly, I would hurl towards the fire.

This was a good life. The letters I wrote to old friends at this time seem funny, hopeful, self-mocking. Was there an emptiness at the centre?

We had come to North Wales to get away from our pasts – from attitudes such as those of my father who saw salvation in commitments to extravagant political causes; from people who accepted the conventions and ambitions of the traditional social world. Such attitudes had seemed to us false, and we had got away: but to what? In North Wales we had wanted to put down roots; but was a hill farm in North Wales a place for us to put down roots? Such beautiful but stony ground! One of my favourite novels just before this time had been E.M. Forster's *The Longest Journey* in which, after the break-up of an esoteric undergraduate circle of friends, some symbol of renewal seemed to be offered by a young farmer rushing off with his young child to sleep in the woods. But what happened then? This was the end of the story! Novelists did not seem much interested in such questions as – But what happened then?

In the summer of 1949 Rosemary's and my first child was due to be born. Our small farmhouse was in obvious ways not yet suitable for a baby: the only available running water was still that which rushed past the back door in a mountain stream (the local house agent had warned us – When it floods, just remember to open the front door): we were waiting for a grant to install piped water under the auspices of the Hill Farm Act. So we came to London to wait for the birth of the baby: we rented a small house in Chelsea and there met up again with some of our old circle of friends. Had we in fact missed them? (Indeed, what are roots!) While Rosemary was in hospital (in those days newly-delivered mothers spent a fortnight in hospital mostly separated from their babies and with the visiting hours even for husbands strictly limited), myself and some of the friends made a home movie called *The Policeman's Mother* with a 16mm camera – the story of which was based on the idea that oppressive social attitudes arose from the frustrated Oedipal yearnings of those in authority. We laughed a lot, drank a lot.

When Rosemary left the hospital with our baby son she went to stay in her grandmother's huge house in Hertfordshire. Here, while I went back to the farm to try to speed up the work that was now being done, she was provided with what was called a 'monthly nurse' to look after the baby. This was another regular tradition among upper classes at the time – people like Rosemary and I were not considered fit to look after babies. (My father used to say – Leave it to the experts! – 'experts' in his context being sometimes teenage nursery-maids.) Rosemary and I had imagined that we were breaking away from our pasts, but nothing in our present had taught us about babies.

While I struggled with the machinations of the Hill Farm Act Rosemary took advantage of her freedom by going up from Hertfordshire each week to an art school in London. This was something she had always wanted to do, but it had been postponed by her marrying.

We were both still so young! We had had such hopes and ideals. We thought that married couples should both be faithful and be free. This 'freedom' was part of another upper-class tradition; but as rebels against tradition we thought we could manage the fidelity too. But what was fantasy: what was reality?

What indeed is the style of love? Does not each want both to possess the other, and be free?

We had to start from scratch in learning about children.

Here are extracts from Rosemary's letters to me that autumn. They were written from her grandmother Lady Desborough's huge house, which was called Panshanger, and from the lodging-house in London where Rosemary stayed when she went to the art school. (My own letters of this time do not seem to have survived.)

How is the farm? I do hope you are all right and will come here soon. It is so nice here, it is very hot and dry, with a small wind which blows all the silver sides of the leaves up. I spend most of the day trying to get near the duck, and last night a hen pheasant came within 2 feet of me as I sat so still with pins and needles.

The baby is very well and brings up a lot of wind. The nurse is very nice and has been to India and tells me about Ali Khan, I wish we knew him, the people there all bring up a lot of wind.

I've just got your letter. Oh Angel, utter misery, why did 10 more chicks die? I bet Mrs D. never lit the stove. Oh gosh, I'm ruining your life, and you get nothing in return and may even have to tie yourself to your suitcase in your spare moments. Impotent me.

It is *exciting* – Sister C. once nursed a baby that had a pekingese's head – this is quite true. She says it is quite common; and in the Rotunda, a very famous Dublin hospital where she trained, there is a museum of babies – lots of them half Alsatians and horrifying ones which she won't even describe.

Angel, the baby seems very well and the nurse is so nice. I found a little book she keeps about him with a page for every day, saying things like 'Has baby a rash?' And then the answer comes next day, like *Mrs Dale's Diary*.

I do miss you, do write to me. What are you doing? Angelic and beloved you. (Slop to make you reach.)

The baby's Sister has been rude to Mummy; he seems hungry, and it is impossible. She also grumbled to Mummy about not getting enough free time which is ridiculous. He was left to cry by her for an hour this morning and seems very strained and exhausted this afternoon, but better now. When we have him at the farm he could sleep in the middle room till he gets older, where I could hear him from our room and then feed him there at 6 in the morning to save waking you.

There is a teacher at the school who thinks my work is very original, extraordinarily macabre and hideous. So far he has only seen one design for a scarf, but he wants to see my painting *seriously*, which is a great chance I think as he may really be able to help. But he wants to see what I do when I'm alone.

This is a nice life (except for you being away). I cook my food and the gas leaks all night and I walk about when I want to. Have you ever been to the Science Museum? It is shatteringly wonderful with every sort of machine and gravity-escape-contraptions and old cars; and did you know that the towers on Battersea Power Station are only for cleaning gas?

I showed everything to my teacher yesterday. He was flabbergasted by my painting. Here is how it happened. When I first went in he was very sinister and said my drawings were good, but when he came to a coloured design for a room he said the colour was most EVIL and the room only one which 'a certain kind of woman could live in'. He then went on to my 'scurrilous' painting (which I hadn't brought with me) and said it was disgusting, vulgar, and lower than Disney and hideous in colour. I argued a little bit but couldn't make him really understand, so I said he must look at my paintings and try to see what I was trying to do. I think he was very impressed in spite of a very strong natural antipathy. He said they were all very physically degenerate – luckily I never showed the new one of the 2 people dancing. He said he thought it would be *most* dangerous if I went back to Wales and painted in the same way. He said that I am following no tradition, I was completely isolated and responsible. Also that he didn't want to try to stop me being morbid as I might be brilliantly morbid.

The baby is very big and much happier. He really quite seriously is a freak as when the Sister sings and then asks him to sing he does, but not till she tells him to. Also he seems quite certain that his will is stronger than mine, which is a lie anyway.

I do miss you my angel, my love.

The baby's Sister is leaving. I shall look after him myself after the 21st as I think these trained nurses are almost absolutely insane. When you come to London let's get some records so we can have a dance every night in the studio. I have been dancing with the baby this evening. He *is* nice now, and smiles a lot.

—— and —— are both nauseating types who have to grovel about in front of something – either you or God it doesn't seem to matter much – you always find them being towed along by great men (not that this means you are specially great) as they don't exist without some sort of idol to dribble in front of, and which at the same time makes them feel rather grand and superior to other people, which makes me *retch*.

So – fantasy? reality? Love, indeed; but some emptiness at the centre? ('—— and ——' were members of the old circle of friends.)
    We did not seem, certainly, to be putting down many roots.
    There were times when Rosemary and I were alone together when some sort of fear seemed to come down, or to be summoned up, between us: this usually happened at night when conventional protections are less alert. It was this sort of fear I tried to write about in *A Garden of Trees* in relation to Marius and his wife. If there were any difficulties between Rosemary and me then it seemed

that I, just by imagining the projection of fear, could make Rosemary frightened; and then the fear would be reflected back to me. In all love there are battles; and Rosemary and I were asking a lot of our trust in wishing ourselves also to feel free. My literary hero at this time – beyond the somewhat romanticised characters of Henry Williamson and E.M. Forster – was Stavrogin in Dostoievsky's *The Devils*. Stavrogin is the centre of a circle of acquaintances who profess no allegiance to rules or conventions: the 'devils' of the title refers to the parable in St Luke's gospel in which when one devil has gone out of a man and nothing else has come in, then seven devils return in its place.

Rosemary and I had tried to be clear of some devils to do with our pasts: but what else, truly, had come in?

Another literary image that came to obsess me at this time (and has continued, unlike others, to do so ever since) was the scene in Thomas Mann's *The Magic Mountain* in which the hero gets lost in the snow and lies down and has a dream. In this he sees beautiful, serene people walking on a beach; they glance every now and then towards a temple in the sand dunes; he wonders if this might contain the secret, the awareness of which enables them to be so serene. He goes to the temple, and there finds old hags dismembering a child.

So indeed – life might be of a kind to be epitomised by images like this: of the horror which beauty is in awe of. But then – How to bear it! let alone manage it.

This is the way, indeed overblown, in which in *A Garden of Trees* Marius's wife, talking to the narrator, tells how her love for Marius used to make her afraid. (This was my effort to understand how I might make Rosemary afraid?)

'He went away from me, searching for something. I did not know what was happening. When you have put your trust in shadows there is nothing that is real. Have you found this? He went with the fishermen in their boats as they sailed after the flying fish, he went with them into the hills and stayed in their villages. They treated him as their god, their personal god, but he did not do anything. This is what happens when nothing is real. The nothingness destroys you. The weight of it grows. The estate was mine, a huge rotting estate with sugar canes and fruit trees, but it was he who became part of it, who decayed with it, who felt it. He sat with them in front of their huts and ate their food and watched them. He sat for hours with his hand among the grasses and there was a silence about him like death. He never did anything. I did not see much of him then. In the evening it grew cold and I went back to the empty house where no fires were laid and I sat there. I remember the sounds that came down from the hills.

'There was a day when the wind stopped. Marius came down and sat with his back to me on the verandah in the darkness. I waited for him. There was a futility that was deathly. Love, I remembered. Then he went away from the house towards the sea and I followed him. He sat on a rock and dropped stones into the water and he watched them become silver and seem to burn beneath the surface. "That is the phosphorus," I said. I sat down beside him. "What are you going to do?" I said. He put his arm into the water so that it shone like something molten. "Who am I?" he said. I thought he was mad then. I am sure I thought him mad. That is what happened.'

'What happened?' I said.

'I tried to know what he was feeling. Why are you frightened, do you know? It is the emptiness that kills you. His shape in the darkness was like wings, like animals. And it was not he, had he not said so? I am not, he had said. And that is what I knew, that he wasn't, in the darkness.'

'And you hit him . . .'

'There is a fear which is of damnation. When a person is a person no longer there is death in his place. As he sat on the rocks crouched heavy like a devil it was as if he were a mirror and I was he and there was nothing between us except what was going outwards into what was not bearable. All that he had said and not said was a hollow like a skull. What it meant was nothingness. It was not then that I hit him. He dived into the sea and swam away from the moonlight.'

'And you went out on to the sand . . .'

'When he came into the room I did not expect that there it would follow me. He came in with the thing that was not him and the death and corruption and when I cried he shouted to drown me but it was not him that I wanted to kill. I ran for the door and he slammed it in front of me and it was then that I hit him. Whatever it was that was taking me into eternity and would have taken me if I had not run, it was not it that I could kill but rather myself before it could take me. When love is nothingness and words are empty and what you have trusted is a lie there is nothing else to be done. I went out on to the sand where the sea was crying.'

'And you shot yourself . . .'

'Living as we had done what else could I do? With one of us mad and nothing but the two of us I only wanted to end it. There was nothing but the two of us in the whole of the world. With emptiness there is terror and you cannot escape it. Outside it was raining. Everything was a shadow and the shadow was a lie. That is what you must remember when you talk with Marius. That is what you must remember when you talk about love. By the sea there was a wind and I was not good at it.'

'The wind had stopped,' I said.

'Yes,' she said. 'The wind had stopped. The rain was soft and heavy with tears.'

'And is this true?' I said.

'True?' she said. 'I have told you that what is true cannot be told. This is a story of love and Marius.'

So once more – a smokescreen? an effort to break through?

It is true that in such areas between fantasy and reality, between the conscious and unconscious parts of oneself, it is difficult for truth to be seen let alone told.

At this time I was also writing a play called *The Fool's Game* (which, too, was never published) in which a young couple, Andrew and Jane, come home from abroad and Andrew thinks he can somewhat cynically manipulate people – his friends, his mother, the old family lawyer. His young wife Jane fears for him: faced with his arrogance, she fears for herself too. If there is no truth, if all is manipulation, then why should not this be at the heart of the relationship between herself and him? In the end it is Andrew who is destroyed: he is in a somewhat bizarre way electrocuted – trying (like Hilaire Belloc's Lord Finchley) to mend the electric light.

Rosemary wrote to me about this play:

I think your play is really very clever and terribly sad at the end. I think Andrew is very good, but must be acted with tremendous CHARM and very VITAL (like you??). Jane is *exactly* like me, but please make her a little ruder to —— I think the moment he asks Andrew to come and turn the switch on as he can't manage it is

BRILLIANT and very *significant* in a way you probably can't understand – in fact definitely can't.

    We are beastly when we are together, but I like you when you're
away very much.

This —— to whom Rosemary asked me to make Jane a little ruder
was a character taken, at least in Rosemary's eyes, from my old
great friend who had been blown up by one of his own mines in
the war (he was also one of the two referred to by Rosemary in her
letter on page 23). But in fact it was this friend who was now trying
to do something far more decisive than any of the others in our old
'circle' to break out of the nihilism or fantasy in which we were
beginning to feel ourselves trapped. He had just announced that he
was thinking of becoming a novice monk. I thought him mad, and
told him so: surely this was a reversion to a too extreme form of
self-laceration!

    This happened when I was about half-way through *A Garden of
Trees* and my hero was going off for a further period of rumination.

    So what indeed might be self-laceration; or an effort to look at,
to deal with, the dark side of oneself?

3

It is difficult to look back, or down, on one's states of mind. I was quite often depressed at this time. I would sit up suddenly in bed at night with the impression of the blade of a guillotine coming swinging in a horizontal arc to cut off my head.

I had no language with which to try to explain what was going on. The contradictions of society might be impossible, fantasies with friends might be impossible, but I had got what I wanted: I was lucky and in love; I loved the farm with its mountain stream that glistened in sun or rain. And yet from time to time I seemed to be pursued by devils with prongs.

Rosemary and I were trying to live and love with no graspingness, no power-games, no jealousy. Oh this was noble and self-effacing! But then what did one learn about the seven devils that seemed to rush in?

This was how I got my hero in *A Garden of Trees* talking about his despair after he had not made a grab to possess Annabelle:

> There is a donkey, theoretically, who starves to death when he is placed between two bundles of hay which are equidistant from him. He has no means of deciding which way to turn. Now there was no hay, no hay in the world, and the effect was the same. The donkey could not move, I could not move, I was the donkey.
>
> There was nothing I desired. I stood on the edge of a street in which there was nothing, between the ends of perspective at which nothing belonged, and it was no use thinking this or that would

lead me to intention, and no use turning my head in hope. I knew
I was the donkey . . . Now I am mad, I thought; I am finally in hell.

So this was the result, was it, of our thinking in terms of a Garden
outside Eden?

The consequences of this sort of experiment bounce and rebound
between the two people involved. Rosemary and I realised we were
in difficulties at this time. She wrote to me:

> Beloved, I am horrified by our public arguments. Here is my final
> slash. You say that whenever you are in a gloom I don't really help
> but sink into one too. I say that when I collapse you also collapse
> into a disdainful hit-at-any-cost-if-possible-covered-by-guile state
> like Jack the Ripper.
>
> BUT – Do let's be friends?

We had little inherited capacity, Rosemary and I, for dealing with
this sort of predicament. In our family backgrounds depressions and
their attendant troubles had been referred to as brainstorms or
neuralgia; they were to be dealt with by doses, or by efforts of
will. To enquire into psychological causes was considered somewhat
vulgar. Oh indeed we had been spoiled children! But 'spoiled' means
what it says.

In the spring of 1950 Rosemary came to the farm with our baby
son and a nanny. Here there was now the newly-installed bathroom
and a kitchen sink, though our electricity was still generated by a
village water-wheel which ground to darkness in times of frost or
drought. But apart from considerations like this, what on earth was
the point of living in a would-be Garden-of-Eden hill farm if one
required a nanny for one's child? With a nanny, indeed, I could
write and Rosemary could paint. But what sort of stuff would I
write?

In the writing of *A Garden of Trees* I had got to the point where
my characters could perhaps see where they had gone wrong in
imagining they could separate themselves from usual human drives;
they had found themselves cut off from a usual human sense of
reality. It might be a defeat if they tried to go back: but in fact, can
one go back?

On the farm we sowed and reaped and managed to get our corn in, just, by Christmas Eve. The butcher to whom we sold our chickens complained that they had vast legs but almost no breast – presumably as a result of their hopping up to and down from the branches of trees.

I had continued to correspond with my friend who was planning to become a novice monk. He was moving towards this decision from having been the war-time joker: so was this a move forwards or backwards? I had told him of the manifestations of fear, of bedevilment, that sometimes sprang up between Rosemary and myself late at night: he had been saying to us for some time – why did we not come and meet some of the committed Christians who had so much influenced him? Particularly amongst these was a Father Raynes, the Superior of the Anglican Community of the Resurrection, which was the order of monks that my friend was thinking of joining. For a time I continued to be hostile to such an idea, saying that I would rather live with uncertainty and even fear than show respect to an illusion.

What both Rosemary and I objected to about the Church people we had known were their attitudes that seemed to us hypocritical: they appeared to demonstrate almost nothing of what they said were their beliefs. But we did not feel hostile to the idea of God: we recognised that some such acceptance was necessary to explain the existence of so much order and beauty. And had we not experienced something of what seemed to be devils?

So I continued to correspond with my friend; and after a time he was writing to Rosemary:

7.1.50
Dear Rosemary,
    When you talk about the Church it's in terms of whether it's a good or bad thing, thus it's hard to argue with you, as I am only interested in whether it is true or untrue. Let there be drunken padres in Irish messes – God is not mocked. It does not take away from the truth of the Christian faith if the Archbishop of Canterbury gives his blessing to the indiscriminate slaughter of German civilians – although this rightly revolts conscientious people like yourself.

30

The Church has a long history of horror as well as of holiness; but it endures, because it is founded on the truth, which is Christ.

Why I am saying all this to you is that someone who reviles the Church as savagely as you do is likely to have a much closer understanding of the Christian faith than the wishy-washy holy-lifers who pass as Christians. And therefore I do think you ought to meet one or two people who are genuine Christians, as you might find that your own ideas are closer to theirs than you imagine. I suggested to Nick that he come down to South Park in March and he said he'd like to: would you like to come too? It's a weekend party and a man called Father Raynes gives about six talks and tries to answer questions afterwards, and you could learn more about it all there than in a year anywhere else. But don't think I'm trying to 'convert' you, as I'm not that foolish. Only I can't get your painting of that red-haired priest out of my mind, and I'd like you to see the other side of the picture as well.

And to me:

28.2.50
    Dear Nick,
    But of course you can come without praying: how can you pray if you don't believe in the person you're praying to? And how else should you be coming but as anti-Christers? I jib at the word 'Christian' because it honestly doesn't mean anything now. You will at least have honest opponents in Fr Raynes and the Lamberts, our hosts.

It had become difficult to hold out against this proposal of my friend, because almost the only faith I had was that there was virtue in not running away from challenges that were presented to one. And it might be good exercise if I were able to parade the simple questions that I thought were unanswerable: If God is good and all-powerful how can he permit evil? If God's omnipotence is limited by man's freedom, He is omniscient and must have known that the Fall would occur, and so He is still responsible for evil – and thus why should He now demand that mankind should ask for forgiveness when it was He who had put us in our horrible predicament? I did not imagine there could be any exposure of myself in these questions.

So Rosemary and I agreed, yes, to go to this dreadful-sounding

31

weekend party. Years later, when I came to write the biography of Father Raynes, I described this, my first meeting with him.

My wife and I arrived on Friday evening at Mr and Mrs Lambert's house in Surrey and were welcomed by people who were kind and cheerful but who seemed to represent what had made us uneasy about Christians – the way they were secure and jolly in their group. There were about twenty-five of us of all ages and both sexes, mostly upper or upper-middle class. My wife and I seemed the only ones antipathetic to Christianity. We knew that we had come to meet Father Raynes; that my friend hoped he might persuade us. I thought this was impossible, and I would stump him with my age-old questions.

Father Raynes was in the drawing-room among the cocktails like a totem-pole – gaunt in his black cassock with his shaved head forwards and eyes so pale they looked transparent. He seemed to be enjoying the party yet to be quite separate from it. When he shook hands his arm became limp and totally impersonal.

The talks took place in the library with everyone sitting on sofas and on pouffes and on the carpet, and being expected to ask questions afterwards. He was to start with the Christian Conception of God; the next day the Creation and Fall, the Incarnation, the Atonement; ending on Sunday with the Church, Sacraments, Prayer. He sat in an armchair and spoke so hesitantly that I wondered if he stammered. He had a notebook on his lap of which he did not turn the pages.

He answered my questions briefly – the highest possibility for man was to be made in the image of God, the nature of God is to love, you couldn't have love without freedom, you couldn't have freedom as we conceived it without the chance of going wrong, this didn't imply God made us go wrong, omniscience didn't include intention. Love that was freely given and that was incapable of not-love was the perfection of the Godhead itself; if love was to exist outside the Godhead then it had to have freedom of choice – there was no love in a machine. There was no answer to the question why, if He wanted to create anything, God had not created something better of which we could not conceive. We were here; this was what the world was like; this was what we had to deal with.

To those who have faith this explanation makes sense; to those who have not it seems like a dream. And whereas to the faithful the whole scheme of love and failure and redemption is not only true but glorious, to others it seems monstrous – a huge trick of the mind, or worse, a trick of the Creator. How could man believe himself loved if thrown into the maelstrom and then blamed there? This was the great gulf between the converted and unconverted – not just that between sense and nonsense, but between what was beautiful and what seemed horrible . . .

On Sunday morning, in some outrage at all this, I said I preferred a universe that admitted that it was crazy. Father Raynes said, 'You'd better get out of it quick.' I determined to stay aloof from the rest of the party. The gulf seemed permanent, and desirable.

In the biography I tell how I took refuge on my bedroom balcony and how my friend came to talk to me; he suggested that I go and talk personally with Father Raynes – to which I agreed, because this seemed still a reasonable challenge. What I did not tell in the biography, because after all this was a book about Father Raynes and not myself, was that my friend had said to me, as if casually, 'Those frightening experiences between you and Rosemary – have you been having them recently?' And I had said, 'No, it's odd, they stopped about two months ago.' And then my friend had said, 'That's about the time I asked the nuns at Burnham Abbey to pray for you both.' And I had thought – Oh odd indeed! But is it not true that one is touched by just things like this?

In my biography I describe how I went out to talk to Father Raynes:

> After tea he was there, unobtrusively, and I said, 'Can I talk to you?' We went out into the garden. I wanted to explain why I thought the party so awful, but I said, 'I'm not really so awful.' We talked for an hour. He hardly said a word. The landscape became exact, with a different light on it.

I also tried to put this into more explanatory words:

> The process of conversion is different from brain-washing in that it does not seem to happen through planned human agencies. People can bring you into 'relationship'; they can pray (this always happened at these weekends); but they cannot cross the gulf. The gulf is between love and not-love: people can try to transmit love, but only those who have it can receive it. If the gulf is to be crossed, there has to be a movement of love itself.

Oh indeed, these are difficult matters to put into words.

In the biography I said of my further relationship with Father Raynes: 'I rebelled from time to time: the whole thing again seemed nonsense . . . conversion anyway lasts a lifetime.' But with regard to my own story – what terrible to-ings and fro-ings indeed! what desperate diggings-in of toes; what draggings by the hair!

What I had at least got now was some story-line for the last third of *A Garden of Trees*; in which my hero resists, and yet is half taken over by, the influence of priests. In real life I had further meetings with Father Raynes: when one was alone with him he in fact seldom spoke, he was like some rock against which one's complaints and fears broke in waves. But now there were going on in my head not only my own old nihilistic speeches but the voices that I myself could make up against them, as it were as a result of what I was learning from Father Raynes. Towards the end of *A Garden of Trees* there are two priests, one worldly and one passionate, who have come, so the narrator thinks, to ensnare Annabelle and Marius; their voices I suppose were what I imagined from even the silences of Father Raynes. Father Raynes was gentle and worldly-wise and tolerant in his personal dealings; yet, when the situation seemed fitting, he could be dogmatically passionate. Here is the worldly priest in my novel talking to the narrator:

> What I would say to you is this, that it is what a man believes that is important. I would rather a man live faithfully by what he believes than attempt to persuade himself of what he does not. A synthesis of persuasion is useless: an antithesis of truth is not. This is perhaps what you will recognise. There is something of the truth in every man, however contradictory expressions of it may appear. It is this truth that can be respected: I should say more than this – it can be loved. The claim that the Church makes, you see, is a very large one after all – it claims that if every man will observe and honour the truth that is in him, then there is not much more that need be done. The Church, as it were, is doing the rest. It is working for the world in the only way possible for it. There is a good deal of confidence in this, and certainty. This is what you will learn to understand.

And then this is the voice of the passionate priest, a native of the

West Indies. This voice has not got much directly to do with Father Raynes; it has more to do, I suppose, with some voice I was furiously struggling with in my head:

I cannot teach you, teaching is irrelevant to you, what is it that you believe? Teaching is only for those who believe already. You believe in nothing? My friend, if you believe in nothing then death is the end of life and life is nothing and that is not possible, that life is not possible, because you know about this life, you have eyes to see this life, you know the evil of it . . .

. . . You say that you want no salvation, that you need no redemption, that you will take responsibility for what you have done and you will live out each day of your life in misery for it. And I say to what end do you do this, to what end do you desire this misery? You do not desire misery for the sake of misery, you cannot, you desire misery so that truth may come in its place. And I say this is the most foolish dream in the world, it is the mad dog barking for the moon because you have no hope for it, no hope at all, because the mad dog cannot fly and you are human. If you wish to make yourself sufficient for your responsibilities that is an aim as wild as the moon and you will miss it, you will fail, you will end up in delusion which is the greatest sin of all. You will think you have reached the moon because you will have stared at it so long that it will have blinded you, the image that you will hold in your arms will be the deception of your eyes. It is you who have talked of failure and I tell you that this is the most terrible failure of all because it is deliberate, it is the deliberate will to failure arising out of pride . . .

You now have no freedom. You have said that you are a machine. You cannot talk about your failures or successes because you are living as a machine and not as a man. Only a man has freedom who has chosen love. Until you have made your choice this futility will continue, you will never know what happens and what there is to be done. And for us who have chosen, who have attempted to make the choice, do not talk to us about our failures or successes because failures may be triumph and it is not for you to say. Nor is it for you to presume we should live our lives in misery when here, now, there is a joy such as you never dreamed of, once and for all and always there is this joy that was given at a moment in time, the greatest triumph in history that is the whole of history, the point of triumph of eternity . . .

Man does not require comfort, he only partly requires aid, what he requires is absolution. Sin exists and man lives in sin and there

35

is no real aid other than this absolution. And when you have realised this and lifted up your eyes to the light then and only then will you realise what this world is and what is the perfection of it. You will realise then that everything in the world is beautiful, that every horror and every terror and every pain in every corner of the world is beautiful, that it is beautiful because it is known by God, because God himself has suffered it, and then you will undertand. You will understand everything, you will understand even this – that when the lion eats the heart of the deer, yes, that is beautiful; that when the child dies in agony for what it has not done and for a pain that is unbearable to it, yes, that is beautiful; that when the hangman puts the noose round the neck of his innocent victim and the floor drops and the tongue comes out and the neck screams as it is torn from the shoulders, yes, that is beautiful. You will realise that even the hangman is beautiful. Think of that when you talk about misery. Then you will know the meaning of that moment in eternity.

Dear God, what was this: a smokescreen? Surely more of a bombardment, a gas-attack, a frenzy, going on in my head!

So I wanted some absolution, did I – from trying to say the unsayable? This might be some breakthrough!

But then – what in the 'real' world was happening to me now?

In the autumn of 1950 Rosemary became pregnant again and nearly had a miscarriage; our local doctor in Wales seemed whimsical and somewhat drunk. Rosemary was told to stay in bed and I tried to look after her. But by this time her family were understandably becoming anxious, and it was true that in our plans for a garden-farm outside Eden we had hardly considered the bringing-up of children. Rosemary's mother offered us the use of her house in Sussex until the new baby was born, with the hint that some time later the house might be ours. She herself was spending most of her time looking after her own mother in the huge house in Hertfordshire. The offer of the Sussex house seemed impossible to justify refusing – even if it meant giving up some of our dreams. And in fact, might we not after all be grateful to be close once more to the delights (the temptations even?) of the old circle-of-friends life in London?

And were we not told that one did not in fact escape devils by cutting oneself off or turning away?

So Rosemary with the baby and nanny moved to Lyminster House in Sussex; I stayed behind in Wales to pack up the farm. We had been there less than three years. There was sadness; some sense of failure. But perhaps we had always known, Rosemary and I, that for us a search for 'roots' would involve a readiness to move on.

I finished the last sections of *A Garden of Trees*: there was indeed confusion about what the book was trying to do. The chief characters had accepted something of Christianity, but this seemed to have brought them to just a more mapped-out wilderness: what they had gained seemed to be a readiness for death. This seemed, certainly, to be an aspect of traditional Christianity; but the presence of Father Raynes seemed to involve a promise of so much more. I went to see Father Raynes when I could – in his monastery in the north, on his visits to the south. His bright transparency, his authority, seemed unrepresentative of so much else about Christianity. I tried to pay as much attention to what he suggested as I could. And I continued to correspond with my friend who had by now joined the Community of the Resurrection at its headquarters at Mirfield, in Yorkshire, and had thus become a novice monk.

Here are extracts from the letters that my friend wrote to me during this next year. My letters to him (as usual, and perhaps mercifully) have not survived.

10.12.50
Your letter seems to contain one fundamental contradiction. At the beginning you say 'I have got to "judge" Christianity: not feeling it, I can approach it no other way.' At the end you say 'He (Fr Raynes) is consistent, sane, and to my conscience appears right and true. His opinion, statements, behaviour, judgements, appear conscientiously proper. Other people's (and often my own) don't.'

If this is not a judgement, what is? You will say that Fr Raynes is not 'Christianity'? He says that he is. I mean, he says that he is a Priest of the C.R., which is a Religious Order in the Holy Catholic Church, and that what he preaches, by precept and practice, is the Word of God, or Christ, or Truth, as far as that Word has been revealed to him and allowed by him to grow in him. In as much as what Fr R. says and is appears to your conscience to be right and true, the Word has been revealed to you and you have accepted it.

What more is there to say?

The answer to your 'vital question' is – Yes, Christians can be taken as 'evidence' for the truth or non-truth of Christianity. But throughout history you will find evil and hypocrisy and treachery and corruption in the Church: you will also find saints. And, which is odd if it is merely an institution like any other institution, despite the evil the Church goes on. Because other institutions don't: the Roman Empire and so on. From the beginning you get treachery: you also get the other eleven. Is this evidence going to help you make your mind up?

But it seems to me that you have already accepted the Truth and that what you have to do now is to make an act of will, and pray, and use the sacraments. Of course it *seems* false because one's whole outlook, one's ideas, imagination, understanding, are not Christ-centred but self-centred. Conversion is a very slow, painful and yet joyful and exciting business, and goes on all one's life. What would be false would be to deny that to your conscience Fr Raynes appears right and true.

12.8.51

It is all right your writing so much about yourself until you realise that you can tell all these things to a priest and receive the much more solid benefit of counsel and the *fact* of absolution.

I should have been surprised to hear that you *had* received 'consolation' from being 'restricted to good': it is its own consolation, and far from being 'your own fault' it is a blessed state to be in, although one *feels* anything but blessed at the time. You say that 'it is hell' being 'restricted'; all right, accept it as your bit of hell – or as someone else's, for one can never tell for whom one is suffering. But of one thing there can be no doubt: GOD is drawing you closer to Himself all the time. Your remarks on grace are beside the point: God is not thwarted by your stubbornness, and if you do not pray or go to Church He still finds means to touch you and draw you even though your resist. It is His nature to give, so it is quite foolish not to ask of Him simply because you don't like asking things of people (anyway prayer is not, basically, asking: when you say 'you get something from worship whether you ask for it or not', what you get may be something very unpleasant – like being restricted – not what you asked for at all).

'The real war as it affects you' – the real illusion is not that you are capable of winning this war on your own, but that you are on your own at all. And a very nice illusion it is, because it means that you are only responsible to the god you have put your faith in, the god you have hammered (or are hammering) out for yourself. Of the countless implications of this illusion, *qua* responsibility for others, real relationships with others, in fact *qua* love, you do not seem to have taken any account; you certainly do not reckon on any final decision in this war. 'It is proper for us to be involved in the war on our own even if we are defeated in it. The question of winning is not really significant.' By Heaven it IS. This is not a game, it is a war of life and death: not a war which involves only temporal life and temporal death, but the real life and the real death of eternity. That is the issue, and until you have realised a little of what that thing called eternity is, you have not grasped at all what the war is about.

But you know all this, Nick: but do you believe what I tell you, that it is an illusion that you are on your own? Religion (*re-ligio*) means that which binds – hence your sense of being 'restricted to good'. It is rather like that Chinese thumb-screw one used to find in crackers: once it was placed on your finger, the harder you tried to pull it off the tighter it gripped: the grip of love is apt to be intolerable. You have given me no cause to think you do not believe it, or that you are denying it. But you do seem to be tugging rather hard?

You say – 'Is anyone ever really converted without *being lost*? (i.e. passively, it happening to them, rather than by will).' In a sense this is quite true: i.e. it is the Holy Ghost who is the active agent. But then it is *in* you that He is acting, and He cannot act without your consent (even the Lord had to wait upon the consent of a young girl before He could clothe himself in man's flesh). So although there is nothing you can do to affect conversion, there is much you can do to hinder it. You have to will to submit to His Will. But think of it less now as a conversion and more as the growth of the Kingdom within you – 'as if a man should cast seed upon the earth: and should sleep and rise night and day, and the seed should spring up and grow, he knoweth not how'. Judging by our weekend here, your letters, and accounts of you from others (whose judgements you may think superficial, but I believe they are not) I should say all was going well and according to plan (does this make you cross? let it not) and that you are at worst only hindering things by refusing the help that's offered . . . He is already in you, and you in Him; you have only to become in Him what you are always, and eternity is now, here, always.

27.8.51

You say 'I don't know anything about anything': and on the next page 'I have these feelings, and feelings they are – love is a feeling,

39

responsibility is a feeling, *they exist*, this I know.' And here I could write a long essay about the distinction between οἶδα and γιγνώσκω, but as you are going on holiday and I am going to a lecture on 'Disintegration' by Prof. Mackinnon I will spare us. But you do affirm knowledge here, knowledge of love as a fact which is, of responsibility as a fact which is, both of them really existing – really existing, I am to infer from earlier remarks in your letter, whether you exist or not. Love and duty as objective facts – known by you and in you admittedly, but not created by you and subject to you: the reverse rather.

Your 'agnostic' passages are wholly subjective – 'I don't know anything about anything ... I don't know what "I" means, what "good" means ... I am impressed by certain people, certain occasions, books, music – but impressions are not knowledge.' Quite. But 'impressions' can illuminate the objective knowledge that is already 'there' and become, if you so choose, part of that knowledge.

The facts known, your two facts, tell you a good deal – that GOD IS, and furthermore that He is Love and He is Moral.

4.11.51

What you are going to do – 'to go ahead quietly, undramatically, trying to do what you say hopefully, not forcing myself, not prating about battles, above all *not thinking about myself*' – is good and sensible. And if the greater part of this letter seems dogmatic, that is only because I do not see how else one can write about these things, and the last thing I intend is to force you into anything.

Since you have mentioned the sacrament of Penance ... I feel I can say I am sure it is time you made your confession. I think I said this when you were here in April ... but I have always been and am still diffident and reluctant about making an explicit exhortation because I believe that the Lord the Holy Spirit is much better left to work on His own by Himself. Still, the fact that you feel you are 'at the moment incapable of saying anything about myself that is true' shows that perhaps at the moment it is difficult for you to hear what He is saying to you internally, and for that very reason He may speak to you through another.

8.11.51

It is very wonderful, dear Nick, is it not? and why so improbable? Others had prayed, and you had prayed – for a long time, as it seems to us, tho' to Him so short. But I am so GLAD, so very glad. God *is* extraordinary, isn't He, and it would be just like Him to act at that moment thro' one of His saints who doesn't even consciously believe in Him. Truly there is no end to the wonder of Him.

4

So this is an embarrassing part of the story. What on earth was this that was so 'very wonderful' of God – the activity 'through one of His saints' who did not 'even consciously believe in Him'?

God works in mysterious ways, all right. But what is tragedy; what is farce. (Much the same thing?)

Rosemary and I had found ourselves, in spite of love, in some solipsistic wilderness. Then we had been told – If you face truly even this emptiness, this arbitrariness, then something different may grow.

Growth usually occurs after some crack-up; some pain.

One of the presuppositions of the way in which Rosemary and I had been brought up was that after marriage each one of a couple should be free within limits to lead his or her own life in relation-ships with other people: marriage was seen as a practical enough institution for it not to be considered as an imprisonment or a blight. With some of our parents' and grandparents' generation the convention had been to look on even some sexual affairs as being within socially acceptable limits: these limits were that such affairs should be carried on only between people who would not be socially hurt – that is, between men and other men's wives of the same social standing, but not with unmarried women. Rosemary and I were of the more romantic wartime generation whose revolt against our elders included an objection to what seemed to us such duplicity in sexual affairs: what a farce that marriage should be taken as a signal for promiscuity! Rosemary and I intended to be sexually faithful to one another; but we accepted the idea of a certain freedom in marriage, and this included the possibility of friendships, even somewhat sentimental friendships, with people of the opposite sex.

The circumstances of my life had made me almost insanely romantic about girls (I shall continue to use the world 'girls'; am I not writing of some form of infantilism?). At school I had adopted the homosexual attitudes that were almost *de rigueur* in English preparatory and public schools at that time (there was very little serious sexual activity; it was nearly all talk; and in such homosexual dalliance as there was one learned – what happy lack of complications! what fun!). I had gone straight from school into the army: I had still not come across many girls except the friends of my sister, who were older. Then in Italy there were just a few pretty nurses for whom young officers had to queue up as if for tickets to Wimbledon. There were tarts, of course; but one of my duties as a young officer had been to lecture to my platoon on the dangers of venereal disease, and in Italy there had been an effective travelling exhibition of photographs showing the grotesque physical malformations which resulted from going with prostitutes. The result of all this was that when I returned to England in 1945 aged twenty-two and there was suddenly a host of creatures called débutantes on the scene like a cloud of butterflies in June – I became quite bowled over by girls, I could think of almost nothing but girls; but how on earth was it possible, I wondered, if one was to fall in love at all, to fall in love with just one girl? Surely this sort of eye-opening, heart-opening, marvelling kind of love was a condition to do with almost everyone, or nothing. Paul, the hero of *Spaces of the Dark*, as soon as he had got home had fallen in love with not one but two girls. It was after a year or two of this sort of thing that I myself had felt the urgent need to marry and to be committed to just one girl, Rosemary. Getting away from my past had seemed to include getting away from endlessly haphazard convolutions with girls.

In *A Garden of Trees* my hero feels committed to just one girl. But then what became of him and Annabelle? Their lives seemed to get lost in the wastes of the sea. And what had been my hero's strange obsession with some further understanding that had seemed to be suggested by Marius's dying but visionary wife?

Rosemary and I had tried to escape into, and then had had to get out of, our would-be Gardens of Eden: now here we were, after four years of marriage, come down to Sussex, to a house not unlike those in which we had spent our childhoods. And Lyminster was only an hour and a half from London. And it was in London that there were what had seemed to be the hordes of butterflies so beautiful and desirable; but which as caterpillars can be the destroyers of gardens.

However, it had been our very aloofness within our Garden that had recently seemed to contain neurosis and danger! And did not my friend the novice monk seem to be saying – It is no use trying to protect yourselves: you have to become exposed for this or that voice, or experience, to come in.

And what was all this stuff about being pursued by love as if it were a thumb-screw?

Lyminster House, near Arundel, is a fine Georgian house on the edge of a village. It had a large walled garden (so we thought we were getting out of Gardens?); there were a gardener and a cook already in residence when we arrived. Rosemary's mother said she would help us with expenses. It was a perfect house for children. But it was not the sort of place about which we could any longer pretend we were cutting ourselves off from our past, or from society. And indeed, I could whizz up to London.

By this time I had finished *A Garden of Trees*. This was turned down by Rupert Hart-Davis. David Garnett said that he found the story rambling and the stuff about priests distasteful. The book went a lengthy round of publishers; it was eventually accepted by Weidenfeld & Nicolson. But by this time I was well away on my third novel, about which I was much more excited and was keen to have published first.

The story of my third novel, which was called *The Rainbearers*, is as follows:

A young man, Richard, is heir to an estate in the north of England.

He has not wanted at once to settle down to the life of a bourgeois country gentleman, so he has enrolled as a somewhat dilettante student at an art school in London. There he becomes involved with two girls. The first, Mary, has during the war been in a concentration camp in France; she bears the psychological marks of her suffering. Richard falls in love with her because she seems to be in touch with some authenticity; but she does not love him, because he seems to her a dilettante.

The other girl with whom Richard becomes involved is Elisabeth, who comes from the same background as Richard and whom he loves because he feels he can build a serious life with her – though it is Mary perhaps who has made him dissatisfied with his superficiality. Richard and Elisabeth marry and try to put down roots as conventional country landowners in Northumberland. They have two children, who are largely in the care of a nanny. After a time both Richard and Elisabeth feel that life is running down; they seem to be out of touch with whatever might be authentic.

They go on a smart social holiday to the south of France. On the way back from this Richard, on his own, again meets Mary. She is in Paris working for an organisation which helps refugees. But by this time Mary has become wearied of trying to deal with the pain of a senseless world, and now she does fall in love with Richard, who seems at least to have a foothold in a stable society. So Richard becomes torn between his love for Elisabeth, with whom he has built a life with their children, and his love for Mary, who seems to turn up at moments in his life to point him towards, indeed to pierce him with, some vision of a larger reality.

Elisabeth becomes angry with Richard's irresolution and embarks on an affair of her own; Richard uses this as an excuse to go off with Mary. They go to the Mediterranean and lie about in the sun. Richard hopes to do something to repair Mary's suffering; but is he not also using this as an excuse for himself? And what is all the talk about a larger reality? With Mary there seems to be no chance of settling down; she is at home only in suffering or ecstasy. So the relationship between Richard and Mary after a while begins to run down too – or perhaps to run towards something further? Richard begins to feel, in fact, that what he may be learning is something necessary about himself and his marriage to Elisabeth. But then if he returns to Elisabeth, would not Mary once more be being cast in the role of sacrificial victim? And anyway, might not any such move, or idea, still be just an excuse for someone like Richard to go selfishly on his way, using people as he wants and then leaving them?

Richard goes back to see Elisabeth, promising to return to Mary. Mary, following him, thinks she sees evidence that he is simply betraying her. She feels she is back in her prison camp; she becomes ill; Richard does what he feels he has to do – he leaves Mary in the care of an older man who has always loved her and who will look after her, and then he is reconciled with Elisabeth. At the end of the story there is some evidence that he and Elisabeth have learned something about themselves and their marriage. But this has been at the cost, indeed, of a betrayal; and a sacrificial victim.

During the latter part of the book there is a lot of talk about God. Mary and Richard argue about God: is the 'love' of which God is said to consist something that can be held, encapsulated, between two people; or is it always a pointer to something further?

And is it then unavoidable that there should be sacrificial victims?

This was the story that I started to write not long after Rosemary and I had moved to Sussex. We had known there were dangers in this move: but might not good of some kind come out of danger?

The time-scale of life is different to that of a novel. A novel has to have an end that is seen. This is why novels are for the most part to do with tragedy or farce.

What matters in life for the most part goes on secretly; and a pattern emerges only later.

I was up in London on my own one day – there was a lot of to-ing and fro-ing concerning the move from Wales at this time – and there I came across someone whom I had known briefly at Oxford: she had been, as a young girl, yes, in a Japanese prison camp during the war. It seems to me now (it had not struck me at the time?) that I might have had my passing acquaintance with this person in mind (as well as Rosemary) when I was writing the character of Marius's wife in *A Garden of Trees*; she had seemed to carry within

46

her something of the suffering of the world. In *A Garden of Trees* my hero became obsessed with trying to make some reparation to Marius's wife: but then Marius's wife died, and my hero's own sacrifice seemed useless. But when I met again this person, whom in *The Rainbearers* I called Mary, she wanted to live. She had suffered; but she wanted no more sacrifice.

In London I asked her out to dinner. There was nothing unusual in this in Rosemary's and my scheme of things. After dinner Mary and I (I shall call her Mary) sat in my car and talked. After a time we decided that we should not see each other again.

We imagined we knew what we were doing? Indeed, how ludicrous life is! It was this meeting, and this decision, to which my friend the novice monk referred when he spoke of the wonder of God's activity 'through one of His saints' who 'did not even consciously believe in Him'.

What my friend the novice monk was referring to was the fact that I had been so ravaged both by the meeting with Mary and the decision (mainly hers) not to see each other again – ravaged by love, that is, and compassion and desire and the apparent impossibility of doing anything proper about any of these; by the overwhelming impression that I had no means of handling on my own the terrible ambiguity and tragedy and pulling-in-two-ways that seemed to constitute life (I loved and wished to be faithful to Rosemary; I loved and desired Mary; I did not want to cause anyone pain) – that I had gone, as my friend the novice monk had for so long said I should go, and even had seemed so oddly confident that something would eventually happen to make me go, to a priest to make my confession. (This was a recommended ritual in the Anglo-Catholic world of Father Raynes.) And then I had written to my friend about what had happened; about how indeed I hoped that such a jump in the dark might be a way of handling the impossibilities of life; and he had written about the extraordinariness (to be sure!) of God's ways.

The priest to whom I confessed (Father Raynes was away) was a dry and doleful man: he seemed more censorious of my confusion than filled with the wonder of God's ways.

But it did seem to me, yes, that this might be a step in learning further the complexities and ambiguities of God's ways.

47

I began to write *The Rainbearers* that long winter. This was a difficult time. I was trying to discover, to create, patterns. But in real life, of course, these are only glimpsed after a journey in the dark.

And in the end what happens is different from what one has imagined?

One hopes so; or what has one learned?

Here are extracts from the letters written to me during that winter and spring by the person who in *The Rainbearers* I called Mary. (What happened to my own letters, again, I do not know.) This is an ordinary, even banal, story of a kind that is usually put only into fiction. But such a story is often at the centre of a person's life; and fiction does not deal with the question – What happens then? Nor indeed does it include the realisation that there may be no end to the working-out of patterns.

31.10.51

All I can say at the moment is that I love you, and you have gone, and I am only half alive.

This will pass. I know it will. It is what we must both remember – one doesn't love for ever.

I wish I knew you were safely at home. Anything rather than wandering about the streets. I hope you sleep tonight.

Darling, I can't write to you very well. I should send you little mathematical formulae; with words I am lost.

It will be all right with you. It will.

There is nothing I can say.

4.11.51

Here is the proof –

Let $a = b$
Then $a^2 = b^2$
and $a^2 - b^2 = ab - b^2$
therefore $(a - b)(a + b) = b(a - b)$
or $a + b = b$
or $a + a = a$
or $2 = 1$

Was this your proof too? Is this to be our only proof that I love you, that you love me? For the first time I see sterility in logic. I cannot write tonight. I think I was mad. This awful negation.

I had dreamed last night of Camp – and woke to find myself in an imprisonment as bad – because it is of my own making, and because you are there too.

5.11.51

I wish so much I was a Catholic – that would make it clearer. All I can do is pray for you – to a God I do not believe in. This shows how much I love you. This shows my weakness; my ultimate dishonesty. But I must do something for you. Your letter has made me cry – I who said I never cried.

19.11.51

Nick – whatever next step we take must be decided by you, not by us. This is the hardest thing I have ever had to say.

What I did three weeks ago I had authority to do. I can do no more. I have no right to encroach further on a side of your life in which I have no place. I must not say do not come, or come.

I pray God that you understand this – and with it all its implications – not only half, one-sided, but all.

Because if we stay apart it will be because of your life. If we come together it will be in spite of your life. No blame. No blame.

When one is younger one believes that somewhere, if only one could find it, there is a solution to any problem. I am not sure of this now.

My life is empty without you.

I do not think we are trying to forget each other by writing three times a week. I am not sure that it is not better to know the pain, and love. If I forgot, half of me would die. I suppose if one solved this problem, one would have solved all.

28.11.51

Yes, of course I will. I had reached *exactly* the same point. It is the only thing to do. 3.00 p.m., Friday 30th November, on the verandah place outside the doors of the National Gallery.

5.12.51

All I can say is what you have said – that this happens very rarely to anybody; that it is more valuable when it happens than anything else; that we stand on the brink of it.

Oh Christ, darling, I know you love your children, how could I not? I am all right. I have been a little ill. I was more ill in the month we did not see each other.

10.12.51

I feel I have grown up ten years since October 30th – there are so many things I have made myself think about that before I did not believe were worth consideration. You have made me see the importance and the prevalence of the second best – for this I hate you a little – I don't know why I didn't see it before – I think one doesn't if one wants to die.

But I think that if we stopped completely now it would not kill either of us. Later I think it might truly kill.

I think that if we decide to stop completely we will regret it for the rest of our lives. What I do not know is how strong the regret would be; it might be as strong as any other power of destruction. We have only seen each other five times, my darling.

If only we could be together somewhere quietly for a week. I would not become your mistress then because all the searching for the right decision would be nullified. We would have begun the new world and nothing could stop it.

I feel an inevitability in what has so far happened. You may say this is the cowardice of determinism; it is not quite like that.

For me it feels as though God is in it. Perhaps all lovers feel it. It does not stop me wanting to have died after all in Camp, but it does stop me regretting – since we had to meet – anything that has passed between us.

11.12.51

This is absurd. I am 25, quite acquainted with life, a fellow of a learned society, a don working in a loony bin – you would think I was a sensible woman, wouldn't you? All I can do is sit about and smile vaguely – feeling absolutely gay and about seventeen.

Friday – Isn't that the nicest word in the English language? Friday, at 11.00 a.m., at the Hyde Park Hotel – in that lovely anonymous lounge on the left at the top of the stairs.

Lots of chairs to rest our aching knees, and *Tatlers* to soothe whoever gets there first. So sobering, the *Tatler*.

25.12.51

I love you all the time, you are always with me, and still very near to me. I pray for us with more faith and belief – and I think of your saying that to pray for each other is like praying with each other and this makes me happier.

30.12.51

A short practical letter.

I would like to see you – preferably on Tuesday. There are things I want to discuss – mainly my going abroad within the next few weeks.

This is a problem first shelved, and then forgotten all about in our days together – but plans are being made around me.

This has been perhaps the worst ten days I have known. I know what it has been for you.

1.1.52

Thank God, my darling, thank God I have heard from you. You will find a silly letter from me – ignore it – I have been ill for several days, that is why I wrote so coolly. Don't worry about me going abroad at the moment – this is minor compared to the rest. It was only an effort of mine to try and hold on to my external world.

My darling darling love, I do pray, that is all I can do since I have been ill, I pray and believe somehow we will be together, we will laugh together, we will lie together at night. I believe it – or else why should we have this?

Yes, write soon but don't write anything except love, and when you will come and see me. Anything else would be meaningless – apart now we are not quite ourselves, only together are we wholly ourselves and then there is sense.

A silly letter, my love. I am perhaps still a little ill. But I will be better. I love you so much.

The first overpowering relief has faded, sense (?) is beginning to return. I reread this and consider it *undoubtedly* a good example of a Reserved and Remote letter.

26.3.52

I am so happy that the first time there was so much love. Thank you for not frightening me at all. I am so happy that it was good for you. It will be better. I am glad that your birthday is the 25th.

I am so tired that I do not know if I will ever not be again. I had drinks with five different lots of people after you had gone. I did not drink. I wore the black jersey and padded skirt and every time I walked into a room people stared and said I was beautiful and stood away from me a little. It has never been like that before. Perhaps I should not tell you this, it is not vanity, I want you to know.

Tomorrow I will be worried for you: tonight I am not. Tonight I am a woman writing to her lover.

I sit by the fire and remember how it was, and see that now I know how it will be. Almost the first thing you said to me was – now you are mine.

My beloved, understand that this is a formal letter with a formal ending. Take care of yourself.

9.4.52

I don't understand your letter. I will try and be well. Why now, your talk of getting tough? It doesn't matter.

I know your speeches, the hope, the promise – your new speech about going back in order to help the hope. These I keep always with me.

I may go abroad rather quickly – in 2 or 3 days – if so I will let you know when I get there. I don't know where 'there' is. I don't know for how long. *Don't* let's write dramatic letters full of meaningful spaces and full stops. If there is anything of that sort let us say it. That I *ask* you.

I have been thinking so much of you and the war. I was thinking about us talking about the nuns who came out of convents into Camp. They were very frightened of death. They lay under their beds and pulled their mattresses down over them when the Americans bombed us – which, when you consider they bombed us from Oct. 17th to Feb. 1st almost every day from 7 a.m. to 6 p.m., was a bit boring for them.

I was thinking how in 3¼ years I spent one hour and ten minutes by myself in a room with the door shut. Even in the lavatories we weren't alone. After hunger, that was much the worst – worse than imprisonment, or boredom, or stupidity, or being cut off.

1.5.52 Geneva

My darling, I hope so much that you had a good flight back and are not too tired. Did you sleep or read? Thank you very much for coming. I love you so much for it, and it did make a difference. I think you were absolutely right to go when you did, but I wish you had stayed.

Such a funny house. I sleep in the top floor in a pretty room: lots of lovely Victorian chairs, a writing-table, a big walnut sofa covered in pale blue velvet on which I am sitting now, a dressing-table with a squinting looking-glass, twisted little glass bottles, a long vial of perfume, and tiny scissors and button-hooks and things that must have been here for 100 years. And all along one side books and books and books, everything one should read and never has – Maeterlinck and Molière and Pascal and Balzac and Heine and Pierre Loti – and Proust by my bed. Did I ever tell you how in Camp there was a sweet little Frenchman who, because he had once written quite a funny little article before the Japanese war about the Vichy French, etc. was blinded by the Japanese and then brought in to us – he used to sit for hours and recite French poetry till we learned it by heart. He *was* a nice man, with nice 19th-century tastes. I find that I can remember so much and so correctly – do admit, jolly clever – of Lamartine, and Sully Prudhomme, and de Musset.

So doesn't it sound a nice room? You would have slept next door in a bigger and barer room; so you would have come into me in my big walnut bed.

?.5.52

Listen, beloved – I have spent the last three hours trying to write to you – such an awful letter, so now it is just notes.

I am here *only* because you wanted me to be: because you wanted me to make my own plans. I write you gay letters and try to lead a normal life because I do not think I would be doing what you wanted unless I did, but only pretending to. Nothing else keeps me here. I can scarcely endure your unhappiness in the letter you wrote yesterday. But with your dear speeches, I can bear yours and my own if that is what you want.

Thank you for willing me not to sleepwalk. I know it helps. There are nights when I don't. At least I suppose I don't. Sometimes I wake out of bed and that is not so bad, but sometimes I wake in bed and see my gloves and bag put ready on the table, or the light on and all my books in neat little piles on the floor. And that is rather unnerving. But *don't* worry about windows and things. I don't any more. I sleep with your telegram.

Tell me about the children when you can.

I think you are turning into an old Sgt Major.

5.5.52

I leave Geneva on either Tuesday or Wednesday, fly either to London or break my journey for a few days in either Paris or Brussels. I shall have then been away a month, or almost, which is what I planned.

Do you want to meet me here, where you have a definite invitation, or in Paris or in Brussels? It would be such heaven to be together in the sun. All I shall say. I left England because you asked me to. I do feel well. I shall not ask you to – but it is a practical time if you want to come.

Don't forget – there is a point beyond which one cannot go in sadness or in gloom. I get frightened, as you know, for you sometimes.

Oh my darling, Nick, I am laughing with tears pouring down my face. Of all the absurd ways to write – you have tied me in knots, my darling!

27.5.52

Hold on to something, hold on.

We are not well you know.

A letter from you tomorrow perhaps – like the telephone perhaps, or worse. I will not mind it very much until I see you – because until we see each other we cannot know whether what you may have thought, what I may have thought, is true or not.

I am not well. Nor you, my darling heart. The symptoms I could not tell you, that worried me so when you were ill before.

This is important.

Your play. Finish your play.

I remember always your saying – Whatever I say or do I will come back to us, never forget this, my darling.

I will not forget it. Never forget that you have said it. You do not feel it now perhaps.

Don't worry about the telephone last night. It was cruel for both of us, from both of us? Unreality. You were wrong to say that I was doing harm more quickly than you believed possible. There was not much to harm between you as you were and I as I was last night. Unreality.

Compassion for you, for us. Because I am trying to help you.

Suddenly I remembered that you made your speech about promises. Darling love – to help me: whether you wanted to help or not. Darling, thank you. I keep it. I know it is there.

I am so utterly utterly tired. I am not well.

3.6.52

My very dear love,

I am sitting up in my bed – white shawl and nightdress – leaning against the quilted back – after such a delicious breakfast, dreaming away. The only time I ever eat breakfast in bed is in other people's houses. I do enjoy it.

No more dreaming for a little. I want to answer as fully as I can your letter. I loved you as you wrote it very much.

This telepathy – absurd in your letters. You wrote to me – 'nothing calm and reasonable can come out of the demands of sickness, sadness and hysteria.'

The same day I wrote to you – 'everything is meaningless while we are sad and ill and faintly hysterical.'

Darling – eh?

With this I agree entirely. I agreed that we had to be as well as we could apart from each other when you asked me. I have never believed that we could be entirely well apart from each other because by definition if we were, this *histoire* would never have arisen.

For this reason, my darling, I went abroad as gaily as I could, I lived a normal life and wrote to you cheerfully. This you have got to admit.

Your letters – 'I can't say there is not a gloom when there is, because you know there is anyway.' – 'Then I heard from you and wanted to cry, what else can I do.' Sorry to copy this, but you must know what you said. With these things, my darling, I had every right to believe you were not quite well. Not ill, but not well. And this you must also admit.

So that was why I wanted to see you, why I telephoned, why I got so worried and began to feel ill again. I do not believe that when you are like that it helps us to keep apart. I entirely agree with you also that it is not a good time to meet – that we may very easily hurt each other, and have tears. But I believed with my *intelligence* it is better to be together. There are things that I know technically, because of my work.

I would *not* have asked you to come up just because I was feeling ill and being sick. I *will not ask* you for that reason. I quite agree with you over that.

Blackmail. We have both said that the other used it. In fact we have both used it. I feel very deeply that we will not use it again. I am your dear mistress. I promise you I am trying to act with dignity and sense. I know I am not always successful.

So that has answered your letter that I loved.

Please please be sweet and answer this letter.

I felt so flat when you finished your play. Gosh, you did work.

9.6.52

I am writing a book about Camp – because you are my only beloved exorcist. Did you know your love has eaten tree-trunks and roots? Is intimately acquainted with cat-skinning? Did you know that your love was photographed with a number two feet wide hung round her neck? That we had one coffin – and it used to go out in the afternoon not quite closed?

Oh darling, do laugh. With you I do laugh about it. That is what is so extraordinary.

?.6.52

Before I answer your letter I must write something very hard for me to say. Please read it with as much love as you can. Please read it over and over and try to understand it.

Before last October my spiritual welfare was of great importance to me. Because I could not accept the outward and visible things of any one Church I think the other ones were more with me because there was nothing else to carry them. The last six months has not altered this. Did you realise that?

Because we love, your spiritual welfare is of equal importance to me. And that is that.

This you will have to take on faith, as you take my love. You do not *know* I am not a wicked woman using you for my pleasure (darling, such pleasure, not enough, she says) or for the presents I can get out of you.

In October *I* made you go, and it did not work. I had to think again – and realised in time that you only found some belief when you found you loved me. I found something too, and you knew it. We were and always would be tied together and would never escape from each other – those implications – deadness of one sort or another.

This is all with my *intelligence* – not my heart. Our welfare and its *complexity* over time. Which is what I carry always before me. I say 'ours' because this is the one and only place love comes into the whole business. 'Ours' because if I ignore your welfare I am lost: if you ignore mine yours is finished.

I cannot talk to you much about God yet. You hurt me so much in Jan. when you rejected what I tried to tell you, that I cannot yet talk about it. I will be able to in time, I know. I do not make a god of love. I do not make a god of *anything*. I understand now that God can be perceived with love, and I understand now that this is for me necessarily a mystical experience *only* gained through love. Perhaps in time I shall understand that God is love. Read the N.T. more carefully: it *never* says God is loving other people or God is self-love or God is love through self-sacrifice (these last two only inversions of each other) but that God is love.

I did not think that I should ever gain this much understanding even, because I felt it was so much not my cup. But this much I now understand because of us loving. And you learned to believe, because of us loving.

Forgive me. I cannot write more. I am not yet sure enough to write more. I do not think you can say 'God to me will always be more in terms of conscience.' You have only been acquainted with belief for six months, and that you didn't get through conscience. The N.T. does not lead one to think this is true.

My problem is straightforward, yes. What I want is simple and definite – a life together. From this we deduce that my problem is your problem.

A Worthy Thought

If you're not lighting any candles,
don't complain about the dark.

Anonymous

Lord, open my eyes to opportunities to
share Your hope with others. Help me to
see when You have already opened the
door and someone is standing near me with
a candle that needs to be lit. Help me to
always carry a light and be ready. Amen.

making some definite progress though the specialist says it will be a long time before she is quite well. She had a complete breakdown and had I not called in the specialist when I did she might have died. There is no doubt in any of our minds that her illness was due in great measure to the shock of hearing unexpectedly that you had planned to go off to Spain without telling her, and to the cruel and many of them untrue things you said to her during that terrible night at Arundel. These have gone round and round in her mind ever since, torturing and bewildering her beyond endurance. You must try to understand the agony of the past four or five months in case there is any way in which you can help her. She could not and cannot still understand how you could keep on telling her that she would always be your responsibility, and yet go off without any explanation or expression of regret. It is not as if you did not know what you meant to her. I know that you did, and that you and she had shared a profound experience. The disillusionment and destruction of faith in everything and everybody is tragic, and she has a dreadful sense of failure.

It is very hard for me to write this letter, but I feel you should know what has happened – I think you do realise your responsibility. The conviction that you could not be leading a genuinely Christian life while hurting her so much seems to have been one of her great anxieties all these months – a fear for your soul.

I have asked Fr —— to let me know when Fr Raynes comes to London: it may be advisable to see him.

24.11.52

Dear Nick,

Thank you very much for writing to me so fully. I don't think it will help at present if you see each other. If later, however, I think it might, I will write to you again.

She is a little better, but progress is very slow.

Yours sincerely,

5

Oh yes, one of the oldest stories in the world: a maiden betrayed; a would-be Faust staggering off to new lacerations and self-lacerations.

Or – out of a maelstrom of love and desire and despair and pain and savagery – what indeed in time might be the workings-out of a pattern?

When one confesses to God one tells only the bad things about oneself; one does not give one's own side of the story, as it were: it is presumed that God knows this anyway.

To reproduce Mary's letters is some sort of a confession.

But what of a reader?

Every time – whether for virtue or self-preservation – I tried to stop seeing Mary, she became ill; people let me know she was ill; she could not eat, which was for the most part the result of her experiences in the wartime prison camp.

If I went to see her then she could eat; she got well.

So what is virtue; and what is preservation or self-preservation?

The 'promises' that I made to her were aimed at reassuring her that I would try to see her get well. Oh of course there was (is?) self-delusion and self-justification in this! What were the conditions of her getting well? We indeed managed often enough to have a good time. And then with such love and passion all things might seem possible – or even right. But then again this seemed deception.

In the course of the confusion I myself took on the trappings of becoming somewhat ill.

What sacrifice, I wondered, might I ultimately make for Mary, who seemed to have been so much of a sacrifice herself – the child in *The Magic Mountain* torn apart by hags? I felt I might be ready to die, oh yes, if she were able to get well. But what fantasy: and what good would this be for others?

All this is the stuff of fairy stories. And fairy stories tell of fearful journeys in the dark: of sorrows, pains, break-ups, that have to be undergone if, in time, there is to be healing, change.

But what of others caught up on the way?

Rosemary herself had once been to me the agent of pointing, of change. I told Rosemary such 'truth' as seemed to be proper about Mary. But the words to describe truth seemed to be now one thing, now another. I did not want to break or indeed damage my marriage with Rosemary. But had not Rosemary and I reached a state of some unreality? Perhaps things had to get somewhat out of control (did Rosemary and I both glimpse this?) for there to be learning, change.

Rosemary was hurt. But she said – You must do what you think proper about Mary.

Sometimes in later life it seemed that if at the beginning it did not appear possible for me to abandon Mary, then it would have been better if I had tried to conform to the conventions of my parents' generation and had had no scruples about setting her up as my mistress and we had all tried to lead conventional double lives. Mary herself at moments had suggested this. But then, what we all seemed to be trying to learn was something opposite to duplicity.

I should never have asked Mary out to dinner? But what had such conventions to do with efforts against duplicity?

Of course, it could be said that in spite of the pain it just suited me for a time to keep, like a juggler, all my implements as it were up in the air at the same time.

It seems to me now that the characters of Richard and Elisabeth in *The Rainbearers* had little in common with myself and Rosemary – except in so far as they were representative of dreams of Gardens of Eden running down. Richard and Elisabeth were too passive: it is a common experience amongst novelists to make characters representative of themselves too passive: like this perhaps they hope to avoid a sense of responsibility and shame. But we were all of us, in reality and in the fiction, involved in journeys to do with change; and were concerned with what might be the agency of change.

From the beginning the business with Mary had got mixed up with God: my friend the novice monk had referred to Mary as a 'saint'; she herself, after a time, reluctantly spoke of God. As the real-life story went along I told it to Father Raynes. He did not comment much except to show concern, especially for Rosemary and the children. He said he would do what he could for Mary. As for me (though this was hardly spoken) – Well indeed, what might I learn?

Always with Father Raynes there was the impression that what mattered about human tragedy or comedy was the chance to see the place of these in some cosmic pattern that was being worked out (that had been worked out?) as it were round some corner.

One of the more bizarre and mundane bits of business that turned up at this time was that as a result of what seemed momentarily at least my step towards a deeper Christian commitment by the act of confession, I had been approached – just after my meeting with Mary when we had decided not to see one another again – by some friends of Father Raynes with the suggestion that I might become the editor of a Christian magazine they were thinking of starting – a sort of Anglican counterpart to the Roman Catholic *The Tablet*. They were trying to raise money for this, and perhaps their thought of such an unlikely candidate as myself for editor was not just because of my mysterious 'conversion' but because I was someone to whom they might not have to pay a salary. Negotiations about all this went on through the winter. For committee meetings I had to make frequent journeys to London: and would it not indeed have been showing a cowardly lack of faith if in these circumstances I had refused to visit my sick Mary? Oh justifications! But still – what of truth? It did not seem possible by reason, by efforts of will, to disentangle truth, self-delusion, charity.

What I was learning, I suppose (though in turmoil and misery I was hardly aware of this), was the way in which a true Christian (to me, Father Raynes) seemed to see things in quite a different style from that in which other Christians and non-Christians (and indeed my old self) seemed to see things. Father Raynes seemed to take for granted that God did not make use just of pious human behaviour to do His will (how indeed, it seemed to me later, could anyone reading the Old Testament imagine He did?); God might use any means that seemed available, within the human set-up of free-will. And the qualifications for a person to be available to be used by God – either for His own sake or for the sake of others – seemed to depend just on His choosing, in spite of confusion and wrong-doing, to watch, to listen, to remain open, just to whatever is occurring or has occurred. In the Bible there were the morally ambiguous stories of David and Bathsheba, Jacob and Leah, Rachel and Bilhah. I had once thought I could score off Christians by saying – But the God of the Old Testament is so immoral! Now it seemed that a true Christian could say – Yes indeed God can be what humans call immoral! the pattern of redemption so evidently does not depend on what is conventionally held to be moral or immoral.

The plans for the Anglican magazine did not in fact come to fruition at this time: they stayed like seeds under the earth, along with other more heartfelt matters. I hid myself away to get on with *The Rainbearers*; I was also writing the play that Mary had referred to in her letters. This was a weird drama in verse (hardly shown to anyone, let alone not published) about Savonarola, the monk-dictator in fifteenth-century Florence. I suppose I felt Savonarola was somewhat like Father Raynes. In my play Savonarola's followers have faith in him, lose faith, then find it again – but only always in terms of their or his immolation. I suppose I had no faith at this time that there could be any visibly worked-out pattern in terms of life as a going concern in relation to myself and Mary. Certainly in *The Rainbearers* I felt it was my job to be as mournful, as self-lacerating, as I could. Here is a scene in which Mary's old friend whom she ends up with, Mr Gabriel, talks to her about the character of Richard –

'I hated him the first time I saw him with his dog face waiting for temptations and disasters and I hate him now when he has got them and is licking his teeth about the bones. I hate him for being an idealist without strength and a hypocrite without ability. I hate him because now he has hurt you like the dog that kills the sheep he comes crawling back to his master and whines there at his feet. I hate him because having eaten his carcass he needs a God to purge him of it.'

'I only know,' Mary said, 'that it will make him rotten.'

'Good God, Mary, need you worry about him? He had no God before. He has been rotten from the start – a man with no hope of anything but rottenness, someone who preys upon what is given him and then smashes it and runs in fear. Didn't I tell you this? I told it to him, even when I hated him. He will go back to his wife's bed and he will beg her cold forgiveness and then he'll be off again for another bed to make filthy. He's finished, empty, someone with too many curses from the beginning, a wastrel rich and impotent on the edge of the world's decadence like a plant that goes to seed without ever flowering. He and his wife are like that, predatory without giving beauty, introverts and outcasts with no actions to fit their dreams.'

This might be a display of penance, all right. But I had imagined *The Rainbearers* to be some paean or love-song to Mary, and how did I think that such displays of self-laceration could be of help to Mary? This was a delusion, I suppose, I had picked up from conventional Christianity.

There were obvious senses in which Mr Gabriel's imprecations against Richard might be relevant to myself: I was indeed perhaps at this time in danger of being 'a plant that goes to seed without ever flowering'. Sometimes the feel of this comes out in the writing of *The Rainbearers*: the style becomes stifling, overblown; it swirls and eddies, flies off the handle; there is a yelling like that of a victim in a burning room. At the end it is true there is some stillness, listening. But did I know for what, in unconventional terms, I might be hoping?

Perhaps when I had told Rosemary about Mary I had hoped that she would fight; would take responsibility away from me by saying – Of course you must never see this woman again! But still, I probably would have done: and Rosemary, like me, had faith in the idea that if one is not to be trapped one has to take responsibility for oneself.

I wish that Rosemary could have told her own confessionary stories of the time. Rosemary was always brave enough to take responsibility for herself.

I sometimes heard news of Mary through one or two friends and through members of the Community of the Resurrection who went to visit her. Father Raynes was dispassionate and practical – for instance I might indeed be able to help her in the matter of money. This I did. For the rest, he seemed to be saying – There is no point in guilt: you recognise what is your responsibility and what is not; then indeed others may have the chance to do this, and something may have the chance to go its proper way.

But I was writing *The Rainbearers*. Good heavens, was not much of Western literature to do with laceration and self-laceration? Could I really write a novel in which all characters might be seen as being responsible for themselves?

It sometimes seemed that Father Raynes, by his silences when one was with him, was saying just – It's difficult, of course, to see things in the pattern of what they are –

– Let's wait, and be still, and listen; and then we may find out what really is happening and has perhaps been happening all the time.

The time came when *The Rainbearers* was finished and was ready to show to my new publishers. They agreed that it was better than *A Garden of Trees*, and should be published first. And so now I was thinking – For Mary, will this not be like the bird coming back to the Ark with an olive branch in its mouth; will she not see it as a monument to love? (I really thought this? Well, monuments are often to insanities that seemed glorious.)

Then I learned that Mary had heard that *The Rainbearers* was to be published and had got one of her literary friends to procure a proof copy; and now she had gone to a lawyer who had written to my publishers to say that if the book was published she would sue for libel.

(A monument on a battlefield? Mary! What do you mean? Mary!)

(Should I not have remembered that love, indeed like a thumb-screw, can be vengeful and pursuing?)

My publishers explained that there was a routine concerning such threats of libel against novels: the publisher's lawyers wrote to the complainant's lawyers and asked exactly what details in the book were objected to; the complainant had to specify these, and then it was usually not too difficult for them to be changed. But when I talked to the friend of Mary's who had got hold of the proof I learned, of course, that this was not the point: it was not this or that part of the book that Mary objected to but the whole thing, the fact that I had written it. And still, of course, mainly what she minded were the facts of what had occurred. So if I went ahead and published the book even in an amended form I would just be dropping another load of pain upon Mary – casting her endlessly in the role of sacrificial victim. And this was just what I had said I wanted to help her to escape from! All right, so what was I going to do? It was understandable, this friend suggested, that I might have had a personal need to write the book, but how in fact was I going to demonstrate the 'love' that I kept on talking about? Was not the choice quite simple: I could either go on hurting Mary, or I could stop the book and hurt myself.

And indeed, what should a good Christian do?

So I told my publishers that I would withdraw the book, and would reimburse them for their costs.

This was a serious business for me because I was now thirty and had only published one book and that was three years before. And my publishers were now not all that eager to publish *A Garden of Trees* and I myself no longer had the stomach for it; it was to do with things now so distant and shadowy compared to *The Rainbearers*. This was a bad time for me – with regard to my writing, to my marriage, to my family, to love. But still – look, listen (but do not talk about this too much!): might I not after all, the way things were going with this libel business, have a chance after a time of talking once more with Mary?

But in the meantime – oh indeed a long winter! with nothing much seeming to be growing.

Father Raynes came to stay with Rosemary and me. Rosemary's

grandmother had now died and her enormous house in Hertford-shire had been sold and some of her marvellous paintings and pieces of furniture had filtered through to us. So we now lived in some style behind our high brick walls – with our two children, nanny, a cook and a gardener. Father Raynes would sit in our elegant draw-ing-room in his black cassock and with his gaunt and shaven head; he was like some figure of death-and-resurrection in a Bergman film. The children liked playing with him; when he was with them his face would light up as if a candle had been placed within a Hallowe'en pumpkin. Father Raynes had no small talk; he liked to tell stories about his time in South Africa where as a missionary he had spent the central part of his life; he liked to grumble about railways. But for the most part his presence was such that people found themselves asking questions of, and answering, themselves – questions that they had hardly thought of asking; receiving answers that they had not expected. It began to dawn on me that although Father Raynes seemed pleased to stay with Rosemary and me, there were things behind his silences that needed to be enquired into as if they were rooms that had never been explored in our own house. In *The Rainbearers* I had seen what might be some lack at the centre of a life such as Rosemary's and mine; but it was typical, I suppose, that I had not seen an aspect that later seemed so obvious. However, the time came when in Father Raynes's presence I found myself asking – Did he think, by any chance, that there might be anything that might be called 'wrong' about Rosemary's and my style of life? I think perhaps even then I did not expect much of an answer; I had indulged in conventional self-lacerations about my egocentric behaviour, had I not? But now Father Raynes said, hesitantly – as if he were indeed feeling the burden of taking other people's responsibilities on himself – Well, yes he did think, as a matter of fact, since I had asked, that there might be something wrong with our relationship with the children.

It seems to me now extraordinary that in all the putting-up of smokescreens and the efforts to break through in *The Rainbearers* there was hardly anything said about Richard's and Elisabeth's children – they were shadowy creatures existing in parts of the house as it were occupied by servants. This was how Rosemary and

I had been brought up: we had tried to break away from our pasts in ways that were not too difficult for us, but it seems that our early conditioning was so ingrained that it never occurred to us to question this style that we were perpetuating. (Nor indeed did it yet strike me that my own early conditioning behind green baize doors with nannies might have something to do with the hungers and pursuits and confusions concerning love that I was finding myself involved with; but this realisation belongs to a later part of the story.) Now Father Raynes just seemed to suggest – well, he did not really seem to suggest anything, it was just that Rosemary and I now found ourselves having to look at the question – what on earth were we doing in this upper-class business of handing children over to nannies?

So after a time we got rid of Nanny. We took on more responsibility with the children, though other lesser helpers came and went. To learn about love – love of children, love of loved-ones – is a long hard process if one has to go back to a new beginning – a learning about love that was hardly provided for one at the right time. Even then what one learns is that there are no exact answers: there are only the questions that endlessly have to be looked at – questions concerning the particular conflicts, impossibilities, predicaments, that each person finds himself involved with at any time.

All this was happening at the same time as the miseries and difficulties attendant on *The Rainbearers*: it seemed an endless winter with old energies cracking up and old assurances dying; new comforts not yet growing. I hoped perhaps (though this was what could not be talked about) that there might be connections between what on the surface seemed so lonely, and that which underground might be growing.

When I had withdrawn *The Rainbearers* from publication I had asked doctors and mutual friends that if ever the time came when Mary might be able to envisage an amended form of the book, then perhaps there could be discussions about alterations. I did not know if this time would ever come. But then in the summer I was told by her friend – Yes all right, Mary was now well enough to discuss changes.

So in the end *The Rainbearers* was published. Of the changes that were made some were trivial, a few weakened the book; but it did not seem to be exactly this that mattered.

So what did matter?

Here are extracts from the letters that Mary wrote to me at this time – beginning two years after the last time I had heard from her, and moving ahead of the time here reached by the rest of the story. Some pattern begins to come to fruition – a pattern that might perhaps be thought too contrived for serious fiction – to do with life and change.

2.7.54

Will you send me the galleys of *The Rainbearers* in order that I may re-read them please. I will not be able to get in touch with you about them until after July 20th, but I will do so after that.

11.8.54

Thank you for the proofs of *The Rainbearers*. I have re-read it, and now can discuss specific omissions and alterations with you.

I could meet you next Tuesday 17th at 2.30. This will involve rearranging some things, so could you let me know as soon as you can if this time is convenient for you. I gather from your last letter to —— that you would prefer to see me without lawyers.

In that case I think the best place to meet would be at ——'s house. I will of course be by myself.

18.11.54

Thank you for your letter. I quite understand that you were anxious to hear about the book. I am sorry I have taken longer than I thought I would.

If you publish the book I would be glad if you would delete –

1. Descriptions of clothes – grey skirt, black trousers, etc.
2. Dark blue writing paper.
3. The 'matches'.
4. Phrases in Mary's letter that are the same as phrases I wrote to you.

I believe we discussed these points, and you agreed to remove them.

I said 'if you publish' because it is now up to you to decide whether to go ahead with it. I will not make any effort to stop the amended edition if you believe that in it you have met all the objections that I have any right to make.

The changes made appear to me superficial.

Here in effect is still the story of a girl who suffered rather particularly during the war, who was hungry and ill-treated, who lost a parent, who was crippled emotionally by this suffering, who did not want to go on living, etc. etc. Some years later she had an affair with a married man. When the man shattered their relationship very suddenly she broke down completely (I do not think that you can really believe you have got rid of the atmosphere of mental collapse).

I will not attempt to stop you publishing this version, but I believe you will be acting both wrongly and cruelly if you do.

I do understand you had a very great need to write this book, and now a very great need to fight for it. I am certain this need arises not simply out of wanting to write a novel, but also out of a great desire to resolve something within you. It seemed very clear when we talked that you recognised this at least partially. I do not know what will resolve it, but I am certain that to publish the book as it now stands will be no resolution, but will only deepen the muddle by adding to it something more of deliberate cruelty and misconception.

I would be glad if you would later let me know your final decision so that I shall know what I must expect.

22.7.56

I never answered your letter about the book because there was nothing at the time that I thought it would help to say.

But now I would like to see you very much. Will you let me know if this can be arranged? I shall need to know a little in advance because work must be reorganised.

30.7.56

I have been thinking a great deal about our last meeting. My strong inclination is to postpone another till the later autumn, unless you are yourself confident that something helpful would come of a meeting next Wednesday, in which case of course I would be glad to see you.

I feel that a number of things were said which, as you readily agree, were true but which you hadn't really been able to take into account. Hence, perhaps, one or two of your curious little volte-faces. You may need time to assimilate these things, and I would like you to have this time, there is no particular hurry.

I need to know – for reasons which you said you understood – what you are and how you are capable of acting, both inwards and outwardly. Circumstances have made you appear in one light; I have always believed in you (not in what you did) in another. Now that

I am well, it is time and very necessary – before I move on to other things – to know whether I was right to hold this belief in you.

Try not to muddle this with talk of my becoming 'positively' involved with you. That was inappropriate and rather indelicate. I am inevitably 'dependent' on you in that the shape of my life today was fixed by your actions five years ago. And this is a shape utterly unlike the shape – both present and potential – it was. You can't avoid that, but words like forgiveness, expiation, responsibility, redemption, do have meaning, and these we can't avoid either – nor, I think, do we want to. Bless you.

27.11.56

Thank you for your letter which made me very happy.

Because of it I can perhaps say more clearly what I was struggling to say when we met – We have a common problem (though its aspects are very different) rising out of events and actions that occurred and occurred irrevocably. We cannot solve it together but it can be solved apart if we both admit it and work with it. What was making it incapable of solution was a denial of its existence.

Now I feel that together we have accepted and defined it, and each in our own and separate ways of life can get on with solving it.

As for the money – I need nothing at the moment and am well. If the emergency arises you have now placed me in a position where I shall have no compunction but great confidence in asking you, and I promise that I will. For the rest that we discussed in the summer – this probably is one part of the solution and lies, I think you will understand, in the next positive step (whatever it may be) being taken by you.

Bless you, darling.

14.4.58

Your letter has moved me deeply and made me very happy.

Thank you, darling –

– on the practical level, for making possible a freedom that I now need very much. I am grateful.

– on the other level, for this next step, and for all it implies.

Of course there is hope. I am so utterly and profoundly glad that you feel it. I have never wished you other than this sort of hope – I know that I have learned in the six years that there is always at least some hope when a problem is acknowledged; but without this recognition, no real choice and hence despair – much of it, I should imagine, unconscious.

Of course, too, I see the difficulties of being avuncular to your anima. That did make me giggle. The first time I have ever known you flippant about something of great seriousness. I *do* approve – the implication being that it is manageable (where have you found your Jungian jargon – at Kramer's table?).

But understand what it means to both of us for me to write about gratitude (truly felt) when there was and could only have been grief at things done. This is not the same as forgiveness (which for the original act came earlier than perhaps you knew) but it is as necessary.

My feeling is still that after that it will perhaps be more difficult to go on communicating than not. Do we envisage a time when we meet without behaving like two badly set jellies? Bless you, darling Nick.

5.5.58

We both remember it slightly wrong: it is –

> Peace I leave with you, my peace I give unto you: not as the world giveth, give I unto you. Let not your heart be troubled, neither let it be afraid.

I always pray for you (not quite as you do – I try to be clear here only to avoid the cosiness of shared mysticism, etc. which we talked about the other evening). But I will now remember in my prayers your present fear of 'means'.

Darling – to be intimidated by means is an almost universal condition of human existence. That they are frightening need not mean more than that.

It is good of you to arrange to see your accountant about the money so quickly. Thank you.

Regarding this, I am touched by what you tell me of Father Raynes – you never told me that before. Obviously this makes a difference to my assessment of the part he played as an individual. Probably not, though, as a symbol of authority.

Some day I would like to discuss with you the part symbols played in both our lives six years ago.

6

So (God help us) what might have been the patterns being shown to each of us through these years? That at the heart of love there is perhaps after all no impossibility? Or rather – of course there is! but if you look at this, hold on, trust – then in spite of what seem to be terrible dead-ends, miseries, illusions, there is – what? – just this which there was after a number of years!

One turning-point in this story seems to me to have been, roughly, when Rosemary and I tried to become more responsible with our children. Nanny went; we looked around; what on earth were we supposed to do? We played games with them and read to them in the evenings; we took them on holidays abroad. We ourselves read John Bowlby's *Child Care and the Growth of Love*; Ian Suttie's *The Origins of Love and Hate*. We learned – how frightening is the relationship with children! what power a parent has over love and hate: what power children have over one's own self-love or self-hate! No wonder people run away from, are savage about, their children. And indeed about my own conditioning as a child – my mother's not trusting herself to look after her children even on Nanny's afternoon off – might it not have been this that led to myself in later life looking for love like a hungry cat under dustbin-lids in alleys? I do not suppose I saw this clearly even then: but I saw that whatever I had inherited had given me little confidence with children. Confidence had to be learned, inch by inch; both in the time we spent with the children, and through what we could gather about why this seemed so difficult.

We read Freud, Melanie Klein: they explained what might be at the back of fear and inability; they did not say much about how things might be better. I read Jung; he seemed to agree – of course a proper life is like a tightrope! regarding children – too much care can be stifling, too little even worse. There are no answers, no; only processes of constantly changing discovery. For everything learned, there is probably a harder task which follows.

Rosemary and I continued to go to the weekends at South Park where we had first met Father Raynes. We took friends and relations; some were affected, some not. I struggled to try to observe some of the routines of an Anglo-Catholic life; occasionally I seemed to succeed; more often not. Rosemary and I said prayers with the children at night; on Sundays we took them to church where the services went so slowly that the children slid under the pews in boredom or despair. But we still wanted, needed, to get away on our own to work. Rosemary did for a time almost give up painting: this was a time of hardship for her. But then there were the helpers, au pairs, to share the day-to-day business with the children.

Rosemary would get up at dawn to paint the sunrise over Worthing beach. I embarked on my fourth novel. In the afternoons I set about clearing a large silted-up pond at the bottom of the garden in which a cow was reputed to have drowned. I stood up to my waist in water and flung shovelfuls of mud on to the bank. I thought – Perhaps the cow was trying to work out something about life.

There were still the delights which were the chasm, as it were, on the other side of the tightrope – the tightrope that seemed to be the path between self-discipline and spontaneity. We often enjoyed the trappings of country-house life; we had friends to stay at weekends, we ourselves played childish games and talked and danced into the night. These were the days when there was a grown-up craze for acting-games – charades, 'in the manner of the word', the game in which someone makes a list of things like the title of a play or a book and then one person from each of two teams has to mime these in a guessing-race with the other side.

'Fun' was pretending to be something other than oneself! and others having to guess who you were.

In London there was still the easy conviviality of just-post-war life: pubs and restaurants and night-clubs were cheap: it was understood that those who could pay would pay for friends who could not. There was a magic area of Soho which contained the Gargoyle, the Colony Room, the French Pub, the Stork Room: in any or all of these one would be likely to bump into friends. This was before the time when money and snobbery pushed people back into privileged compartments. When feeling energetic one could venture to 100 Oxford Street where Humphrey Lyttelton (with whom I had been at school; when he had joined the army he had for a while left in my care his marvellous collection of early jazz records) was introducing traditional jazz to an audience of ungainly Londoners; we hurled ourselves into the dance; we spun and lurched like gyroscopes running down. Rosemary and I rented a flat in which we could stay when we were in London; here the revelry could continue to the tunes of old favourites on the gramophone – 'If You Knew Suzy', 'You're Driving Me Crazy', 'You Ought to See Sally on Sunday'. There were times, indeed, when in this part of life it was all too difficult not to topple off one's tightrope; there were evenings when I felt I was like the drunken man looking under lamplight for the key he has lost in the dark. And in the mornings – could it really be true that this sort of thing did not matter very much so long as one saw what one was doing? that things would be worked out if one could clamber back on to one's tightrope? I continued to wonder – Is all this some sort of romantic fog I have been enveloped by; or through it am I really learning what human beings are?

After one long night I was rung up by a gossip-journalist who asked me what I was giving up for Lent: I said – Talking about God in night-clubs.

But indeed what might it mean being, or trying to be, a Christian, if one accepted that it did not mean simply sticking to given routines? St Augustine had said – Love and do as you will. The implication seemed to be that in time, if one tried to love truly, one's style of love would change. But was this true? (Or indeed – what was truth?)

Once during this time there was a renewed attempt to get me to be editor of an Anglican magazine. Just before I was due to be interviewed by a panel of Church dignitaries there was a night of particular revelry in the Gargoyle during which dancers had wheeled and gyrated to a point of Dionysian exhaustion; some onlooker had telephoned a Sunday tabloid and a photographer had turned up and taken pictures; these had included one of myself propped up like a dying swan on the supportive shoulder of Sarah, the wife of my great friend Raymond Carr. The pictures appeared in the tabloid in a centre-page spread, headed – 'The Chelsea Set at Play'. Perhaps my panel of Church dignitaries did not read tabloids; anyway, a few days later they did not seem to blink. I had wondered if this might be the end of my candidature for the job of editor of a holy magazine – but no such chance.

This sort of life was spasmodic; it occurred in intervals from work. Sometimes it was patently overdone. One summer I was staying with friends in the south of France while Rosemary remained at home because she was again pregnant; I and the friends made a home movie called *The Grave-digger's Mother* which was even more indecorous than *The Policeman's Mother* of seven years before; we got close to being arrested for unseemly behaviour in a local cemetery. I was taking care not to fall off the tightrope on the side of piety all right! But from home, Rosemary wrote me a letter about one of our children:

> He desperately needs a father to be with him or about actively a lot and for discipline, as a man and head of the family is a vital influence for a child like him and he can be safely disciplined by you without resentment and resulting cussedness, as the mother is still there gentle and firm. He is a problem in one's life and is very rude to Mrs —— and I do hope he won't call —— a smelly worm or she may leave. I think that this father-influence and time given to it are infinitely more important than getting —— to South Park (I mean re your time this should come first, or we are all going to suffer) and it should be only a matter of time before home becomes normal again and then excessive demands on you should cease. I don't know how we are going to manage this, but I think it is the most important thing in our lives at the moment, which must be faced up to. Do think it over.

I keep dreaming I am going to be hung, except for 2 nights ago when I was in a small boat and a whale swum under it.

To people who knew us in the country we did seem to have the reputation (or so they said) of being a dutiful and even unusually happy family; and it was true, indeed, that we were often having a shot at this. Weekends with friends from London were tailing off; neighbouring families liked to come to the house. There was a new game I invented which was a mixture of fives and real tennis and was played by four people round the three sides of a courtyard of farm buildings; sometimes at crucial moments the ball had to be pursued into the bull-pen in which there was either a bull or knee-high manure. This game became very popular with young and old.

But there was a central difficulty, it seemed to me, about trying to be a good husband and father-of-a-family and at the same time trying to be what was seen as a 'good' writer. To be a novelist one had to observe life, not to turn away, to be attentive to what turned up: how else could one imagine that what one wrote might be 'true'? Of course, this might give licence for any sort of ludicrous behaviour; but this was a tightrope on which novelists had always trod. To be a novelist one had to observe the multifariousness of experience rather than to be committed to one view of it; but how could this be reconciled with the Christian idea of 'good' – especially with the idea of a good family? For this it seemed that there had to be limitations, disciplines, a special commitment. And indeed, what good novelist had been known to be a good father of a family? Oh I remembered Father Raynes saying that there was freedom in true Christianity! that one had to trust, and then what happened would be taken care of. There was even a true Christian tightrope – 'Whosoever will save his life shall lose it', and so on. But I was beginning to feel a compulsion to end my particular precarious balancing act; to face what did seem to be a rottenness in the old style of romantic dalliance or agony and the use of this to write novels. I felt the demand to be more obviously committed: but then I did not see how to go on writing novels. But at the same time there seemed to be creeping in on me some dissatisfaction with novels: or at least with the way in which I had been following tradition in writing novels.

The elaborate, somewhat turgid operatic style in which I had been accustomed to write had been suitable it seemed for characters (or indeed for authors) who felt themselves trapped in a smoke-screen or fog; who sang sad songs in the gloom or who shouted to get out. But was this really the style of what I felt was now happening in my life? Was I not now more interested in looking and listening for what might be a way through – or at least in the sort of character who saw that he might have been conditioned into thinking he was trapped in a fog, and by just the ability to see this might be begin-ning to get out?

The novel that I began writing after *The Rainbearers* was called *Corruption*. People used to say – But it is not about corruption! I would say – Corruption is the illusion that one is in a predicament in which one is not.

The story is as follows:

My hero, Robert, is someone who from the beginning sees himself as a victim; he is the poor relation of an aristocratic family and since childhood he has harboured a starry-eyed but apparently hopeless passion for his cousin Kate, who is two years older than he and comes from the rich and powerful branch of the family. In childhood he and she had both been members of a gang that played games together – on one occasion sexual games. Later, when Robert is sixteen, they find themselves together in the country and they have a brief sexual encounter while exploring a cave. But Kate then elopes and marries and has a child; Robert is left nursing his hope-less passion. Some years later he comes across Kate yet again and he finds that she has been using his name as a cover with which to deceive her husband while she has been going out with someone else; her husband apparently thinks that he, Robert, would be a harmless companion. Kate does now agree in fact to go off for a weekend with Robert – but then it seems that she is doing this so that her husband may have grounds for divorce. Her husband does divorce her, citing Robert as co-respondent. But by this time Kate has gone to live with the man with whom, presumably, she had been going out when she said she had been going out with Robert.

So indeed Robert feels a victim. But he knows he has chosen this. So at least he feels an ironic, rather than a tragic, victim.

Years later Robert comes across Kate yet again in Venice: she is living in a palace with the multi-millionaire to whom she had gone after her weekend with Robert. Robert becomes friendly with Kate's child, now nine or ten; Kate tries to be friendly with Robert but his bitterness and wariness are like a shell. He says – No more betrayals! no more so-called love! Then one day there is a political demonstration and riot in Trieste; Robert is there with Kate and her millionaire lover and child and in the ensuing violence the child is in physical danger and in order to stir Robert to action Kate has to tell Robert (but this give-away is the point of the story!) that he is the father of the child. The child was conceived the day in the cave: Kate could hardly then have told Robert, who was still a schoolboy. She took responsibility for the child and married: and then when she wished to divorce, who better to turn to than Robert? And might not things have gone differently if Robert had not chosen even then to be so wary and bitter? Perhaps she might then have told him about the child. But still, it seems now to Robert that scales have fallen from his eyes. These scales are to do with not only the present but the past – his view of the universe is reversed in a moment of illumination: what was fog becomes bright-ness – it seems that Kate might even have loved him, as well as have been using him, all the time. The 'corruption' of the title has referred to the way in which people choose to feel at home in self-laceration and confusion rather than to look for what might involve them in acceptance of responsibility and care. At this point in the story Robert and Kate, together, rescue the child.

But then at the very end of the story Robert finds himself involved once more with renunciation – now consciously and in the light of facts to be sure – but still, this part of his pattern has not changed. He wishes to do the best for his child who hopes for a reconciliation between his mother and the man who he thinks is his father. So Robert says goodbye, romantically and ecstatically, to Kate and her child, and is once more left on his own. He has broken through some smokescreen of illusion and with Kate has recognised some sort of love. Nevertheless – here I was for what seemed to be the umpteenth time ending a novel with an act of immolation.

In the writing of *Corruption* there is some development from that of *The Rainbearers* because although it is in much the same elaborate (what reviewers called 'baroque') style, the emotionalism is for much of the time as it were turned against itself – the story is deliberately about the propensity of humans to put up smokescreens and about the toils that result from this – and because of this irony the style does have some authenticity even if it slips over all too easily into exaggeration and disarray. The sentences wind in and out of each other like snakes, like filigree, indeed like strands of fog; but then do not humans often live much of their lives in a fog of illusion, projection, self-blame, denial – and is it not only by recognising this that there is some chance of breaking through? Stories that present the minds and experiences of humans as resolute and all-of-a-piece are (so I could well argue) not much to do with human life at all.

My favourite authors at this time were Proust and Henry James and, above all, William Faulkner. Regarding the first two – did they not spin their magnificent filigree-screens with words so that through these, by such filtering and focusing processes, there might break through – aesthetically, morally – some profound illumination? And with regard to William Faulkner – the first novel of his that I had read had been *The Sound and the Fury* which I had come across in the Red Cross library of a liberated prisoner-of-war camp in Italy: this had opened my eyes to what truth-to-life in a novel might be! The first eighty pages or so are told by a congenital idiot; it is only when the reader is about two-thirds of the way through the book that he sees, in a flash, not only the present but the past – So this is what the whole story has been about! There has been ignorance and confusion; then suddenly there is pattern, meaning. I had thought – Yes, this can be a way of writing about what experience is truly like. How arbitrary and imposed is the form of most traditional novels!

But moments of illumination in the books that I loved were still usually to do with self-immolation; they did not seem to represent life as a successfully going concern. There is self-immolation in Proust's idea of redemption through memory and aesthetic vision; in Henry James's unravelling of moral conundrums as a result of which his heroes and heroines accept responsibilities on their own. My favourite book of all at this time was Faulkner's *The Wild Palms* in which the hero – facing life-imprisonment as a result of his unintended responsibility for the death of his girlfriend, and being offered the chance of suicide, utters a line which seems to have become a talisman for others besides myself – 'Between grief and nothing I will take grief.' But what a limitation of choice! My problem about how to write a 'good' novel that would be 'good' in a Christian sense had been further complicated by the conventional Christian emphasis on suffering and sacrifice: Christians claimed that a cosmic battle had already been won, yet much of so-called 'Christian' literature itself depended on the portrayal of nobility in defeat. It seemed to me suddenly vital, at the stage (whatever it might have been) that I had reached on my journey, that I should write no more books except ones that might talk, however obscurely, of life as a going concern; of battles, although containing tragedies, in some sense winnable or won. For life did go on, did it not? Almost the only good books that seemed to portray life explicitly in this way were children's books and those about animals.

Oh there were writers such as Jane Austen, to be sure: but in her books the portrayal of life as a successfully going concern seemed to depend on the convention that the achievement of a marriage might represent this; but at the same time her portrayals of older married couples seemed to demonstrate that it did not. There was of course, uniquely, Dostoievsky's *The Brothers Karamazov* in which at the end a group of children cry 'Hurrah!' for the good brother Alyosha for the help he has given them; but it seemed that readers and critics hardly paid attention to this, so caught up were they in the attractive and desperate travails of Dmitri and Ivan. Oh yes and indeed there were Shakespeare's late 'miracle' plays – but then in these the portrayal of human life as a successfully going concern seemed to depend, precisely, on miracles.

My own early writing had been like the cover for a military attack

– with just the distant hope that when the smoke cleared something might have broken through. Passages in *Spaces of the Dark* were like a bombardment; those in *The Rainbearers* were like groaning rocket-launchers at night; *Corruption* had suggested some breakthrough, but only in imagination at the end. There still remained the question – What in practice might happen then? It seemed that the limitations of traditional novels were partly a matter of the nature of language: language seemed structured to describe bombardments, attacks, sacrifices, self-immolations: it could touch on moments of illumination, but after that – what has language to do with calmness, stillness, comprehension, with awareness of the whole?

Here is the description of Robert's moment of illumination in *Corruption* when Kate has just told him, in the street-riot, that he is the father of her child, so that the whole way in which he sees his life is altered.

> There was a blindness then. I remember her eye like the edge of a moon and a wave obscuring it. Then the wave withdrew and with my mind I saw the whole of it and it was clear and exact like the bed of a blue sea and I understood it. Another wave came and broke against my sight and in the wake of it there was darkness and a roaring like that of blood and then it withdrew and I understood it. There was the whole of my life there and everything I had done and it was as if I were a child that only waited to be reborn and there were the waves and the dead membranes to prevent me. I saw it in coral and crystal on the bed of the blue sea and I had to fight to give it life and to be forgiven it. I began to go back to where it should have been born before and her eye stretched again like the opening at the end of a cave and I let my arms trail away down the length of her. And as I moved away from this eye into which the light had suddenly come there was a pain and a desolation such as there always are in births when things are born into the necessity for forgiveness; but I left her, and I went back to where there was a tunnel of tall trees and somewhere, like a bird, the sound of crying.

Well, perhaps a plunge through a gas-attack all right: but afterwards in what manner might an illumined life go on?

When I had finished *Corruption* I was pleased, but I did not see how I could go on – go on, that is, writing in this style. To Robert the smoke-screens were revealed as illusion: so might not this style be something that I needed to break away from too? And was not involvement with turgid emotion representative of what I was beginning to want to get away from in my life – towards a more alert or constructive understanding? So indeed it seemed that this might be an added reason for giving up writing novels – the realisation that serious novels seemed incapable of representing life as a successful concern.

Spaces of the Dark and *The Rainbearers* had had some good reviews; so, later, did *Corruption*. But the publication of the latter came at the very end of an age in which there was easy sympathy for romantic stories of self-immolation: this was the beginning of the age of the 'Angry Young Men' – of *Lucky Jim, Under the Net, Hurry on Down, Look Back in Anger*. It suddenly became the fashion in novels and plays to see things simply in terms of 'us' versus 'them' – to get rid of any tendency to guilt or self-questioning by cocking snooks at others. In my present mood I was able to appreciate the point of this: but still, it hardly seemed a lively way through to portraying life as a going concern: it was a turning away from agonised battlefields perhaps, but back to a world of playing-fields.

The one fellow novelist I became great friends with at this time was Hugo Charteris, who came from a background similar to my own. He had been at Eton with me although I had not been friendly with him there – he had seemed an aloof figure and somewhat contemptuous of the whimsicalities of me and my friends. He had gone into the army at the same time as me and then to the war in Italy and had had much the same experiences as I had had; but I had not begun to know him well until after the war when he had married the sister of one of my oldest friends. His first novel – *A Share of the World* – had been published at the same time as mine and had been about – guess! – a tormented young man coming home from the war and finding himself at odds with the society around him. So we began to correspond with each other – he lived in the north of Scotland and I lived in Sussex so we did not at first often meet – but we were able to talk about each other's and our own writings; also to grumble about the writing that was becoming fashionable and from which we both felt alienated. I on the whole admired Hugo's writing and he on the whole did not admire mine;

but he became important in my life because he had the straight-forwardness to say what he felt and he said it with affection. He could also take me on on the subject of religion. I found myself defending my writings: but at the same time Hugo's strictures ran parallel with my own dissatisfaction with, and desire to break away from, my old style.

Here are extracts from letters between me and Hugo from 1953 when I had finished *The Rainbearers*, and 1956, when I was finishing *Corruption*. Hugo worked on and off as a journalist; he had no private income; he hoped one day to earn a living by his fiction. This was the style in which we both liked to write letters at this time.

Dear Hugo,
    I've read *Under the Net* and enjoyed it – it rung a small bell with a small clear ping! but had no overtones nor undertones nor echoes at all, like a correctly tuned triangle being tuned by a triangle-tuner in the Festival Hall.
    Also *Hurry on Down* which is absolute silence.
    A brilliant book I'm on at the moment is *Cards of Identity* by Nigel Dennis. The whole thing has the smell of an enormous highbrow joke, but even so – in places it reminds me of your stories.

My dear Nicky,
    Some of *The Rainbearers* is to me deeply impressive – above all the last two pages. But some of it, to me, is too antipathetic and even meaningless for my opinion of it to have any significance for you. As far as the character of Richard is concerned my reaction cannot get past the fact of knowing you. Any would-be biographer of your father should certainly study the book – because it contains another attempt to sublimate – 2nd generation – that before which I raise the hand with the outer fingers extended prong-wise.
    The anonymous scenes are remarkable, but the characterisation is too often palpably projected.
    Richard on compassion is to me nauseating even when he doesn't nauseate himself – and in the end the catharsis is not of him or of the book's situation but a sudden abstraction, a flash of pure beauty, unrelated. Richard never really traced his tension honestly – his mazes of emotional pressure are camouflage and again camouflage. Nihilist to the spine, even when dealing with natural scenery. But you have power, and that is what literature has.

Dear Hugo,

We seem to be representatives of an inflexible opposition in ways of novel-writing. You try to take characteristics straight with no twisting (true?) and thus to get a 'reality' which is directly relevant to the 'reality' of life. But I don't think this is possible. I think the only reality one can hope to get is of a separate order, the order of storytelling – and to try to get any other is the mixing-up of two worlds, like the hope that by getting a portrait 'accurate' enough it will suddenly come to life and speak, which it won't.

Tolstoy got it by insight, he didn't get it by taking one oddity of character on its own and inflating it in the hope that by being blown up enough it would be the whole.

Richard's emotional camouflage – why not? Isn't this what people do?

Dear Nicky,

I read again some of *The Rainbearers* and was distressed by the letter I wrote – not because it was dishonest but because of the zeal with which it shaped the honesty in one distasteful direction – and because I had said no word about the general level upon which comment was made at all – by which I mean that I should have pointed out – the very highest.

I revolt against Somerset Maugham's objectivity in exactly the same way as I do against your subjectivity. The undeniable compulsive fluidity is there in each case – but in each case I go forward like a dog dragged from where it wants to pee. Only with the added determination, in your case, of the emotion which is always provoked by emotion. And then suddenly you stop pulling frantically – and I can widdle away for three pages amazed.

I doubt if you are hurtable, or if the machinery would permit admission of such an event even should it take place. But in case you are, please forgive in my first letter a kind of spleen which was really a sort of compliment – and known to be that even when indulged.

Dear Hugo,

I'm muddled about subjectivity-objectivity: any writing about events seems to me 'real' – i.e. I see it happening. But what I jib at in novels is when I can't make out *why* the people are doing what the writer says they are doing – which is why I don't like pre-Proust French novels. I see Mme Bov. rushing through woods but I never know why she's rushing, I can't make out why she isn't at home thinking of something more sensible. And if she's too stupid to sit and think then I want to be told this, and to be told what she is thinking if she isn't thinking sensibly. And so on. Otherwise I see it clearly but I don't understand it, like looking through a microscope at an unknown species – fascinating, but only for a very short time. And de-humanised: this is the point. It seems to me that all interest in human action lies in what a person is intending, fearing, hoping, while he's doing it. Otherwise it's a description of unconsciousness, of inhumanity. Animal books.

I think novels too often don't know what they're up to. We're past the instinctive stage when society was a structure in which you could just let talent rip and you got Art. Structure's gone, and you have to build it.

Dear Nicky,

The spine of my hobby-horse is that man has made an environment which, commute as he may, he can never be reconciled with on a level that will save his sanity. Therefore I believe there will be a bang – to be Jungian – from inside himself, thought *apparently* in cobalt mushrooms. All this is rather stale stuff and I see a rather good but not very poetic poem about it in the last *London Mag.* from Roy Fuller who often speaks my mind for me – 'frontal lobes bad, possessing society – rear lobes good, neglected'. Jargony as any thirties' stuff and no art – but *true*: from the bad, inartistic front lobes as they wait for a life-line – that life-line you rave for in *The Rainbearers* and Virginia Woolf rocks to and fro in exacerbated consciousness of being alive: and Proust too – as time shrinks sharply from infinity to the moment. Nietzsche writes, 'Aren't we sick of this confounded ipsimosity *but* . . .' a big but! He feels its inevitability like a noose round his neck – and has in fact the courage which Sartre has not – more popularly Schweitzer has not – to be *engagé* – I don't say with complete and enduring Truth (that anyhow wouldn't be to be *engagé*) – but with this moment which we are living now, which for him was already there. Religion – if I may invent a jargon – is the civilisation and exteriorisation of the rear lobes. Nietzsche entered them without it – and was consumed. In the end today we must have faith in un-reason – but refusing at every stage the weapons it puts in our hands. You say – Why don't I climb on to the religious bandwagon? I would answer (only since you make the statement) that I have been on it since I could think – separated from the drill and the practice only by laziness and other failings – though I have prayed nightly all my life. As to joining a particular band of it – the RC for instance – it has always seemed to me much simpler than all that theological stuff you gave me two letters ago (which began to sound like the march-past of an armoured division while Ayer's jets pined slick as farts overhead). How can a thinking person be an RC after understanding – feeling that they understood – Dostoievsky or *Christ*? Christ was an anarch- ist – God or not God – and He didn't require people to come to terms with Society – God in them was strong enough. But He had himself crucified as a great cross-girder from the rear lobes sticking out into the front – and round which whole frontal systems would form – amongst them the Inquisition . . .

Dear Hugo,

I might have known my front-lobe intellectual slogging (Farm St Black Sox) was no good – I have learned this now – no more pitching of dogma balls. And yes, yes I have always known that you were a one-man band with drum, trumpet, violin and cymbals when you moved your ears; but the point of the bandwagon is that it's the wagon show-boat style – if you *can* clash the rear-lobe cymbals with your ears, OK. And yes this is what Dostoievsky did etc. etc. and it may be true that it's what a writer should do (I never know about this) but I know that I can't. If I could I would. But Dost. was a shit and Nietzsche went mad (good luck to them). They also wrote the best stuff for 100 years (good luck to them). Perhaps on the bandwagon one hasn't got a chance of good stuff – I don't know. But I know I'm not tough enough to stand the racket till I go mad, nor to stand the racket of being a lonely shit. This is weakness, OK. But my one-man playing produced such discordance as pierced me, so I chucked it. I hope I can still produce good stuff, but I don't know.

The exteriorisation of the rear-lobes – but then this is angels, and can I talk about this? Christ wasn't a one-man band, he didn't play with himself but with things outside him: he lived with God and angels and what He fought were devils. These ARE externalisations: they are nothing to do with the anarchy of oneself, as Jung would know. And God knows it makes me sweat to say this, but what I would try to play with is angels and nothing else. But you've got to find your angels, you've got to find out HOW to externalise lobes. When migraine turns to terror – that's the time. Or when sentiment turns to love. Then (as they say) you're on the wagon.

The point about Dosty is that he knew that Alyosha existed but he couldn't write about him. Ivan, Dmitri, Raskol, Stavrog, etc. etc. – he knew more about them than anyone, but they are all men crucified at various stages between front and rear (as you say). But Christ resurrected and this is what Alyosha should have shown but Dosty never did it. There was to have been a 2nd vol. of Karamazov about it but there wasn't. So Dosty never bowls on the Catholic wicket at all – there's only Zosima who might be any mystic anywhere and Alyosha in that pantheistic earth-kissing scene, and then Ivan. All the stuff that people quote comes from Ivan, and why they quote it God knows, because Ivan is straight character stuff. Ivan's an intellectual front-lobe article. The Grand Inquisitor character stuff – simple front-lobe attack on an imagined rear but wide of it – people who are bowled over by the Grand Inquisitor are Katherine Mansfield, D.H. Lawrence, Middleton Murray, etc., and whatever wicket they're on it's not Catholic. Internal – 22 yards between lobes. So they had a good game with Ivan. But neither side reached Lord's, where the big games are played. They thought Lord's was a cricket ground – good luck to them.

And so on. God knows, as you say, I couldn't write this stuff to anyone but you. I'm a novice: the death of the old self is bitter and often absurd. My rattle and gyrations make me weep. But I'm far enough gone to know – I can smell it dying and although I cling to it like a necrophile because I love it, sooner or later I'll be driven off by the very smell. Then I think it's either suicide or OK.

Dear Nicky,

Thank you for your real vintage Nicky-Faulkner letter. Most un-Christian style you know. *Caecula caeculorum* on the tom-tom. You've got me a bit wrong. I don't at all want to be a one-man-band and I'm so acutely susceptible to the psychological benefits of mere company that even to provide five paras of trash cribbed from *France-Soir* and see it next day in the *Daily Mail fed* me – not merely literally. So you see . . .

Our correspondence is reaching the gate in by which we went . . . don't beat your tom-toms at me again. There's no need. I'm on your side; and I'm sure you'll need a side having within you a real corker of a prodigal son – to come home. All the bigger and better banquet for that. Such a lot of black is needed to eke out even a little white. It all seems to hang on how much Chaos can one stand. With an infinitely deep attachment – an infinite amount. Some hang by dressing for dinner and a rolled umbrella, some by butterflies or prize leaks (sic); and some much deeper by the Catholic Church. But Christ by nothing, nothing – till with His last cry admitting defeat He gave a life-line and a victory to millions for thousands of years. Even on an almost infinitely removed and smaller scale it seems it is the amount you can go before admitting defeat which conditions the extent of victory. I half admitted defeat when I was twelve, and half not. This sounds galled, which I promise is misleading.

When I say Christ hung by nothing till He hung by his nails – I mean merely that He hung by no Church – and by paradoxes, than which there is nothing more. Nothing – unless changed in essence by faith. Real faith, that is: faith intransitive: I believe – verb, intransitive.

My dear Hugo,

I think *Marching with April* [Hugo's second novel] is brilliant – bursting at the seams, compact like a peak-fit boxer; every paragraph a potential knock-out. Criticism would only be of what you set out to do – sweat down to the lightweight level so you could move fast and surely round a definable target and knock it cold in a couple of rounds. But then this poses the damnable question – What is Sugar Robinson doing among the lightweights anyway; and why isn't he making more bloody and painful hay of a 22-stone Carnera?

It seems sometimes that you are fighting no opponents at all, but just trying to give the best display of shadow-boxing yet seen.

What I mean about shadow-boxing is a matter of what view – and therefore what description – can be said to be true about people. I'm prejudiced both as a person and a writer: people say that my view and description is shadowy – both in life and in books – and it may be so. I see everyone in the same predicament as myself. But perhaps it's true that people become this, literally, when they are with oneself; and then not when they are not – so the question of shadows does not apply. What I feel about your shadows is only what I have said before – you don't describe people as if they suffered. To me, with my prejudice, this seems the ground upon which they become human.

I once said in a letter – à propos I can't remember of what – that when I came into a room of strangers I floated like a balloon. And it strikes me you do this with your characters – you float about between them and see them with brilliant clarity but through a telescope. And why not? except that they remain, perhaps, as distortions through lenses. I'm reminded of our discussion re the photographer as artist – but I don't mean that here. I only mean that you aren't perhaps fond of the touch of them for simply being human.

I am poorly at the moment, not writing and without a sentence in my head. When in this state I dissolve faster than your bricks in the rain. I know the cause and I know the answer – the cause being spring and whisky and London and girls who live on pills and will one day die of them and me like a stomach-pump to get them fit for the next attempt. Also like the character in *Point Counter Point* who massaged his secretary for her tired heart and talked about God while his hand got nearer to her you-know-what. And the answer is to sit in front of my typewriter biting my fingers to the bone and to say No to everything suggested from tea with the Vicar to a cruise round the world on a raft; and then slowly with bleeding fingers I begin to type again and my bricks re-form and my house is set in order. I go a bit mad within a week when I'm not doing my eight hours a day in my room.

But what does one do about this power-in-a-vacuum? One floats into the attitude of aboveness inevitably like a balloon. And the greater the natural powers, the greater the appearance of absurdity.

The hero of *The Rainbearers* should have been a stammerer. I funked this. What started that back-to-the-womb drive was when a comparative stranger laughed very lovingly and copied me when I stammered. This was a shock which burst me at 20,000 ft and brought me down in a limp heap. It had never happened to me before. But a womb? A few days later I was at my first confession. Which is how things work, I suppose.

One day I'll write a book about a stammerer. But then no one will see that it's only an extreme case of the common vacuum predicament.

Dear Nicky,

Come to Africa with me and leave your stammer there. A lion might suddenly say *Gurrrrrgh* in your face – and you would come home clear. To see the Gargoyle from mid-Sahara would be an event in your life – particularly if it was the last, ha ha.

7

The plan to go on a trip through Africa had been thought up first by Hugo and a friend; this friend dropped out, and the opportunity for me seemed too good to miss.

I would get away from the dead-ends after the finish of the writing of *Corruption*; and surely smokescreens would be seen for what they were in the clear light of the desert? And Hugo and I could rattle on about subjectivity/objectivity under the stars in the evenings.

The original plan had been to get a Landrover and drive across France, land in Algeria, cross the Sahara to Nigeria, then head west to the coast at Dakar and come home across the desert again by the route behind the Spanish territory of Rio de Oro. But the French were now making arrangements to test their atomic bombs in the Sahara, and crossings had been banned. So our plan was now to go by boat to Dakar and then head east along the southern edge of the desert – to wherever fancy and local information might lead us. Hugo had been commissioned to write articles for the *Daily Mail*, and I was to try to write a travel book. We did not think we would undergo the rivalries and quarrels that seemed to beset most travelling companions, because our disagreements as well as our friendship were so well aired.

My journey through West Africa with Hugo was of importance to me because he did indeed teach me something about objectivity: I learned to look, to listen – to people, at a landscape. Hugo was a passionate countryman; he knew about birds, animals, trees. Sometimes when he was driving and we were travelling across arid scrubland he would stop with a jerk and point; and there was the tail of a distant warthog disappearing behind a bush.

There was such brightness and colour in Africa: it was not difficult to learn to look.

Hugo was also a good and practised interviewer; he spoke fluent French. Listening to him talking to administrators, merchants, tribesmen, odd travellers picked up by the side of the road, I thought – Good heavens, such chat can actually be – interesting?

West Africa was still mainly under French colonial rule, with the British territories carved out here and there. In French territory fraternisation with the local people was carried on with badinage and good spirits: however, the French encouraged the Africans to continue to see themselves as children. In British territory the ruling race usually segregated themselves within wired-off compounds like animals in a zoo; but still, Africans perhaps thus learned to cater for themselves.

But humans were anyway often just dots on the huge green-and-gold landscape. Solitary figures would stand like statues just off the edge of the road; a line of women with cans of water on their heads would move elegantly on the horizon like a frieze. There were huge thick and knobbly trees like things growing under the sea; bushes as spiky and delicate as fans of coral. We carried a shot-gun and a rifle with which to procure food; occasionally when hunting guinea-fowl I would find myself half lost and alone in the landscape. By a small lake perhaps there would be butterflies like blossom flying from trees; huge white birds like ghosts; fish making plopping noises as if the lake were on the boil. This was a landscape into which it seemed proper that man had not come.

In Guinea we went on a trek to outlying villages with a French administrator; we travelled to the diamond mines in the hills at the back-of-beyond in Sierra Leone. We began to follow a diamond-smugglers' route into Liberia, but this was outside the safety-net of colonial administration, and when a customs officer in a torn vest and patched shorts fingered lovingly our shot-gun and our rifle we decided to turn back, and managed this with difficulty. In the evenings Hugo and I sat round our camp fire and talked.

Hugo was a devotee of Jung; I was making what I could of orthodox Christianity. Hugo had disliked the subjectivism of my writing but he also saw my would-be objective view of Christianity as bizarre: I was at the stage of saying – Either Christ is what the Church says He is, or He is nothing. Hugo had Jung's idea of Christ being 'the answer to the dream of the western world'; of Christianity as 'a piece of vast subjectivity which became a piece of objectivity – cutting across nation, class, sex, age'; (these are quotations from Hugo's letters). One night we became entangled in an argument about Jung's *Answer to Job* in which, it seemed to me, Jung assumed the Book of Job had been written by God in order that he, Jung, could say how unpleasant and inadequate was this Christian God, whereas in reality the Book of Job was an expression of humans' struggle to understand God – but then what on earth subjectively or objectively was I calling 'reality'? This was the one night on our journey when it could be said we quarrelled. In the morning it was not too difficult to make things up: surely when it was necessary, you could choose what would be reality?

The highlight of our journey through West Africa was our visit to the Toma tribe who lived in the mountains on the borders of French Guinea and Sierra Leone. There was to be a big festival in one of the villages; we could not reach this by Landrover so we set off with porters on foot. We walked through the forest for a day and the best part of a night; when we got to the village it was crowded for the festival and we had to squeeze into a visitors' hut and find a place to lie down in the dark between bodies. There was a terrible smell, and in the morning I saw that this came from the severed head of a bull propped just next to my own – a next day's sacrificial offering.

This festival took place every four years, when the young girls of the tribe who had been undergoing initiation ceremonies returned from the forest to their homes. These ceremonies centred round the ritual of excision; this operation involved, we understood, the removal of a girl's clitoris. We had learned what we could about the background to this on our way to the forest: a conventional explanation had been – Of course it is men who wish girls' clitorises to be cut out, so that men but not women can get sexual pleasure and so wives are likely to be faithful. But in the tribe it was evident that the men had almost nothing to do with the excision ceremonies; it was the old women who went about brandishing their primitive surgical instruments in celebration. So perhaps the business was just to do with the age-old jealousy of the old for the young – the old women had suffered, and so why should not the young suffer too? But the knowledgeable French administrator who had taken us on our trek in Guinea, and who himself had a beautiful African mistress, had told us – Don't believe stories about African women being made frigid! the excision of the clitoris offers them in fact the chance of a deeper sexual pleasure. In the end we seemed to be learning – Humans explain mysterious human drives in whatever way suits them.

During the day in the village there was ceaseless drumming by individuals and groups; in the evening the girls came out of the forest in a long line. They were naked except for brief cloths round their loins, they had bells and trinkets on their wrists and ankles and behinds, they wore tall conical hats like witches beneath which their hair fell in masks over their faces. They came into the village dancing, they broke up and danced in groups and on their own, and after a time their families joined them. The dancing was a jerking and a shuffling and swaying with angular movements of the neck and elbows and knees; they danced for hours, only occasionally pausing to rest on an older person's lap. Sometimes a face could be seen peering like something forbidden from behind the mask. They seemed totally absorbed in what they were doing. We took photographs and cine film; they hardly seemed to notice us. It was as if we were almost invisible, being non-members of the tribe.

We asked our questions of whomever we could – What did this or that totem or ritual signify? Such questions to the people involved seemed to make no sense: how could 'meaning' be separate from that which was or that which occurred? The dancers, the celebrators, were doing what it seemed to them it was necessary to do; what questions need be asked?

The tribe had a god, it appeared, who might be that which told

93

them what to do. Who was this god? He was a spirit, the totality of the tribe, a mask that was kept secretly in the forest. Yes, but which of the three? This was a question above all that to them made no sense. Should not God be everything?

It was the children of the tribe who seemed bright, individualistic – like children anywhere. Perhaps, we wondered, the aim of the excision ceremony was to cut individuality out, so that grown-ups would be merged into the tribe. And indeed might not this be the aim of the rituals of many so-called 'civilised' families and schools – that children should have their individuality cut out, so that they could become part of the tribe.

After our stay with the Toma tribe Hugo and I did not spend so much time talking about subjectivity/objectivity. Things were what they were: you looked, listened: you felt – such connections as there might be just beyond the scope of language!

We went up to the edge of the desert again where villagers lived in dwellings cut into the faces of cliffs; where gods were phallic fetishes streaked with feathers and blood. We went down to the coast for the Independence Day of Ghana where tribal chiefs were carried to and fro on elaborate litters with coloured umbrellas flapping above them like wings; where the British looked on from behind the screens of their verandahs. We went north again in Dahomey to where a hundred years ago British travellers had watched the king offering human sacrifices for the 'feeding of his people'; where sixty years ago the French had fought with an Amazon army of razor-women. Our journey ended in Nigeria.

In Kano I hoped that there might be a telegram from Rosemary who, we had planned, might fly out to join us for a brief holiday on the coast. There was a telegram, but it said – Afraid cannot meet you Kano, could you possibly come Kampala? Kampala was in Uganda, some two thousand miles away over the impassable mountains of Central Africa. I had been travelling far and fast: I was tired: I said to the man behind the counter of the Poste Restante – Where did this telegram come from? He said – Ambassador. I said – Where is Ambassador? He looked this up in a big book and said – Saskatchewan. I said to Hugo – Rosemary is in Saskatchewan, and wants us to meet her in Kampala. Hugo said – Where is Saskatchewan? The man behind the counter said – In Canada. And then he added, because I suppose we both continued to look bemused – To the north of the United States of America. I thought – Well indeed, one watches, listens – and things happen.

What had happened, it transpired (Rosemary's telegram had said 'letter to follow' and this did arrive later) was that her telegram had, of course, been sent from the telephone exchange in London that was called 'Ambassador'; she wanted to meet me in Kampala rather than Kano because she had unexpectedly had an invitation for us both to stay there with the Kabaka of Buganda, King Freddie; and she thought, quite rightly, that once I had recovered my wits, this was the sort of invitation that I, even after a journey across West Africa, would not want to refuse. So she had taken the risk of accepting the invitation for us both and in fact now it seemed was already in Kampala; where, her letter said, she so much hoped I would hop over and join her. She held out a bait:

> The Kabaka's court sounds wonderful, his sister or wife wears a Jacques Fath dress back to front, and when a crocodile got into his private pool all the court thought it was his wicked uncle, who is dead.

I still was not sure if my wits were about me. I had been looking forward to meeting Rosemary in Kano.

But how wonderful! Reality is what you make of it? reality is what turns up?

Hugo had to fly home, so I left him to sell the Landrover, and I scrounged a place on a pilgrim plane to Mecca which had wooden benches instead of seats and seemed ancient enough to ensure the faithful a quick passage to heaven. It stopped for refuelling at Khartoum, where I got off, and picked up a regular flight to Nairobi. By the time I reached the Silver Springs Hotel in Kampala where Rosemary was staying I was in a ravaged condition, I felt, like that of Speke when he discovered the source of the Nile. I found Rosemary sitting in evening dress in front of a mirror and putting on the diamond earrings that she hardly ever wore. She said 'Oh hullo, I'm so glad you're in time, the Rolls-Royce is calling to take us to the Palace in twenty minutes, have you got a clean shirt, can we talk about things later?' My spare shirt was not quite clean, and the Rolls-Royce from the Palace somehow managed to get stuck in the ditch at the end of the hotel drive; but oh yes, yes, in these sort of circumstances it is worth seeing reality as what turns up, and indeed one can talk about the ins and outs of it later.

King Freddie, the Kabaka of Buganda, had been exiled to London some years before after a quarrel about the constitution of his country with the British Colonial Governor of Uganda. In London he had become friends with Francis Wyndham who was a friend of Rosemary's; the Kabaka had recently been allowed back to his capital, Kampala, and he had asked Francis and Rosemary – and myself if this was possible – to visit him there. He held court in the Old Palace which was a set of buildings with mud walls and thatched roofs and was guarded by ritual stranglers as sentries at the gates. There was a more conventional New Palace next door which was where the Kabaka's wife and children lived and where the Governor sometimes came to tea; but King Freddie just before this time had run off with his wife's younger sister and had set up a separate family life in the Old Palace, the atmosphere of which he seemed to prefer anyway. He had been at school in England and then at Cambridge; now, in the Old Palace, his subjects had to remain on their hands and knees facing him when in his presence, and to crawl out of the room backwards. However, there was an air of extraordinary elegance and sophistication about life in the Old Palace, which was in contrast to the ungainliness of much of the colonial life outside. I wrote to Hugo:

> The palace is full of children who never cry, gramophones playing Schubert, and philosophical doctors on their hands and knees discussing politics. The Kabaka is the most aristocratic person I've come within a mile of; he makes Rosemary and your father look like Dr and Mrs Dale.

One of the highlights of Rosemary's and my stay as guests of the Kabaka was (I wrote to Hugo) 'the arrival in a 40ft Cadillac of the King of Urundi, the best ballroom dancer in the Congo'. This King was a huge man who, at the state ball in his honour, swept Rosemary literally and for considerable distances off her feet.

Another highlight was a three-day trip in the Kabaka's yacht to shoot hippopotami on Lake Victoria. I wrote to Hugo:

> Hippo shooting is not what it might seem. You sit in canoes and shoot from the shoulder without support and the canoe rocks and the hippo only sticks his head up six inches at a hundred yards and then only for five seconds, so it is like snap-shooting. We got so tired of missing that the bodyguard, a policeman with a sten-gun, was called in to try with a whole magazine. This became all the rage, and was very dangerous.

From Uganda Rosemary and I set off home by paddle-steamer down the Nile. For six hundred miles the steamer chugged and wended through a swamp of reeds, bouncing off banks to get round corners. The twenty or so passengers, dining in a temperature of about a hundred in the shade, had to hang on to their plates of steak-and-kidney pudding. From time to time the steamer stopped at a fuelling station to take in logs, and there would be the very beautiful men of the Dinka tribe standing on one leg with their spears like flamingoes, naked except for a plaited sheath round the penis.

From my trip round Africa I learned – to look and listen, oh yes: not to talk too much! What were words doing anyway? In tribal Africa there had not been much talk; people had made cooing noises to and fro – for greeting, for harmony – like birds. Individuals might have to break away from tribal identity by means of words, all right. But then – what about a conscious breakthrough to some more universal sense of wholeness again?

Corruption had been published while I was away: the reviews were not too bad, not all that good: Hugo did not write to me about it. But before I went to Africa I had known I did not want to write another book like *The Rainbearers* or *Corruption*. And now I had my travel book to write. But after that – I did not want to be involved with any more smokescreens, with fog; I wanted to get out; but for this, would I not need some further commitment?

Hugo and I had sent a trunkload of paraphernalia home from Nigeria by boat; this tin trunk, which French-speaking Africans referred to as '*le canteen*', contained books we had carried with us and fetishist objects we had picked up from strange tribes. From Sussex I wrote to Hugo:

> The customs officer at Liverpool, having discovered *The Memoirs of Fanny Hill* in *le grand canteen*, seems to have confiscated our entire baggage. What he's doing with the wooden penises perhaps his wife alone knows. What I'm now waiting for is the charge of importing pornographic objects being publicised just before my second appearance before a committee of bishops as the proposed editor of a Holy Magazine. My first appearance was a week after the *Sunday Pic* photos.

There seemed to be some fate in the persistence of the efforts to get me to edit a Christian magazine. Father Raynes from the beginning seemed to have set his heart on it; and now – was I not myself insisting that I needed some commitment other than that of writing in the style of my old novels? Suddenly coincidences seemed to converge.

There was already in existence a small Anglican monthly called *Prism* which had been started the previous year by two young men from Cambridge – Christopher Martin and Robin Minney. They had now run out of money and had appealed for funds from The Society of the Faith – a charitable institution which had already been involved in discussions with the committee that had its eye on me. The Society said that they would put up £1,000 if I did too and if I came in as editor of an enlarged magazine. This I now said I would do – there seemed to be too much coincidence and persistence to avoid this fate. But nevertheless I was in some despair. How does one change a lifetime's attitudes, propensities, by deciding that change should occur?

First I had to finish the travel book. I tried to keep this to descriptions of events, shapes, colours, sounds; to keep away from sentences weaving in and out like fog. It was to be called *African Switchback*, because of our roller-coaster ride between the desert and the sea.

While I was writing this, and having discussions about the magazine, I carried on with my old life in something of the style, I suppose, of a man who has been told he has just a few months to live. Hugo had written to me before our trip, 'To see the Gargoyle from mid-Sahara would be an event in your life'; and perhaps it had been, but not yet in the sense of stopping me running there. The Gargoyle was above all the place where one went not only to meet old friends but to dream of picking up new ones. I was there one night just before setting off on a brief trip to Berlin to pursue an idea I had had for a play (even when I was in what seemed to be death row, I dreamed of new possibilities of writing) and there was a girl whom I had come across once or twice before and who was one of those miraculous girls who seemed to live, as we are told to live, like a lily of the field: and I said to her – Why don't you come with me tomorrow to Berlin? and she said – I will! and she was on my doorstep at dawn. We had a lovely time in Berlin; it was very cold, so we spent much of the time in night-clubs or in bed; and she rang up her regular boyfriend each day to let him know she was all right. Then some time later in London she came to tell me she was pregnant. There was no question of her leaving her boy-friend. So I gave her some money and said she might use it as she liked: I said that I hoped she would not have an abortion. This was just before I was to start editing my so-called Holy Magazine.

I dragged myself off to confession to a strange priest in an Anglo-Catholic Church; this was the Thursday before Easter and there were people queuing up outside confessionals like refugees seeking last-minute exit visas from hell. This was a strange priest again and not at all like Father Raynes; he seemed to take violent personal umbrage at my story – for a time it looked as if I would be refused absolution, like a character in a Graham Greene story about to be consigned to hell. I could not explain – But this was the last fling of an about-to-be committed man; and anyway what do you know about heaven or hell?

The next day was Good Friday and there was the first enormous meeting of the Campaign for Nuclear Disarmament in Trafalgar Square (this was 1958); the meeting was to be the prelude to a march to the Atomic Energy Commission's headquarters at Aldermaston. I thought I would go to this meeting because, although I thought the attitudes of the CND people were too simplistic, I admired the emotion behind their protest – and in what other style might lilies of the field simply wish to stay alive? In the square there was a huge crowd and the speakers were on the plinth from which my father sometimes spoke; the speakers told of the terrible threat of annihilation; the crowd contained many mothers and fathers with children in pushchairs. While I was listening, the boyfriend of the girl with whom I had been in Berlin bumped into me and greeted me; I asked him how she was; he said that the previous day, Thursday, she had had a miscarriage and was now in hospital but she was all right. I said – A miscarriage? He said – Yes. The march to Aldermaston began and we both, myself and the boyfriend, marched for a time side by side. It seemed as if we might be on some pilgrimage. Much later the girl assured me – Yes; she had used the money that I had given her to put down a deposit on a new flat for her and her boyfriend.

On the evening of the first day of the march I was walking with a group of young men and women who were carrying a banner saying 'Let's Go Back to Bows and Arrows'; I had continued to march because I had needed something to do; life seemed overburdened with oddities and ambiguities and wonder and connections. Somewhere beyond Hammersmith there was a group of young right-wing toughs on the pavement who were shaking their fists and shouting abuse at the marchers: one of them, I recognised, was my half-brother Alexander. I had not seen much of Alexander since he had stayed with Rosemary and me a year or two before when he had had to leave the school in Germany to which he had been sent by my father, and my father had asked me to find a place for him in a public school in England. This I had done. Alexander at sixteen had been one of the most remarkable boys I had known: he had been able to explain to me something of the mysteries of Husserl and Heidegger. And now here he was shouting slogans in the style of the most simplistic followers of my father. Alexander saw me marching under my banner at the same time as I saw him: he shouted – 'You!' I called to him to join us on the march which for a short while, bravely, he did. We promised to be more in touch with each other: to be sure, there were coincidences here! I myself did not continue on the march after the first day: there was too much coming in – into my life, my understanding: like seeds, like pollen: 'take no thought for the morrow' indeed! And then one thing rather than another might come in? Easter seemed to be a time for all sorts of miracles. For Easter Day itself I hastened back to my family. Perhaps things would calm down when I edited the Holy Magazine.

PART II

It may seem that to present this story I have arranged facts, picked and chosen. In a sense, of course I have! All remembering, speaking, writing, is a matter of choosing – of giving shape to what is otherwise inchoate.

But what writers find – providing that they are aiming to present what is 'true' – is that they are not so much creating a pattern, a shape, as uncovering one that is already there: and it is this experience that gives validity to their impression of what might be true.

Philosophers have seen that what we know as the world is what our senses permit and arrange: there is little sense in the idea of apprehension of things-in-themselves. Wittgenstein put it – 'One thinks that one is tracing the outline of a thing's nature and one is merely tracing round the frame through which one looks at it.' But still – To realise that this is the nature of things is to realise something-in-itself.

Physicists have said that experiments at a basic level of matter show that the description of an occurrence depends on the way that it is observed – even on the fact that it is observed. Scientists coined a phrase – 'Reality is a function of the experimental condition.' But still – reality is such that there is such a functioning.

So why should not a writer say of writing a life – Of course I have picked and chosen! but I have hoped and trusted that, through knowing this, I may be finding what is there. And there can be a 'sound' of truth that goes between writer and reader. You call this illusion? If you so wish! But in experience is it not an illusion that 'truth' has any other meaning – or none?

The philosopher Nietzsche suggested that a person might see his or her life as an art-work – in the looking back on it and the discovering of what has been there; and by this affecting the future. For it is in the nature of pattern, shape, that the observance of a past forms a future. You watch, listen; if you do this 'truly' a future unfolds in a manner in which it is seen that you are a partner.

There remains the question – What can be said about the every-day style of human conduct in this process of creation; a voyage of discovery having by its nature to go on largely in the dark? What is it that distinguishes that which seems random, from that which a human might be a partner in shaping?

Criteria regarding art-works have been called 'aesthetic'. This word has little practical meaning except with reference to a relation between a work of art and what is felt in the outside world to be 'there'. This is a matter of evaluation, as well as of observation. Of course, everyone will have their own assessment of this relation; but in the end that which is 'there' will be that which has survived.

Nietzsche announced that God was dead – 'God' having been a word for the experience of what is other than oneself or one's assessments. Nietzsche seemed to mean – Now humans can know themselves to be in the business of discovery and creation.

For the experience of making patterns the word 'God' is useful, but not imperative. God was said to have taken rests. But for anyone looking – and it should be useful to look from time to time at what on earth has been meant by such a word – then God, after all, does seem to be there.

8

So in the spring of 1958 there I was, in a tiny room like a cupboard
on the top floor of a gaunt Victorian building at the back of
Westminster Abbey called Faith House; from here for the next two
years I was to edit the monthly magazine *Prism*. I sat behind one
table and my secretary, Anne Holland, a friend of Father Raynes,
faced me from behind another, and there was just enough room for
a visitor to squeeze in between. Christopher Martin and Robin
Minney dropped in from time to time; we had two young and
helpful priests as theological advisers; Robin Denniston, then managing director of the Faith Press, kept a fatherly eye on the enterprise from downstairs; but for much of the time Anne and I had
the running of the business to ourselves. The first week of each
month would be spent in gathering contributions, the second in
getting these into a state for the printers, the third in correcting
proofs and getting these back to the printers, the fourth in address-
ing envelopes and posting them to the several hundred subscribers
and carrying bundles in my car to selected bookshops. We were
usually in the office for not more than three days a week, but I
wrote a lot myself for the magazine and it seemed almost like a
whole-time job – perhaps because for me it never ceased to seem
like going against some grain. No one was paid anything either for
their work in the office or for what they wrote, but this did not
seem to prevent contributions coming in.

I had imagined that *Prism* would be guided by Father Raynes, but in the event he died soon after the appearance of the first number. This was a blow, but not in the practical way I might have feared. In fact many people who had been used to depending on Father Raynes found that they were able to carry on without too much difficulty after he died: it was as if he had given to them before he died whatever was necessary for them to be on their own.

The first number of *Prism* under my editorship – one that was aimed at setting the tone of the enterprise – was entitled 'What's Wrong with the Church'. This led off with an announcement – 'We think it necessary that Church writers should write critically of their Church because our faith tells us to look for the distortions in our own eyes before complaining of the blindness of others'; and then in my leading article continued with what had been a bone of contention from the beginning in my relationship with the Church – my feeling that the behaviour of Church people had little to do with what they professed. I wrote:

> Today in England the façade that the Church presents is one of a vested interest in patterns of mind and habits in which people to whose advantage it is to be churchmen are churchmen and those to whom there is no advantage are not. By 'advantage' I mean the chance to satisfy a desire for a function and a hobby in society in the manner most gratifying to the person's character and tastes.
>
> It is this appearance of the Church that explains its almost total lack of contact with any part of the country's life except its own. It is imagined to be something in the nature of a trades-union of the lily-livered and respectable, and as such to the general public its affairs are as of little interest (or even less owing to the dreary qualifications for membership) as would be those of a trades-union of boilermakers. The only times that outside interest is aroused are when there are squabbles within the union of a faintly ludicrous nature – disagreements between 'high' and 'low' factions which are viewed with the same amusement as are those, in the parallel with boilermakers, about who should drive rivets through iron and who through wood. These quarrels cause passionate feelings among the participants, but to outsiders bring the whole institution into contempt.
>
> It is the tragedy not only of the Church but of the whole life of the country that this divorce from popular consciousness should occur and continue in an age when for the first time this century

there is a demand for religious thinking and religous understanding among the younger generation. This fact says nothing about the merits of the younger generation nor about the validity of religion; but the failure to do anything about it does say something about the Church.

I do not know where I got the idea about the current 'demand for religious thinking' – perhaps this was an impression left over from my own wartime generation. The title of my leading article was 'For Heaven's Sake Repent!': but what on earth did I mean by 'repent'? Were not Church people always droning on about their sins? What I meant, it seemed, was that although Church people uttered incantations about their sinfulness, these seemed to protect them from looking at what in fact might be their case – which looking alone could make sense of concepts such as 'sin' and 'repentance'. Church people seemed to feel themselves able to be virtuous simply by means of formal statements; whereas in fact (it seemed to me) this attitude itself was a sin – virtue depending not on statements but on the relation of these to attitudes and behaviour. The human situation was one in which there always was 'sin' – the failure to be and do what one would wish to be and do – and it was in the holding of this condition in the mind that there was the possibility of repentance. There were paradoxes at the very heart of the Christian faith: we had to do what we could, yet trust that with this trust it would not matter too much when we failed; we had to believe that forgiveness was being done for us, but that at the same time we were responsible for ourselves. 'Repentance' in this sense became the experiencing of some tightrope-walk in consciousness.

I wrote:

> What is required is a new attitude and a new way of talking about this attitude in the Church's *consciousness*. We have got to have new eyes, new ears, and a new ordering of what we see. This attitude we have got to admit is superhuman. We have got not only to understand but to *live* in a state of being wholly responsible and yet not responsible, loving persons and yet fighting what they do, caring passionately about our failures and yet not worrying about them at all. We have to understand and to live this attitude so well that

when non-Christians say we are crazy we can be both concerned and unconcerned at this opinion, and know that it is both inevitable that they should hold it and yet imperative that we should change their minds. We've got to suffer for the sufferings of others and make this compassion evident, and yet be joyful for suffering having been defeated and try to transmit this joy. We have got to be confident we can do this although it is superhuman, for the reason that the superhuman is what the human is given to do.

There was something a bit strident, over-the-top, here: but one of the suggestions being made was – should not Christians become more exposed? This first number of *Prism* laid us open to charges of arrogance (what about the beams in our own eyes?) and even blasphemy (the Church was the Body of Christ; how could it be called 'wrong'?). But the message for the ensuing numbers of *Prism* was set: faith is held and demonstrated, and perhaps grace is transmitted, not so much by the use of words as by what people are, by their efforts to see what they are, and by the interactions to and fro.

We did manage, soon, to be less inward-turning. In September we ran a special number on the H-Bomb in which the Bishop of Willesden defended possession of the Bomb on the grounds that this was a necessary acceptance of human responsibility, Father Huddleston argued that the very existence of the Bomb was a betrayal of Christian morality, and I suggested that the possession of it with the intention of not using it was neither irresponsible nor immoral nor indeed ineffective – there it could be, like some fearful totem or indeed Old Testament God, which just by the fear of fire and brimstone might encourage wisdom. But of course this sort of wisdom would require a state of mind different from that which demanded a logical either/or. And so here I was back on my hobby-horse again, arguing that what a Christian required was a way of seeing and bearing a situation that was essentially paradoxical.

The New Testament gives us no help about such political choices as between peace and war, order and freedom, means and ends. It talks about the encounter of the individual with God, and was written at a time when few Christians did or could have temporal power and thus were not faced with large-scale temporal responsibility. But it is of the very nature of the world that we should not be 'helped' in this way. What Christians are given instructions about is how to try to get to know God's will and to have the courage to do it. The world is just the circumstance from which the attempt is made – from which God's will is learned and upon which it is practised. For the Christian the large-scale choice is of the same nature as the small-scale – a matter of getting to know what God wants us to do as persons. We may indeed be required to order the world; but our success in doing this will depend on our success in having ordered ourselves.

This begged questions about the use of the word 'God': but the message went banging on – Humans look after the means; then the ends look after themselves.

But could nothing more be said about what might be proper means?

By the New Year we were producing a number called 'The Church and Art'. I wrote:

The parables of Our Lord are art: they tell of things that can be told in no better way. Their effect on the hearer or reader depends not on argument nor on reason, but on their nature and quality as stories.

The Gospels are works of art. They are not biographies or histories, but impressions by writers, the validity of which does not depend upon historical proof but upon the reader's experience of their authority.

The Epistles are art. They are written in a certain style, and it is the style that holds the attention and conveys the meaning.

If the churchman of today wishes to get back his voice and means of action it is just this that he has to recognise – what is the nature of such art, and what are its disciplines.

The disciplines of art are the same as those of religion – that you not only have to believe it but to live it. It is this which will determine 'style' and 'authority'. The authority of a religious person depends on his integrity – the conjunction between what he believes and what he does. The authority of an artist depends upon a conjunction of what he most deeply knows and what with cost and effort he makes – it is this that will result in the style that conveys his meaning. Every man is a particular kind of artist: everyone has something to do, or to make, in the life to which he is called. Art is the true pains he takes in doing it.

In this article I seemed to have begun by telling Church people that they should have a respect for art and I finished by telling them they should see themselves as artists – that humans should order their lives by the sort of 'means' by which an artist orders his art. Most of my messages in *Prism* came back to this: that one should see one's life as some sort of trying out, testing, discovering – of something which, if one does this (and this is the miracle!) is in fact there.

The fact that I was writing all this stuff about integrity and the relation between what one says and what one does meant that I had to do something about it at home. I had already resolved to give up the style of my old London life: in the country, I now became churchwarden of my local church; I tried to plunge into parish affairs. Lyminster was a pleasant, rather somnolent parish occasionally bedevilled by Barchester-type rows between an ex-church-warden and the vicar and the rural dean. I began by imagining – I can of course get this sort of thing sorted out! also, for instance, get the main altar moved down to the centre of the church and the Eucharist rather than Matins to be the main service on Sundays; and, oh yes, get goats to deal with the problem of the long grass in the graveyard. But soon I was confronted with – But people don't want change! and – You know what goats do in graveyards! Realities of parish life were brought home to me over the question of the annual fund-raising church fête which traditionally took place in the garden of our house; each year helpers were hard to find and they grumbled about the work involved. So I suggested at a parish meeting – Why don't we each of us here just fork out a few pounds – I'll set the ball rolling – and just by this we'll have raised as much money as we usually do at the fête? The vicar took me aside and explained – But you see, people like the grumbling almost as much as they like the fête.

There was a new housing estate on the edge of the parish and here there had arisen a group of boys and girls who called themselves The Young Communicants' Fellowship. It seemed that here there might be something useful I could do. I became some sort of uncle-figure to this group: we used to have meetings at first in the Church Hall, and then they came up to Rosemary's and my house. We sat around and talked – about personal problems, about current affairs: we found it difficult to talk about religion. One summer evening we had a barbecue in a field at the back of our house and this was gatecrashed by a gang of slightly older toughs who threatened to break the party up. They said they felt left out; we called ourselves Christians didn't we? And weren't Christians supposed to be people who asked outsiders in? So here was a real problem for a would-be integrity-monger who saw Christianity as a business of doing what one professed! Should we not indeed welcome in these strangers from the highways and byways however dangerous they seemed? As usual, the New Testament appeared to be ambiguous on this point: was there not also the example of the man who turned up at a wedding party without a proper garment and was hurled into outer darkness? I went between the two groups of guests and trouble-makers trying to make peace; but before long a fight started, and what had the New Testament to say about that? As it happened a massive farmworker who was a neighbour arrived on the scene and, after a brief warning, knocked the leader of the gatecrashers flat. The latter and his gang retired, vowing that they would return with reinforcements; the Young Communicants went off to summon their own older brothers and cousins; it looked as if we were going to have a full-scale 'rumble' in our back yard. This never quite materialised. While waiting we busied ourselves in arguing about the nature of Christian responsibility; about how parables seemed to say both one thing and another, so that one still had to make up one's mind.

Occasionally it struck me that perhaps our own children felt left out of all this: might not the Young Communicants seem to them like gatecrashers invading their home? There were conundrums here all right. But then there would always be – about the weird business of trying to love one's neighbours as oneself.

I once suggested to older members of the parish that they might like to come together and talk about such riddles; after hesitation some of the men said that at a pinch they would not mind talking about religion, but not in front of their wives. At the time I was somewhat scornful of this. But then I felt – why in loving one's neighbours should one imagine that they are like oneself?

There were some riddles I was involved with that were more like beds of nails. I had forsworn the style of my old London life; but there I was, usually up in London two or three nights a week working on *Prism*, and staying on my own in the flat where Rosemary and I had once entertained so raffishly. Ghosts from the past sometimes seemed to haunt me – to gibber and tweak like the incubi of witches. These were the days when in the streets of Mayfair there were tarts like full-rigged sailing-ships: phantoms perhaps to lure poor sailors to their doom. Walking back from a cinema at night I would think – Dear God, I understand how clergymen find themselves in the *News of the World*! or how Mr Gladstone said he only wanted to chat. And then there was the magic area of Soho where lurked so many old friends, and which beckoned to me like the garden of the wicked magician Klingsor. Indeed one might be lost if one went in; and yet – might one not be lost if one did not? Without some would-be Parsifal, that is, could there be any re-discovery of the Holy Grail? And what about Christ's own preference for the company of publicans and sinners? Oh there were a lot of riddles like bats or broomsticks flying around at night! What a goading, as well as a wonder, that the point of parables and riddles seemed to be that one had to learn for oneself.

In an issue of *Prism* entitled 'The Church and Sex', I wrote:

> To say that there is an opposition or at least a separation between sex and love and that it is love that matters does not imply (as some people would suppose together with the early Fathers) that sex is an evil or something to be ignored or repressed. To suggest this would be to fall into the very error that we now claim the Fathers perpetrated – that of using rationality to make patterns where the disciplines of reason do not apply. The whole business of personality, of relationship, is beyond the rule of reason which cannot tolerate paradoxes but only the demands of 'either/or'. The proper way to look at the separation between love and sex is rather one of seeing that although love is what fundamentally matters and sex does not fundamentally matter, yet there is an area in which sex can very powerfully affect for good or ill the requirements of love: and the proper way of seeing a hostility between sex and love is one not of fear or repression, but of sensible efforts to find the actions whereby the hostility can be dealt with. All this may seem obvious . . .

Obvious indeed! But what a balancing act to learn – a clown on a high wire in the streets at night.

Many of my old friends must have thought I had gone mad when I began to edit *Prism*: they did not talk to me about it much. Hugo Charteris wrote to Rosemary, '*Prism* keeps me young.' My stepmother Diana was amused by an article I had printed by the Bishop of Olympia, 'who I suppose serves great Zeus'.

It seems to me now that much of my antipathy to rationalisation, and my hobby-horse about the necessity of words being related to deeds, must have had their roots in my relationship with my father. His genius was for the forensic manipulation of words; he imagined that by this he might make his politics effective. In the early fifties he had started up his own monthly magazine, *The European*, which was intended to be a forum in which political and theoretical debate could be conducted. My father trusted his power with words to win in debate; but at that time he did not find many people ready to take up the cudgels against him. I myself had sometimes written for his magazine – literary articles on pro-Christian themes that were by implication anti-Fascist – these my father had said he had enjoyed, but they were not of a kind he thought he had to answer. He was probably disappointed that I had not written more, and more politically, for his magazine; and it must have seemed I had moved beyond the pale when I began to edit *Prism*. But the story of my relationship with my father must be kept for the next chapter.

For most of my time with *Prism* – I had never seen myself as being editor for more than, say, two years – I continued to stress my line about integrity; also about this being a more far-reaching business than it might appear. I seemed increasingly to suggest that if this complexity was recognised and held within oneself, then just this might be effective in the outside world. I became involved in a debate with one of our most skilled and forceful contributors to *Prism*, Valerie Pitt. She had written advocating what she called a Christian Social Contract, by which a Christian's proper attitude to social and political matters might be clearly defined. I replied:

The social abuses of this age and country are not primarily practical ones of injustice and squalor, but more ones of the spirit, or psyche, manifested personally and in the community. This is the age of untruthfulness, or double-think, of loss of integrity and a profound lack of courage. It is not nowadays that we are deliberately wicked; we are simply mad. The significance of our attitude to such things as the H-Bomb, Apartheid, Suez, does not lie in a wrongness about them (to such questions there can properly be two sides) but rather that even on our own sides we do not make sense. Everyone told lies about Suez, few admit their real feelings about Apartheid, about the H-Bomb we are as frivolous as hysterics. What the world has now denied is the importance of truthfulness and integrity and honour. We are in a moral vacuum with no values, and idols of publicity are in the place of God...

I think that because the present abuses are those of dissolution and moral chaos then our remedies must be in this sphere also – in a concentration not on political and social lobbying, but on demonstrating personally and in groups what the godly life of integrity should be.

To this Valerie Pitt replied that personal integrity was all very well, but it had little effect in the dire battlefields of contemporary politics. To this in turn I replied:

You say – 'The fact that Father Candid of St Faith's is a shining example of honesty and kindliness will not, I fear, prevent Mr Julian Amery from stonewalling in the House of Commons nor shame Mr Lennox Boyd into doing what he has been begged and prayed to do for years.' But my contention, on the whole, is that it *will*: or, to put it another way, that nothing else will – least of all the arguments of, for instance, Mr Brockway. One just doesn't know what effect Father Candid's example might have: he might even convert Mr Amory; something fearsome might happen to Mr Boyd in the middle of the night. I am writing this somewhat frivolously because it is difficult to express; but there is a real sense in which I mean it. I believe that Father Candid's example *can* have an effect on the practical world via the spiritual. I don't *want* to believe this because it is disturbing and imposes a considerable strain: if you think it all depends on good works, after all, you can knock off sometimes and take a holiday. But I do believe that the spiritual courage and integrity of a hermit say in Battersea can in fact change the heart or alleviate the sufferings of a crippled criminal in Peckham; and this sort of job is a whole-time responsibility. I believe this because I think it is observable from the evidence, and it seems to me it's the sort of thing that the Christian faith is all about – as opposed to the old Jewish law. Also it seems to be one's only way of demonstrating one's belief in that wholly vital but at the moment apparently forgotten Person of western Christendom – the Holy Spirit.

This was the sort of stuff I continued to put out for two years: because I believed it; because, yes, it was some reaction against the knock-down attitudes of my father. I might have felt some urgency here; my father's return to politics was now gaining attention; he had recently announced that he would be standing for Parliament at the forthcoming election in the North Kensington constituency, which included the black immigrant community in Notting Hill.

With regard to the number of *Prism* about which Diana had made her joke concerning the Bishop of Olympia, she had also noted that it had an article about Notting Hill which said that the Devil had chosen it as his place of combat. She joked further that my father would of course be delighted to be the devil with a capital D.

9

My in some ways idyllic wartime and just-post-war relationship with my father, during the period when he had been imprisoned and then had led the life of a retired country gentleman, had come to an end in 1947 when he had gone back into politics as the leader of Union Movement and I had married. Union Movement was intended to 'go beyond' the pre-war British Union of Fascists; there was to be no more simple nationalism but rather the formation of a power-block composed of Europe-with-White-Africa which might be on equal terms with the other superpowers America and Russia. This in theory might make some sense – my father had been able to rationalise even many of his pre-war attitudes and for a while I had been impressed by these – but with regard to how human life in fact worked or could work his policies seemed to have less and less to do with reality. My father imagined that humans could be arranged and re-arranged like words: the problems of Africa could be sorted out by vast re-settlements of black and white populations. To me it seemed that humans were not so much interested in rationality as dependent on often unconscious needs and passions.

During much of the fifties, however, I remained on good terms with my father; he had sold his farm in Wiltshire and was basing himself abroad in France and in Ireland. Rosemary and I spent two or three summer holidays with him; later he rented our London flat from us when he came to England. This was a time when my father became involved with a girlfriend much younger than himself;

they visited us at Lyminster; his cavortings and mine would overlap in London – even once at the Gargoyle Club, of which my father had been a member in the 1930s. He was contemptuous of Christianity but he expressed fellow-feeling with me in this sort of life: he wrote – 'I defend you triumphantly against the charge of hypocrisy by saying you have left Orwell's double-think far behind with a great new system of double-fun: we have only the fun of sinning; you have also the fun of repenting.' And indeed one did have fun with my father when one bumped into him in this sort of life; and he appreciated the idea of at the same time hoping to remain true to loved ones.

The letter from which I have quoted went on: 'Really, however, I am afraid you are all too sincere. Don't go and cut off the offending member or some other masochistic Protestant trick. I so much prefer the Catholic sense that a healthy lapse can bring you nearer to a state of grace.'

During the 1950s my father and I did have shots at carrying on serious discussions; we exchanged letters which were extensions of the literary essays he wrote in *The European* and my occasional contributions. Such letters were also extensions of the correspondence we had carried on when he had been in prison and I had been in the war. But their style now became increasingly bombastic as we fell out of sympathy with one another. (Had I been copying his style? Was it this I was now trying to escape from?)

[Oswald Mosley to Nicholas] 27.1.52

In Paris you will find great effervescence for instance in their plays: Sartre – welcome, welcome, welcome! After Shaw in *The Apple Cart* and Gide in *Thérèse* the last of the great lefties came to judgement in a queue of reluctant Daniels! But if they have any brains at all and intellectual integrity it is in the end inevitable. Now at last we understand why all the bright young things from St Germain des Prés were wearing blackshirts when they took their vacation at Antibes two summers ago: it was not thought but premonition! The thought of *Le Diable et le Bon Dieu* remains, of course, infantile.

But the theatre sense is superb – he may one day rank as one of the greatest dramatists of all time. Perhaps as Macaulay observed of epic poetry – it is necessary to be naif to write great poetry or drama. To such types a man rolling on the floor in agony with sweat pouring down his face is possessed by devils or inspired by gods: I and my friends have reached the sad stage of saying 'appendix or duodenal; operation or castor oil?' So we admire Sartre's theatre with a tired sigh as we hear him groaning and grunting towards the posing of the question to which Plato essayed the first theoretical answers 2½ millenia ago and to which we essayed the first practical answer some 20 years ago – with results which have led us strenuously to revive both theory and practice in our present preoccupation. Anyhow it is all great fun and a good time is had by all. First the killer, the brute, the wanton lust to destroy and the will to silly power – ourselves as others see us. Then the light – the soul-groaners and self-tearers – five acts of having one's bottom soundly kicked while the world goes to pieces in the attempt at brotherhood and love. Then, as this has caused far more blood and suffering than the previous rigmarole, a universal demand for the return of the hero. So he makes the supreme sacrifice – desists from being flagellated in monasteries by beautiful ladies and enunciates certain simple verities which we learnt without the extremes of either pain or delight – order is necessary, also authority; men have not yet reached the stage where love is enough. Power is a nuisance but a painful duty (no acknowledgement of course of the Philosopher King – anyhow, whoever heard of Plato in St Germain des Prés?). So – on goes the helmet over the tonsure, the most tiresome of the anarchists is knocked off in double quick time, Oedipus complexes fairly cop it in the collapse of society. Forth steps again the dear old Dad – rather baffled and bewildered but ready to do his stuff with a newly acquired restraint. Beaten the Boys – not a man more than really necessary to be killed this time, of course! So, wiser and sadder – well whacked, well kicked, but still game – off we go again! Finally ourselves as we see ourselves – the difference between the first and last act reached by a rather circuitious, just as it was superfluous, route. Welcome Sartre!

[N.M. to O.M.] Feb. 52

Your Sartre and Gide business – but Wagner at least was trying to be one jump ahead of them. The old order muddles itself into chaos, all right; brotherly love eventually beats itself into insensibility, all right; and up pops Siegfried. But what happens then? This is the question that was so fashionable twenty years ago when there was no need to think about it and is so unfashionable now that there is. Siegfried gets bored. No more running around blowing horns and lifting shields from recumbent goddesses: he finds himself in an armchair with a rich man's wife. So he flirts with her. So he is stabbed in the back. So everything is in chaos again, and quicker too – the peculiarity of the new order is that it can destroy itself in half an hour. At least the old one bounced a few times before it burst.

The horrible thing about the 'all power corrupts' maxim is that it has never been shown to be untrue. And if it is admitted that men have not yet reached the stage when love is enough, is it likely that they have reached the stage when power is enough? I should have thought, paradoxically, that the two went together: when power is enough then love will be enough and you won't need power anyway. But, as things are, power will fail for exactly the same reason that brotherly love will fail – we are all too stupid and irresponsible; i.e. all-too-human.

This is foreseen, of course, by the best power-advocates. That is why Nietzsche had to call his man a god – i.e. a Superman. This has been misunderstood, yes, but one can't get away from it. If man is naturally chaotic then order can only be introduced by something more-than-a-man. This is the point upon which the whole question rests: can man be more than a man?

If he can, then no philosopher has ever said how. By breeding like bulls? You can breed a bull into the biggest and most beautiful bull in the world but you can't breed it into more than a bull. By Platonic training, selection, seclusion? A man is still a man. How then?

This is the point at which, with that intolerably seraphic smile, the monk comes in and gives an answer: 'How? It's all in the book.' And the awful thing is that it is – not so easy, but still a precise and relevant answer. And this, instead of being the position to which one is driven after 2,000 years of chaos, is really the starting-point of the whole Christian argument.

Well, what a style! I was trying to out-do my father? I suppose we were both showing off.

My father did not read my novels. He did not talk about them; he thought novels were a waste of what might be a talent for polemic and rhetoric. Years ago he had written to me when he had heard of my intention to write novels – 'It is like entering a horse for the pony races at Northolt instead of the Derby.' But there was one work of mine that he did read and said he liked; this was a play I had written just before I had begun to edit *Prism*. It was called

The Good Samaritans. The reason why he liked it was because it was, indeed, some effort to portray a synthesis (a favourite word of my father's) between his hobby-horses and mine. The story was as follows:

A group of passengers flying across the Atlantic have to make an emergency landing in the Azores. They realise that among them are two Russian security men taking home what seems to be a political prisoner against his will. While the other passengers wait they are faced with the question – is there anything they should or can do to help this man, who seems to be like the man in the parable who has fallen among thieves? One of the passengers is a priest, and another a German ex-SS Colonel. These two become involved in a dispute about the moralities and practicalities of the situation: how in fact could a good Samaritan, such as presumably the priest would wish to be, help? Would this not in fact, in the situation in which the man was still in the power of the thieves, be the sort of job for the ex-SS officer? By the end – out of pride? out of humility? – these two find themselves in some joint rescue operation which is successful at the cost of the SS Colonel being killed, and the priest giving him absolution.

When Hugo Charteris read this play he wrote to me that he saw it as – 'a son bending over his father via a priest and saying – "He was a human being with more courage and intelligence than most: forgive him/me!" '

But for what might I think my father and I should be forgiven?

When my father had started Union Movement it had for a time made little impact; there were meetings at street corners in East London and one or two in Kensington Town Hall. During this time my father kept clear of remarks that might be taken to be racialist or anti-Semitic. But then – where in the rationalisations about Europe-with-Africa could there be the rhetoric that had once lifted people out of their seats? He had written to me, 'My chief fault as a politician is that I am too near sane: keep it dark! All that moves men is black and white.' Perhaps he hoped for a time when he might be able to move men again.

My father's association with the Notting Hill area of London began in 1958 when considerable numbers of immigrants from the West Indies had moved in and there began to be street fights between gangs of black and white youths. My father announced that he would mount a political campaign in the area with the aim of bringing order to a troubled situation. His policy was that the recent immigrants should be repatriated – as a last resort by force, but 'with fares paid . . . and to good jobs with good wages'. What was required, he argued, was capital investment in the West Indies: 'I say – Let the Jamaicans have their country back and let us have ours.'

Such a policy could sound reasonable except the bit about forcible repatriation, but even about this my father could argue – What reasonable person would in fact have to be forced back to the land of his birth if there were good jobs there and good wages? But as usual my father's arguments seemed to take no account of an actual human situation – in this case of the reluctance of people to move back when they have made a decisive break with their past; of the difficulties, indeed, of doing much about conditions in the West Indies.

Union Movement's weekly newspaper, *Action*, for the most part maintained a reasoned tone, though Diana wrote a memo to my father quoting unfortunate examples of *Action*'s more virulent style that might make people think its policy was concerned more with racialism than with economic sense. But in the current situation any speech pressing for repatriation, however muted any reference to the possible use of force, seemed to be playing into the hands of those who might wish to indulge hatred. And anyway, why had my father chosen to campaign in just this area? *The Times* sent a reporter to look at the situation in Notting Hill. He concluded that Union Movement was not creating the disturbances but was obviously making use of them; my father's official policy might be reasonable, but it was not on this account that people were joining the Movement. Such people 'fight because they have an instinctive desire to do so: it is admitted that these elements are out of control of the party'. But then – why did the party let these people remain under its banner?

There had been an incident in the early days of Union Movement which had lodged in my mind (I have told this story before in *Beyond the Pale*: I tell it again, together with other stories of this time, because it and they seem central to an understanding of my father). My father had summoned to him one of his lieutenants who had disobeyed orders that members of the Movement should not become involved in the breaking-up of opponents' meetings; my father reprimanded this man in a room next to where Rosemary and Diana and I were having dinner. My father shouted at the man for a time; the man was saying 'Yes sir, sorry sir'; then my father said to him quietly 'Well, don't do it again.' But as the man went out of the door some wink seemed to pass between my father and the man – some recognition of comradeship and complicity beyond the demands of discipline – and it was as if we all knew that the man would of course do whatever he had done again, he knew it and my father knew it, they each knew that the other knew it, it was as if my father had found some way of letting his right hand both know and not know what his left hand was doing.

When I talked to my father of such incidents he would say – with the half-self-mocking half-smile half-frown of someone who has been caught out in some sleight-of-hand but does not mind – 'It's a rough game': or – 'One must keep the boys happy.'

My father's campaign in Notting Hill came to a head during the run-up to the 1959 General Election; this was when he had announced that he would be standing as a parliamentary candidate in the local North Kensington constituency. This was just at the time when I was writing my stuff about integrity in *Prism*. I wondered – I see that it may be difficult for politicians always to match their activities with their words, but what should I myself be doing in this particular situation? I went to hear my father speak in Notting Hill; I stood at the back of a crowd on a street corner; there he was on top of a loudspeaker van and after a time beginning to shout as if, indeed, devils were prodding him. For much of his speech he had been putting his reasonable case about the need to create jobs in the West Indies; then suddenly something seemed to take over and he was off on some uproar about black men keeping teenage white girls in attics. I thought that at least I should write to him. But what sort of tone might be effective? I wrote:

Your policy regarding black men is to provide jobs for them in their own homelands by providing capital for backward areas. This is admirable. Your intention in general is to have a movement which is 'manly, disciplined, restrained and self-controlled; which never begins trouble and never exults in it, just is prepared to meet it if others insist'. Again, this is unexceptionable. But what in practice happens is that your movement holds a meeting in Notting Hill which is followed by violence.

To say that the speakers never wanted nor intended violence is meaningless. To believe this would be an opinion of such astonishing political naivity that it were surely better to be hushed up – it must still be better for a politician to be thought something of a villain rather than an idiot. It must always be remembered that the struggle is not one of policy versus policy, because no one is fighting you on this level, but one of your opponents accusing you of madness through the evidence of your actions and you, presumably, con-cerned with producing evidence that they are wrong. If you hand this game to your opponents so easily, you cannot blame them for not bothering to take you on in the further battle about policy.

To sum up – Fascism, and therefore Union Movement, has got the general reputation, whether fairly or unfairly, of having to depend on racial hatred in order to maintain its appeal and impetus. It was this reputation that made Fascism so hated years ago.

Now you and your followers say that this reputation is unfair, but still it is in people's minds. Your obvious intention, therefore, since it is so harming your cause, would seem to be to take steps to eradicate it.

One would have thought these steps would have included instruc-tions to avoid, in speech and writing and action, all controversial racial issues like the plague; there would be orders, surely, to hold meetings anywhere rather than in Notting Hill. Failure to take this sort of action seems only to mean that in spite of your words on paper, your intention is not seriously to eradicate from people's minds the impression of your need for racial hatred.

Your reasons for not wanting to do this are beyond my com-petence to guess. But the results of it are that your words seem destined to bluff only yourselves, and not to influence responsible people who will go only by your actions.

To this letter my father replied just that in fact no Union Movement meeting in Notting Hill had resulted directly in violence, and he challenged anyone to produce concrete evidence that it had.

I felt the necessity to have some personal confrontation with my father, though in the area of politics it seemed unlikely that anything I said would touch him. Over the years it was true I had shown little interest in politics; and anyway, my father's skill with words was such that in this area he was used to protecting himself against any influence from others.

But there was an adjacent area where it seemed it might be both possible and indeed necessary for me to get round my father's flank, as it were; this was to do with my half-brother Alexander. In a tabloid newspaper of this time there was a photograph of my half-brothers Alexander and Max in Notting Hill: the photograph had the effect of making them look like local toughs; they were reported as saying they had come to the area to help Union Movement.

After my extraordinary meeting with Alexander on the occasion of the Aldermaston March I had been struck by what seemed to be my responsibility for him. Many years ago when my grandmother (my father's mother) had been on her death-bed, she had made a last request of my father which was that his two youngest children should be baptised; my father had agreed to this, and the children then aged eleven and nine had been hauled off to the presumably rather startled local vicar, and at Diana's request I had agreed to be Alexander's godfather – though this must have meant as little to me at the time as to most of the others concerned. But then Alexander had stayed with Rosemary and me when I had been finding him an English school: and it was then that he had seemed an extraordinary boy, half under the influence of my father, of course, but also half looking far beyond it: and was I not in a position to help about such things? And then there had been the incident on the Aldermaston March when he had come running across the road and had joined me for a time under my banner: but now here he was in the photograph taken at Notting Hill being made to look like one of my father's followers who had been told not to become involved in street-brawls – and so on. But then I heard from Diana that Alexander was now in fact at loggerheads with my father, and was in a state of considerable depression: and so she wondered – could I help?

It seemed that Alexander had been working for a travel-agent who was an admirer of my father, but then had left the agency and at my father's insistence had become an apprentice chartered accountant; it was in this life that he had become seriously depressed. Diana wrote to me that this was to some extent due to my father's attitude; my father was refusing to allow him to go to a university (he was nineteen) on the grounds that he could not write an essay and 'is bound to fail in any enterprise through lack of will-power and by making himself universally disliked'. Since Alexander when he had stayed with Rosemary and me four years before had been not only the most brilliant boy I had known (perhaps in this way he might make others feel inadequate?) but also gentle and kind, it did seem, yes, that there might be something here about which I could help.

So Alexander came again to stay with Rosemary and me. He said that he wanted to get out of his apprenticeship and out of his father's orbit: it was in the latter, yes, that he felt some paralysis and despair. Some months ago he had wanted to get away to South America, but my father would give him no money. So of course I now said that I would give him money. In South America there might still be moments of despair; but beyond these there would be the chance to move into another orbit.

Suddenly Diana was backing the plan for Alexander to get away to South America; my father was washing his hands of the affair; he was too tied up with his campaign in Notting Hill. But then equally suddenly there was the possibility that Alexander might be called up to do his National Service. This was unlikely, since Alexander was a resident of Ireland, and it seemed that the authorities might be wanting to interview him simply because of the publicity about his involvement in Notting Hill. But then my father was saying that of course he should do National Service! and thus could not go to South America. At this point motives and emotions became inextricably mixed. There might possibly be a case for Alexander doing National Service, but this was anyway coming to an end; and how outrageous (it seemed to me) was my father's present complaint that publicity about Alexander not presenting himself for an interview might harm his, my father's, campaign in Notting Hill! If Alexander cancelled his plans to go to South America now he might never escape from the coils of my father's attitudes. But then – was I really fighting just for Alexander – or also for myself in my battle with my father? It seemed that such complexities had to be faced, but in the end decisions had to be left to Alexander – or perhaps to fate, or to whatever it is that looks after ends once one has tried to look at correct means.

As it worked out all the strands of the drama seemed to come together on the same day – a meeting arranged between my father and his lawyer and Alexander to discuss the call-up, the last chance for Alexander to get away, and my own determination to have a confrontation with my father who seemed to have been avoiding me ever since my involvement with Alexander and my criticism of his activities in Notting Hill. Alexander had a ticket to Paris, where he had people to say goodbye to, and from there a ticket to South America. The train he had planned to go on left on the morning when he was due to see my father and the lawyer; I presented myself at my father's office on this morning and said I would wait till my father agreed to see me. I sat in an ante-room where there was a printing-press churning out pro-apartheid leaflets about South Africa; I did not know whether Alexander would turn up or if he had in fact left for Paris; after a time it seemed he would not be coming. I had realised on my way to the office that I was more frightened about this confrontation with my father than I had been at any time since the war. Eventually I was shown into my father's office and he and Diana and the lawyer were in a line behind a desk and my father asked me if I knew where Alexander was. I said I did not know exactly, but I hoped he was on his way to South America. Then I said I had some other things to say to him, my father, and I spewed it all out – He had been a lousy father to his children but especially to Alexander; what did he think he was doing wanting to hold such a brilliant person down? And with regard to his politics in Notting Hill – did he not see that with his racialism he was destroying himself and his policies as he had done before? And so on. After a time my father said quietly, 'I will never speak to you again.' I had expected a thunderbolt. I said 'Well, I will always speak to you.' Then I left.

Later I wrote to him saying I regretted implying that he had been a bad father to me, because I did not think he had. He did not reply to this letter. I telephoned Diana to say I believed Alexander to be all right. I had a letter from Alexander which confirmed that he had indeed been on the train to Paris when I had been having my confrontation with my father, and asked me for the time being not to let anyone know where he was.

What had been, and continued to be, particularly equivocal in this drama was Diana's role and attitude. She was the archetypal mother torn between love for her husband and love for her son; between loyalty to the one and the welfare of the other. She wrote of her gratitude to Rosemary and me for what we had been able to do for Alexander, and she had even chipped in with £75 of travellers' cheques for his journey. But at the same time she could not be seen openly to be going against my father's will. In this sort of situation perhaps there has to be some not-knowing by the right hand of what the left hand is doing; and thus eventually some search for scapegoats.

I wrote to Alexander, 'What matters is for you to get an ocean between yourself and Dad. You'll be able to fight it straight in ten years: till then you won't.' And about myself, 'I had not been being quite honest with Dad, and it was time that I said to his face what I believe.'

As things worked out, Alexander dallied that summer in Europe before travelling further; this was a worrying time, but it was understandable that he should find it difficult to make breaks with the past all at once. This summer saw the culmination of my father's campaign in North Kensington; a poll taken just before the election had predicted that my father would get 35 per cent of the vote; then when the time came he got 8 per cent and lost his deposit. He seemed unable to believe this, and instigated a law-suit suggesting that the ballot-boxes had been tampered with. This case came to nothing. It seemed that what had happened was what indeed had so often happened with my father – people were bowled over by his rhetoric, but when the time came for commitment they turned away.

Alexander eventually caught a boat to Valparaiso in November. I wrote to Diana to say that although this had been a risky and obscure period, Alexander had had to be free to do things in his own time, and now we might hope that he might go ahead under his own steam. Through the summer Diana had continued to seem grateful and to back the plan (my father apparently was led to believe that Alexander was already in Chile): but then when he was in fact in Chile the tone of Diana's letters changed. She was now free to be unequivocally loyal to my father; there was no more need to feel torn.

But what weird bombardments and smokescreens there are when people choose to be unequivocally loyal! What a need for scapegoats!

I had hoped in this book to reproduce letters from Diana to me, but perhaps understandably she has not given her permission. Diana writes and speaks with a distinctive voice, and while often disagreeing with me she is formidable in putting her views. I have had to paraphrase her letters, which I have done as well as I can.

In a long letter to me that she wrote after Alexander landed in Chile she blamed me on several counts – not about my help in getting him to Chile, because this she continued to back, but because I had not pushed him hard enough when he had been lingering in Europe. She held up as an example how she and my father had succeeded in pushing him to become an apprentice chartered accountant. She agreed that my father and Alexander had been getting on badly and were better apart, but suggested I had helped achieve this for the wrong reasons – that it was as a Christian I had wanted to separate him from the influence of my father and herself, and in so doing I had almost handed him back to my father's henchman the travel-agent in Europe – preferring publicans and sinners to more noble company. No harm had been done because Alexander now seemed so well and healthy. But it had been a big risk in her opinion. Christianity was the promoter of much of the evil in the world now.

The tone and content of this letter were those of someone in fairly urgent need of scapegoats; an obvious candidate was myself, who had indeed been vulnerable in such a tricky business. This pattern was to be repeated in a more public and dramatic way in a later part of the story. It is a pattern exemplified by someone who cannot see that there can properly be conflicting drives and passions within onself and those whom one loves – especially with regard to one's relations with those whom one loves – who require that oneself and one's loved ones should be seen as all-of-a-piece, sinless.

IO

During the two years I had been editor of *Prism* it had continued with its message – Christianity is demonstrated by activity and style of activity and not just by words; Christian commitment involves a certain cost. In the last number of *Prism* that I edited I wrote, 'It is true that Christians and the Church will always be hated and scorned by some people: it is entirely right that it should give a certain offence and suffer for it.'

Prism's circulation had seldom risen above 2,000, but people wrote about how it gave them encouragement, and I like to think it had some enlivening effect at a time when there did not seem to be much stirring in the Anglican Church. And of course I liked to think that liveliness anyway happens somewhat secretly.

When Father Raynes had died in June 1958 I had been surprised how I, like others, had seemed to get on without him. In 1959 it was suggested by Robin Denniston of the Faith Press and Father Graham, the new Superior of the Community of the Resurrection, that I should write Father Raynes's biography. I was even more surprised, and pleased, about this. This was a way in which my relationship with Father Raynes could go on!

During the winter of 1959/60 I spent time collecting information and talking to people, but it seemed that sooner or later I would have to go out to South Africa where a vital part of Father Raynes's life had been spent. It was this that determined the timing of my leaving *Prism*. Early in 1960 I handed over to Robin Denniston and Christopher Martin.

Just before I was due to go out to South Africa, on a slow boat which stopped at Ascension Island and St Helena, I became ill with an esoteric form of malaria that had attacked me twice before in the three years since I had been in West Africa; my temperature went up to 106 °F and I had a vivid image of myself on the way to hell prodded by tiny devils with pitchforks. Conventional treatment seemed of no use, so I was carted off to the Hospital for Tropical Diseases where I became an interesting guinea-pig for students: I lay in bed and answered questions and people had to guess what was wrong. I thought I should make use of this time by reading the Bible through from beginning to end. This I did, and it struck me forcibly how different it seemed like this from when people read it, as they usually did, chopped up in bits and pieces. It also struck me – Why do people usually do this? to protect themselves from the real message?

The message that was being conveyed, it seemed to me (being prodded from time to time by students or by devils with pitchforks), was that there had been a time when humans had felt they should live under God's law and had found that they could not, so this attempt had been a failure. Then there was a time when it had seemed that whatever God required for humans in the way of obedience and sacrifice He had done or was doing for them, and they just had to believe this and be grateful. But even at this time there had been a hint – well more than a hint! – that what humans were required to do now was to become agents in whatever was God's further activity; and they could do this because the ability to know truth was now within them. There was the God of the Old Testament, that is, and the God of the New Testament, and humans indeed had to be in relationship with these; but there was also God the Holy Spirit – about Whom not very much had even been said or perhaps ever could be said, because the nature of the activity of the Spirit was such that it has to be discovered and practised by each person on his or her own. But now the Spirit was coming into His or Her own – at the end of the Bible this seemed to be the message – and it was this that humans could trust as they went on their journeys in the dark. All this seemed to me by the end of my reading to make – light! But still not the sort of light I could quite pin down in words: you don't do this anyway with light; you see what it illuminates.

For instance, as far as trust in journeys in the dark went, was there not the story of myself and my family and my half-brother Alexander who was now bravely writing to me from South America of his determination to make good. And was there not the continuing story of 'Mary' from *The Rainbearers* who had come bounding into my *Prism* office one day to let me know that she was well, and was going to be married – she wrote to me later to say she would like to keep the money I was giving her because 'without it I could not have married, I think!' There seemed to be good patterns being worked out here: but not to be talked about much, for fear of distorting the light.

I sometimes wondered – Perhaps, if one so chooses, one can make almost anything seem to come out into the light!

When I had come to the end of the Bible and to the end of my bout of malaria, I flew to Johannesburg early in 1960 and went to stay in the suburb of Rosettenville at St Peter's Priory which was the South African headquarters of the Community of the Resurrection. It was from here that Father Huddleston had until recently been fighting his battles on behalf of Africans; it was here that my old friend the ex-novice monk was now a teacher in the Community's theological college for Africans – he who ten years ago had written me such good letters about the ways of conversion. This was the first time I had stayed for longer than a night or two in a monastic house, but from my visits to Mirfield I had become accustomed to feeling at home in the routine of Prime, Terce, Sext, None and Compline – the short services of prayer at set times each day – in addition to daily Mass and Matins and Evensong by which monks regulate their lives. And it seemed that in South Africa, especially, these disciplines might be means of hanging on to threads of sanity in an otherwise insane world.

Living in the complex of buildings that were the Priory were forty or so African students; these were on easy terms with the white brethren; this was one of the very few places in South Africa at this time where blacks and whites could live side by side. Outside there was apartheid, the results of which for the blacks were that bread-winners were separated from their families, and police had wide-ranging powers to imprison anyone they chose. Father Raynes and his successor Father Huddleston had led the fight against this in Johannesburg; lately, however, there had been the question – Would it not be better if Africans led the fight for themselves? In the Priory there was a feeling – Might it not be 'paternalism' if whites and blacks continued to live as teachers and pupils?

I was taken by the brethren of the Community to the African townships around Johannesburg; I talked to the people who had been friends of Father Raynes. Here amongst rows of houses like transport-containers was the quiet dignity of Africans; also the violence – of people who felt their dignity affronted and betrayed. There were the churches where everyone sang at the tops of their voices; children everywhere with their bright, darting eyes. In one of these townships, Sophiatown, Father Raynes had come to work twenty-five years ago. There had been no churches then and no schools; Father Raynes had run a mission with three other white brethren, and next door there had been four or five members of an order of lay-women led by Dorothy Maud, an upper-class English-woman. This group of white men and women together had formed a cell within the huge black township. In my biography of Father Raynes I wrote:

> In six years they built three churches, seven schools, three nursery schools, and had over three thousand children under their care. They expanded the hospital and built a swimming-bath; they raised the money for all this themselves. In the townships they got water, lighting, sanitation and roads. They fought for the poor and per-secuted in the courts, the police stations, and in the Town Council. They became known to a whole generation of Africans as white people who would go to outstanding lengths to help them. And they became known as Christians, people who practised what they preached, whose beliefs and life were worth following.

Their energy for this seemed to come from some gift of the Spirit; they could love their neighbours because there was love amongst themselves.

They had together the private jokes, the private language, that go with common enthusiasm and affections. Enemies were said to be 'up the pole'; friends, and things approved of, 'edifying'. Raymond (Father Raynes) liked the women to wear bright dresses: he liked the church always full of flowers. A nun from Grahamstown came to paint frescoes on the arch by the high altar; her work was hidden for weeks behind scaffolding and then there appeared – among the packed and worshipping faces of the people of Sophiatown – Our Lady with a look of Dorothy Maud, and St Francis with the head of Raymond.

In 1960 when I visited Sophiatown the bulldozers were moving in to make space for a new white suburb and Africans were being moved to more distant and more manageable townships. I wrote:

Many of the outward signs of Raymond's work have been destroyed. Sophiatown is a waste of rubble like a town in war. St Cyprian's School is crumbling and weeds grow in the playground. Only the Church of Christ the King still stands, and people walk for miles to it on Sundays.

For every growth in value the seed has to die. The work that Raymond did in Africa is now alive in thousands of homes that he never knew and never visited. The churches are in charge of Africans he taught, the schools are run by his own 'children'. The Congregation of Christ the King is scattered after the destruction of its Jerusalem.

After more than thirty years it is still possible to feel the work that Father Raynes did in Africa as being alive. Oliver Tambo, for many years Chairman of the African National Congress, was at one of the schools for which Father Raynes was responsible. At Easter 1990 I met Nelson Mandela in London and I asked him if he remembered Father Raynes: after a moment's thought his face lit up and he said, 'Oh yes, a good man! A very humorous man!'

Before I had set out for Johannesburg I had been given the names of people I might visit other than the friends of Father Raynes and Father Huddleston – in particular, friends of my aunt Irene Ravensdale – people who lived in the rich white suburbs. I had no names of friends of my father's, because he and I were still not on speaking terms. However, I was aware that the name 'Mosley', and my father's pro-apartheid reputation, might make me initially welcome in homes of the white establishment. Thus I was able to move across demarcation-lines that to others were a barrier: in the daytime I would be talking with Africans in the townships, then in the evenings I would sometimes venture into the white suburbs where dinners were served by African servants with white gloves. People would ask me – 'Where did you say you were staying in Johannesburg?' and I would say – 'At the Priory at Rosettenville, you know, Father Huddleston's old headquarters.' Father Huddleston was still an anathema to most whites. But at these parties I found, far more than I had expected, that there were people with whom I could talk and make friends: they knew themselves to be trapped within a predicament: does one run away? does one do one's best under the implacable stare of African servants in their white gloves?

I wrote a report for *Prism*:

> The failure of the Church with the rich white English-speakers is simply that of the Church with the rich anywhere – the Church has never made up its mind about money and prestige and the hell of gracious living, and so it has little chance to do so in South Africa, where if you take respect for Mammon out of the social order you are likely to be left with nothing else. This failure is a failure of Christian culture.

With regard to the Afrikaans-speaking whites, it struck me that none of the people I was meeting – neither the Community brethren nor the English-speaking whites nor of course the Africans – had any social contacts with these Afrikaners; yet it was they who ran the government and whose minds and hearts would have to change if there was to be any chance of political evolution rather than the threat of revolution. Even Father Raynes had had little to do with Afrikaners except in public dispute; it was as if even to him they had been beyond the pale. I wondered – There might here have been some failure of trust in ends being changed by means?

I had a chance myself to have some social contact with an Afrikaner when, returning in a hired car from a trip to one of the Community's houses in Southern Rhodesia, at the frontier at Beit

Bridge I was asked by an Afrikaner farmer if I would give him a lift to Pretoria some three hundred miles away. I said I would, and almost immediately our conversation got on to the subject of whether or not, if this man's daughter had any sort of social contact with a black man, he would have the right (which he claimed) to shoot them both dead. This sort of argument continued for much of the three hundred miles; every now and then he would ask me to stop the car because he could no longer bear to be in my company; every now and then I would stop the car and say he would have to get out. But in addition to the fact that for most of the way we were in a wilderness, there also seemed to be a challenge that we should stick things out. By the time we reached Pretoria we were like two boxers at the end of fifteen rounds; but my companion offered to stand me a drink in a bar, about which I was pleased. In the bar there were a lot of Afrikaners drinking beer, and we were continuing our conversation in a desultory way when a very small old Afrikaner farmer came up and offered to fight me with one hand tied behind his back. But by now I was under the protection of my travelling companion – so I never learned how I would get on in a fight with a very small old Afrikaner farmer with one hand tied behind his back.

I reported to *Prism*:

> The trouble with the Afrikaner seems to be psychological: he won't discuss a question straight, but talks in ejaculatory slogans like quotations from a psychiatrist's notebook. An argument about *apartheid* does not proceed point by point about practical possibilities, but swerves off immediately on to sex, death, communists, Ghana, and interminable warnings about daughters. To a psychiatrist the sex-and-death talk must seem a direct symptom of the speaker's own fear and frustration, and a deep inability to face life as a responsible adult.
>
> Most Afrikaners are members of the Dutch Reformed Church, whose theology has stopped somewhere short of the Book of Chronicles. They see themselves as a chosen people in a chosen land surrounded by enemies. Their national symbol is the laager – a circle of ox-carts out of which bearded men fire fitfully. In this sort of mentality there is a need for embattlement and death in order to feel at home. The organisation for self-destruction is a common

symptom of fascism. Events in South Africa – where in the name of saving white civilisation people are doing everything to destroy it – may become impossible to understand unless the psychology of fascism is realised.

I sometimes wondered – As well as learning about Father Raynes, was I still as usual learning about my father? In his political life had he not had a need to be beleaguered: instead of painstakingly going about the business of getting and ordering power, had he not preferred to be on top of a van hurling defiance at a multitude? He claimed he was not a racialist; yet by gathering racialists around him, did he not feel at home?

But then about Father Raynes – he in fact seemed to have driven himself so hard in his battle with his enemies that he had ruined his health and become ill. During his time in Africa he had often refused to eat proper food; he had lived (so I was told) on a diet of sardines and pickles; when problems had pressed in on him he had just increased his times of prayer and fasting. This might have helped perhaps to give him a spiritual cutting-edge in his dealings with the outside world, but it also seemed to have been self-destructive. By his mid-thirties he was suffering severely from ulcers, and bit by bit he had had much of his inside cut out. He had died at the age of fifty-five – and before this he had been in some desolation. I wondered – Might there not have been some sort of laager mentality even here? Surely the style of the Holy Spirit was more than simple self-immolation!

I had been a month or two in South Africa when there took place the incident that became known as the Sharpeville Massacre: police opened fire on peaceful demonstrators in the black township of Sharpeville and some 70 people were killed. When the news came through I was in the Priory at Rosettenville and we were about to have supper; the atmosphere at the meal was strained. It was as if we all – the white brethren and the African students and myself – were suddenly aware of the inadequacy of our positions: a revolution might be (perhaps should be?) starting; should we not be out doing something or other in the streets? After the meal we were all in the scullery washing up; we were still silent and constrained. Then one of the white brethren, who had once been an actor and who still affected the style known as 'camp', turned to the student beside him and said, 'Oh you terrible old black thing, why don't you go away and wash!' And then we were all suddenly laughing, clinging to each other's shoulders laughing or crying, and the constraint and the feeling of hopelessness had gone. Afterwards I wondered – You mean, the style of the Holy Spirit might be something to do with the self-assurance of wit?

At the very end of my time in Johannesburg there was a wave of arrests of Africans and anti-apartheid whites, and amongst the latter was Hannah Stanton, a worker in a nursery school for African children in Pretoria, who was the sister of one of the brethren of the Community. I went with him to Pretoria to see what could be done. At the police station there were policemen with the sort of blank faces from which the ability to listen seemed to have been erased: they told us that under the emergency regulations it was an offence for us even to ask about Hannah Stanton, let alone for them to answer. It was as if they had found a way by which people might be erased.

When I got home I wrote an article about Hannah Stanton which was published in the *Spectator*; also one about racialism which was called 'The Schizoid State.' In this I wrote:

> The two main convictions of racialism are, firstly, that it is the basis of all human life (Hitler wrote – 'The highest aim of human existence is the conservation of the race . . . the maintenance of the racial stock unmixed'); and secondly, that once a man's mind is made up about this he can never think of changing it ('All ideas and ideals, all teaching and all knowledge, must serve these ends. It is from this standpoint that everything must be examined and turned to practical use or else discarded'). Hitler added that he himself had formed his *Weltanschauung* in his early twenties, and since then had 'changed nothing in it'.
>
> A racialist is thus a person who not only lives according to what other people think is a fantasy, but who tries to allow no evidence of reason, science, observation or personal experience to touch him.
>
> It is easy to see these characteristics in South Africa. If you try to reason with a white South African he still assumes you are criticising his country's material care of Africans – the way they are

housed and fed. He thus answers you in terms of how much the Government spends on new building, or of his personal relationship with some loyal office boy. If you say this is not that you are talking about – you are talking about votes and freedom of movement and trades unions – then a blank look comes over his face and he has nothing to answer you. This is not because you have stumped him, but because he finds you unintelligible. To him it is as if you were talking about horses. This is a situation that has silenced philosophers – the man who looks at a human being and says that he calls it something else.

The racialist won't accept the universal evidence of anthropologists, biologists and sociologists that his racial classifications are nonsense. He prefers his own imaginative analogies drawn usually from bull-breeding. (Hitler had a variation – 'The titmouse cohabits only with the titmouse, the fieldmouse with the fieldmouse, the housemouse with the housemouse . . .') His convictions are stronger than science.

The disease of racialism in an individual, psychologists say, arises from a refusal to face the evil or 'dark' side of oneself, and a transference of this on to some group that appears different in order that one can continue to think of oneself as elect and sinless. This refusal is made when facts arise in one's experience which are painful and frightening to bear. These are often natural and inevitable predicaments, and if such facts are faced, then by the very undergoing of the ordeal there is growth both in knowledge and in further capacity. This is how spiritual growth happens. But if painful facts about oneself are not faced, then there is a blockage in the path of normal growth and a deviation towards some dead end of personality.

The normal growth of human societies, scientists say, depends on their acceptance of ever greater complexities and unifications. If society refuses these, it deviates up some dead end of evolution.

In Africa and in my attempt to be committed to Christianity I was learning about 'society'; I was learning about Father Raynes; I was still trying to come to terms, as it were, with my father. But granted all this – in the matter of 'ever greater complexities and unifications' what on earth (for I saw that this was what was basically required) was I learning about myself?

II

My book about Father Raynes was a show of gratitude for someone who had meant so much to me; also an effort to understand a Christian who had continued to express his religious commitment in dogmatic language while at the same time having such a practical attitude to the promptings and requirements of an actual human situation. He seemed to be someone through whom the Holy Spirit worked: there was a transparency in him through which people seemed to see what was beyond him.

Father Raynes had had a devout Christian upbringing; the language of the Psalms and the 1662 Prayer Book were natural to him. He saw religious language as properly one of metaphor, of poetry. Two phrases occur over and over again in his sermons: 'Life is a love-song we sing to Jesus' and 'We sink down deeper and deeper in God's love and are no nearer the bottom.' This was the sort of language by which one might try to touch what is essentially beyond one.

Towards the end of his life, however, he evolved a brusquer style as if this might be suited to God's demand that humans should in a practical way become more responsible for themselves and learn to listen to what was inside them. In one of his last addresses he had written:

> There are certain things that all men know, and that is the truth.
> What Our Lord said is this – If we face the things about which we

know, then we will hear his voice. But if we are not truthful about the things which we know to be true, then of course it is clear that the things which Our Lord teaches, and the things which Our Lord did, have no meaning at all.

Conventional religion is about as much use to a man as a sick headache, because it disguises truth and never faces facts.

I am to serve God in that state of life to which it shall please Him to call me. In that state of life I am to say 'Yes' to God in every circumstance. I am to fulfil his commands (largely made known to me through circumstance and the demands of other people) 'at once, in silence, and at a run'. By this means I am to save my soul – to be a whole man – and salvation is to be set free into the glorious liberty of the sons of God.

Before I had begun my biography I had become aware of the way in which Father Raynes towards the end of his life had fallen out with many of his brethren in the Community, and had suffered some desolation. I wanted to find out more about this. What had he learned (or perhaps not learned?) about God's commands made known to him 'through circumstance and the demands of other people'?

Father Raynes had been Superior for fifteen years when, in January 1958, he had not been elected again. It had apparently been felt he had become too aloof from the day-to-day life of the Community; he drove his brethren as he drove himself, too hard; he was not a comforter to them, being so often away with his friends in the south where he seemed to get comfort himself. To these friends the attitude of the Community was bewildering: should not monks drive themselves hard? Was it not good to accept comfort where and when it turned up?

During the last months of his life Father Raynes seemed to have experienced some dark night of the soul. From the Community headquarters at Mirfield he had written to a friend:

I feel terribly oppressed by gibbering ghosts and devils and in the dark, and it is not easy to keep cheerful before others which I must do lest I make them worried and distressed. I would like to run away from here, I feel lonely and a stranger. It is so difficult when you have been father of the family and have tried to love and care for and teach your sons suddenly no longer to be their father . . . It makes me so weary in heart and mind.

When I came to write my biography I was given the greatest help by members of the Community, especially the new Superior, Father Graham, who allowed me access to the Community archives. From these I learned how, of course, there were always tensions and antagonisms in Community life; also how in theory it was understood that ways of salvation are sometimes to be learned through suffering. I could talk about this in general with members of the Community; but when it came to particulars about the last months of Father Raynes's life it seemed often that a curtain came down, as if there were something shameful here, which for both their sakes and his should remain secret.

As a young man Father Raynes had written that probably at some stage in spiritual development:

> . . . it is necessary for the growth of the soul that sensible consolations should be removed. When this happens something approaching desolation takes place. There is an aridity of the senses – the ways of prayer and devotion to which the soul had grown accustomed become distasteful and there are temptations to 'throw it all up' or to regard the past as illusion.
>
> But when it is passed through it leads to the beginning of infused knowledge and love and the way of illumination . . . This self-knowledge produces a sort of experimental knowledge of God.

I felt that it was not difficult to understand how Father Raynes, after his active and busy years as Superior, had entered into some desolation; so long as there is life there is something new to be learned. What I found difficult to understand was the way in which his brethren seemed to think that such a process – a journey in the dark which might lead to 'an experimental knowledge of God' – was somehow improper and not to be talked about; also the way in which Father Raynes himself did not seem to see that it might be through looking at such an attitude that something new might be learned.

I wondered – Was it because Father Raynes found himself committed to obedience to the rules of the Community, rather than to listening (as he advocated) to the promptings of a truth that might have been inside him, that he did not find himself 'set free into the glorious liberty of the sons of God'?

– Of course people grow old; have to to die –

– It is often what is passed on that sets people free?

When my biography, *The Life of Raymond Raynes*, came out it seemed at first to be well received by the Community: the Superior wrote that he was 'thrilled' with it; 'the skill with which you cope with Community relationships (and indeed the whole of the life) is uncanny'. But then I became aware that there was some hostility to the book on account of its 'frankness' and 'outspokenness' – not only about the sadness of Father Raynes's last months, but even about what had seemed to me to be the success of his early days as Superior. When there was a question of reprinting the hardback edition I was told that there were objections to the book by members of the Community on account of 'factual inaccuracies'. I wrote to Father Graham, who replied:

> Factual inaccuracies? I expect there are a few about dates, misprints, etc. But certainly insufficient to make it a reason for not reprinting the book.
>
> The commonest criticism of the book is that you have heightened the drama by depicting a Community scene before Raymond was elected which is not easily recognisable by those who were living in it. It had to be rather overdone for this great statesman to put it right. That's the criticism. But pressures to stop it being reprinted, sinister and mysterious, are not emanating from here.
>
> It comes from catching so much of the authentic Raymond that people are really *affected* by the book.

I felt – But I had the run of the Community archives: most of the brethren have not. You mean – There may be the need for scapegoats even here?

When the book was eventually reprinted as a paperback the Community said they did not want copies for the bookstall. The book continued to be valued by individual brethren and by people outside.

I felt – All right, so what do I myself have to learn from the promptings of this experience –

– What are the signs of the ways in which people are trapped: what are the ways in which people are set free?

Is it being protected by obedience to fixed ways of thinking that prevents people from 'saying "Yes" to God in every circumstance'?

After my return from South Africa I had been in some correspondence with my stepmother Diana in order to find out news about my half-brother Alexander who was still in South America. Also, Diana had read my *Spectator* article about apartheid and had taken up the cudgels. She wrote defending apartheid on the grounds that blacks were not fit to have power; someone might coerce them into taking 'some revolting Mau Mau oath', and surely neither I nor Fr Huddleston nor 'that self-satisfied-looking Miss H. Stanton' could wish that, even for our worst enemies.

My half-brother Alexander had had good and bad times in South America, but he had survived. And even my father (so I heard from my sister) was now 'very mellow' about his time there, and now had joined Diana in only blaming me for 'not pushing him harder' from the start – though he, my father, was still 'very ferocious about Christianity'. However, Alexander was now thinking of coming home – this was 1961 – with a view to going later to an American university. I thought this a very good idea; also that there might now be a chance of Alexander going ahead as it were with my father's blessing – there being something stultifying about a father's curse. So I wrote to Diana to say that the time had perhaps now come when my father might show some practical appreciation of Alexander. Diana replied that she was all in favour of the idea of an American university, but my father would not put up any of the money, so she would be glad if I would.

Alexander came back from South America and went to stay with my father and Diana in France. Diana wrote further to say that my father and Alexander were getting on very happily, but my father was still adamant that he would not pay for further education. His argument (half a joke?) was that I had taken Alexander away from him and so should be responsible.

So my brother Michael and myself undertook to see Alexander through university (Michael most nobly, because he had had nothing to do with the original conflict); and Diana agreed to increase the small allowance that she was already paying to both Alexander and Max. About this she wrote that, of course, my father knew nothing. She added that I was being what she called thoroughly saintly.

In her first letter to me to say that my father would not be responsible she had had, however, some cogent things to say about parents and children. Her argument was that when a child reached the age of, say, seventeen, a father should not pretend an interest or sympathy that he did not really feel, since this would be detected by the child and would lead to a recurring cycle of resentment and guilt. This was one of the ways in which, in her opinion, Christians produced psychological cripples. She also argued strongly against the upper-class habit of sending children of a younger age away to boarding-school. And here, it seemed, was something that might touch Rosemary and myself.

It had indeed struck us that one of the impossibilities, or para-doxes, at the centre of human affairs was to do with the relationship between parents and children: children had to be cared for, yet also to be enabled to be free to go their own ways. For a parent, love always consisted of treading on a tightrope – with a chasm on either side of too much control or too much aloofness.

Father Raynes had shown to Rosemary and myself how we were out of balance in relation to our children; we had got rid of Nanny, but what had we put in her place? We had tried to put ourselves; then we had made efforts to find the best 'Christian' schools; but still we were obediently following the custom of our time and circumstances in sending them away, and at least one recommended 'Christian' school turned out to be a disaster. We had read in books – children learn not so much from what their parents tell them as from what their parents are: their attitudes, their style of behaviour, the relationship between themselves. I had entered into God-fearing activities at work, at home; but then, as Diana's letter had said, what good is done to children by parents straining to make sacrifices for 'good': might not these indeed be a turning away from the demands of the central paradox? Rosemary and I had learned a few good tricks on our tightrope – we played games with the children, we read stories, we talked to them about serious things. But in our large house with one or two servants we were not always in easy contact with them. And at the centre of the paradox, should it not indeed be something about spontaneity that is learned?

I wrote a piece on 'Fatherhood' for *Prism*. I said that it was the job of fathers to tell children 'the way life works'. 'We must believe that if we tell children the truth, and take care to try to show what the truth is, then they will be looked after.' But, indeed, how do you put into words what is truth? You learn truth just by being on a tightrope? You learn when you fall off? Is it not by more than tricks, that people are looked after?

There was a time when I took a group of four boys and three girls from the Young Communicants' Fellowship, together with my two elder sons aged twelve and ten, for a week at Butlin's Holiday Camp at Clacton. We went with Hugo Charteris and his eldest daughter (Hugo was to write an article for the *Daily Telegraph*), also with my old friend Raymond Carr and his two eldest sons, who did not want to be left out. Oh yes, we were being good and worthy fathers, were we not – looking after our children on our own? looking at how 'the other half' lives? We had a good time at Butlin's; there were dancing and swimming and funfair activities all day. Once Raymond and Hugo and I were discussing Dostoievsky in the queue at the cafeteria and the girls behind the counter became so doubled-up with giggles that they were unable to go on serving. We went to play tennis with borrowed equipment; when we pointed out to the storeman that the balls had holes in them he replied, 'So have the courts.' There was something enervating, if jokey, about the way the other half lived. Then there was one incident in which our children got involved dangerously in a battle of stone-throwing with a gang of older toughs. And there was an evening at the end of our stay when we were having drinks with some of the 'redcoats' who ran the place and we asked them what they had thought of our strange group when we arrived. They said they had at first thought we might be the winners of some competition (what on earth – Knobbly Knees? Doubling-up with Dostoievsky?) but then they had decided that we three – Hugo, Raymond and I – must have come with the children on the equivalent of a dirty weekend. We were suitably shocked by this. We said – But would you not have objected? They looked blank. Later we wondered – Might this not too have been a joke?

But anyway, what on earth in fact were Rosemary and I doing with our children?

The paradox of caring and over-protection remained. We thought of not sending the younger children to boarding-school: but then it seemed that they themselves wished or needed to get away.

If I do not say much in this book about my relationships with my children – up to this point the children of my first marriage, Shaun and Ivo and Robert and Clare – this is because these relationships mean not too little to me but too much: if there are more stories about them and me to be told, then it is the children who must tell them; they are the ones who will know what has been passed on. This is what matters in any relationship between parents and children – what is passed on – not so much what parents might tell them or indeed might have learned for themselves (though children learn from a parent's example) as the ability for the children to learn for themselves – it is this virtue that might be conveyed by a parent's balancing-act on a tightrope. It seems to me that my children are strikingly better parents than myself: and what greater gift (for myself, for others) could have been passed on? Oh there are regrets, sorrows, indeed: children are our means of our seeing our failures and mistakes. But for both their and my ability to see at least some of these, I am grateful beyond words to –

– Shaun and Ivo and Robert and Clare.

12

What had come to dissatisfy me about my early novels (and indeed increasingly about novels by others I had once loved) was the impression of the author insisting, manipulating, putting something over; his voice being involved in a contest with the world and thus his characters being involved in this contest too; so that in the end these novels became a lament or indeed a fantasy – for in such a contest, how in fact could the world not win? Stories were tragedies or comedies because writers and characters put themselves into a position of being defeated; the more subtle stories were those which recognised that this was so.

But how was it there were so few life-like stories of people who felt themselves to be in some partnership with the world; this partnership – by way of struggle and absurdity and even disaster, to be sure – yet showing itself in the end to be a successfully going concern? For this was what human life did seem to be after all – if just for the reason that it produced creators such as writers as well as creatures such as characters and stories. To admit this might be – too great a responsibility?

I had not tried to write a novel for five years. I had thought – How can one write a 'good' novel about a 'good' life? Or indeed even – How can one write a 'good' novel and lead a 'good' life? These two modes of 'goodness' had seemed to be antithetical: the goodness of a life is quiet and hidden; a good story is of drama. But suddenly it seemed – This is precisely the point! 'Goodness' by its nature is not antithetical but paradoxical; if you try for 'goodness' and 'stillness' directly you fail; but still these can be some sort of by-product, even of drama. To discover what is hidden you have to go on a journey; what uproar, indeed, before you arrive at what is there! And of course, how can this be described except in terms of a story? A story is that which holds paradoxes on a journey.

I wrote an article for *Prism*:

> A good novel is one that tells a story that not only is life-like but seems to illuminate life – to suggest some order and meaning. There is a tradition of novel-writing which is concerned almost explicitly to say that life has no meaning – that man is helpless within chaos. But there is something contradictory at the heart of these novels, in that they suggest by what they say that all is chaos and yet by their very existence – their form and structure as works of art – they seem to demonstrate that it is not.
>
> The novel is a very good form of Christian expression. There are many fundamental Christian truths which are almost impossible to express didactically. There are the paradoxes such as those between determinism and free will, or the way that good can come out of evil. These are admitted to be 'mysteries', and any direct statement about them seems able to be countered by an opposite and equally valid statement. The best that can be said directly about these paradoxes is that they do best express what is actually experienced in life. But Christians are now out of the habit of being interested in life in this way . . . they are interested not so much in observing, learning from, wondering at life, as in exhortations, essays, sermons, which describe what life *might* be.

About the second of these paradoxes – the way in which good can come out of evil – how extraordinary it seemed that so many Christians seemed to think that 'badness' in stories should be censored for the sake of 'good': could they not see that without the ability to look at badness, there was often no sense of the operation of good? that so many of the stories in their own scriptures were about ways in which evil, if recognised, could be used for good – not only in the Old Testament, which was riddled with stories about God making use of evil, but also in the New:

When we read the Gospels nowadays what do we make of the story?

How do we explain that for 90% of the time the Apostles were quite boneheaded about what was going on, that at the Crucifixion they ran away, the whole lot, and at least one denied ever having known Christ? And yet it was these people, and especially the one who had denied him, whom God took over, and through whom the story of the Resurrection began to be spread over the world.

And it never seemed to have occurred to these Apostles – the founders and fathers of the early Church – that there was anything odd in this history, let alone shameful. They were happy to let the Gospels be written about how obtuse they had been. St Peter, presumably, did not try to stop the incident of his denial being published; St Paul did not cover up the fact that he had persecuted Christians, nor that he was always liable, but for the grace of God, to make an ass of himself again. He seems even to have gone out of his way to stress this – though in an unemotional and business-like manner.

I think the Apostles and St Paul took this attitude that their own prestige did not matter because they were so tremendously conscious that what mattered was God's prestige. And they knew, which now-adays we seem to have stopped knowing, that God can work best through people – in fact perhaps can only begin to work through people – if they are being honest with themselves and are not trying to keep truth out.

And about the other paradox at the centre of human experience – that concerning the relationship between determinism and free will – how could this effectively be written about except in the form of stories?

It is not easy at the moment, because we have not found a vocabulary, to describe the relation between the inner choice and the outer event, the personal humility and the activity of grace – a relation not of cause and effect but mysterious, though perceptible, to those who are conscious of it. There *is* a world of meaning here, and there are those who talk of it. But they only talk with difficulty, personally, like all good Christians.

It suddenly seemed not just possible but imperative that I should write another novel. This would not be in the old style, of course – that of someone expostulating, lamenting, spitting into the wind. Indeed, if you spit it can be blown back in your face! But if you turn, hold a finger up to the wind –

– the spittle, flying, might be like a bird: might be something to make the blind see –

(I thought you said you could not talk about it!)

– or like one of those particles that pass through one or another of the holes in a screen; are both a particle and a wave; are now an eye, now a landscape –

(Who am I talking to: myself?)

– providing a style, yes, in which there would be spaces, openings, through which, across which, a wind might blow and make noises like those of a horn, a flute –

(Oh these metaphors! you think metaphors provide openings through which you may see?)

– gaps through which a reader might see –

You mean if you say you cannot talk about it, you may still be talking about it? –

Yes.

I had stopped writing novels because of the sound of my voice declaiming, expostulating; perhaps because of some imagined commitment to Father Raynes –

– But what I had learned from Father Raynes was that, if you watch, listen, you do not stay the same: you can challenge, question, the sound of your own voice; you are led –

– Towards what cannot be said? All right.

So after a time I began to write another novel.

The story of this new novel, which was to be called *Meeting Place*, is as follows:

Harry is a thirty-five-year-old man separated from his wife, Melissa. He is doing social-welfare work for a Samaritans-type organisation which helps would-be suicides and others in distress. He sits by a telephone and answers calls in a room like *Prism*'s office-cupboard. The reason why he is separated from his wife is because he has been having an affair with a girl called Annie, from whom he is also now separated. He is doing good works because this seems to him the only sensible activity left in a world of insoluble dilemmas.

While he is at work he is telephoned by someone whose voice he recognises as Annie's; when she hears him she rings off. Was her telephoning him some move to get him back, or is she in some more serious distress? Harry goes to see her. But what she tells him is how ridiculous his work is; his old friends laugh at him; surely he sees that by doing so-called 'good works' he is running away from his real responsibilities! So Harry is now himself in some distress.

He is rung up at his work by a teenage boy who also seems to be doing this as some sort of joke, to mock him. But in this case the mockery seems an obvious cry for help. Harry gets the boy to see him, and befriends him.

But for some comfort in his own loneliness Harry runs to what has seemed to him a magical haunt of his old loves and passions – a pub in the area of London where he used to meet Annie. There he comes across a girl whom he has not met before; she has a spontaneous generosity and kindness and seems to offer some salvation. She and Harry spend a weekend together. After this, Harry feels more able to deal with the mockery and resentment around him.

A tabloid newspaper runs a homosexual smear campaign against Harry concerning a group of boys he has been befriending. As a result of this his house is invaded by a gang of toughs and in the mêlée his own ten-year-old son gets hurt. So now there is a clearer cause for despair!

But other events have been happening as it were just round some corner. The teenage boy who rang him up is in fact moving away from the self-destructive life he has been leading; Harry and Annie do begin to arrive at some understanding and forgiveness; and from the threat to his own child Harry learns – that perhaps the time has come for him to give up the sort of work he has been doing and to set out after his wife Melissa. She too has been involved in good works – at the site of some nuclear near-disaster in America. Harry searches for Melissa; they meet. The last pages of the book are a phantasmagoria, part-reality, part-memory, part-imagination – an interweaving of strands in the inside and outside worlds, which is the Meeting Place. Harry says to Melissa – We had to get away. Melissa says – How are we going home?

Meeting Place was obviously an effort to make a pattern from experiences in my own life at this time – Annie was the girl whom I had called Mary in *The Rainbearers*; the girl with whom Harry spent a weekend was like the girl with whom I had gone to Berlin; Melissa was Rosemary, who with regard to my gyrations with Church affairs (amongst other things) seemed to feel increasingly alienated and to be getting on with a life of her own. There was the story of the group of boys whom Harry befriended which was taken from the boys and girls of the parish and their relationship with my own children; also the story of battles I had fought over my half-brother Alexander. But whereas my old novels seemed to have been concerned with looking back at my life and striking some pose against it, *Meeting Place* does seem to have been an attempt, yes, to see oneself in partnership with life; not imposing a pattern on experience (and thus experiencing failure) but trying to look for, and proceed in, a pattern that might be there. Also *Meeting Place* was the first of my novels which seemed not to be just looking at the present and past but by so doing in some way to be interacting with the future. The story of the teenage drop-out boy had arisen out of my experiences with my half-brother Alexander, but some of the reconciliations in the story had not, at the time of writing it, occurred. And then it was suddenly as if the writing might be helping to make them occur. *Meeting Place* was the first of my novels that my stepmother Diana said she liked – and this in spite of her recognition that part of the story had been taken from events of the last two years, and that at least one of the characters was something of a caricature of my father – a newspaper tycoon whose slogan was 'Analyse and clarify' when he often did not quite see what was under his nose. But still, what an odd view Diana had of what I was trying to say! She wrote that she admired extremely the style and form of the book and was contemptuous of the reviews that she had read; but she saw the book as mainly a pessimistic attack on the hypocrisy and violence in England.

I was grateful: but what was this about pessimism? the book was supposed to end in hope! It was saying – Oh hypocrisy and violence, yes, but so what? What matters is what might be going on round some corner.

But of course – A person need not be aware, if he or she does not so wish, of anything going on round some corner.

But life goes on – whether or not one sees any pattern.

There was a newspaper report at this time about how my father, aged sixty-six, had been knocked down and kicked at the scene of a political meeting in the East End of London, and my half-brother Max had been arrested when he had bravely defended him. I felt suddenly – But I, his eldest son, should have been there to defend him! Then – But of course I could not have been there: the point is, what happens now. With all this patterning whizzing about between life and novels, might not the time have come for me to make things up with my father? I wrote to him to say I had been distressed at the report of the assault on him; and to Diana – 'Do come and see us when you are in England.' Diana wrote that she often thought of Rosemary and me and our 'wonderful family'. Then suddenly my father was suggesting that we all stay with him in France for Christmas (this was 1963) – 'Spiritual consolation among the pagans is amply provided by the British Embassy Church in Paris, and we all usually go to the midnight mass in Notre-Dame.' This was so remarkable that I wondered –

– Well what on earth is happening now?

To go away for Christmas that year was not practicable, and I did for a while have anxiety about the possible results of being on good terms with my father again: I had been told stories about him saying – Nicky took Alexander away, now let's see what we can do about his children! Oh indeed this was one of my father's typical jokes, but still –

– Is not between twelve and fourteen just the age at which boys are natural Fascists?

But then, what of my talk of its being one's job to look to the means, and then ends look after themselves.

I wrote to Diana:

What if I brought the two older boys over to Paris for two days; could we stay with you? They keep on asking me – Why don't you take us to see Grandad, is it because you're frightened he'll influence us? I say – Yes. So I really will have to bring them over soon. I

156

don't want to have any more rows with Dad, there's no point, I wouldn't talk about politics, but I suppose I might if he went off about Alexander. I think it's worth the risk, and would like to, especially since Dad was so good about asking us last Christmas.

Max and Jean came down for a weekend in the summer and it was all going fine, then on Sunday Rosemary asked down a Communist physicist and the director of the Ballet Nègre, and things got lost.

So Rosemary and I with our two older sons went on our visit to Orsay, on the outskirts of Paris, to my father's and Diana's beautiful house which was called, of all things, 'Le Temple de la Gloire'. There was a big lunch party and my father put my two sons, Shaun and Ivo, on either side of him at one end of the table and I was next to Diana at the other; and I could hear my father talking, talking – ah, how he could talk! – about the union of Europe, the annexation of much of Africa, about how of course with such a gigantic undertaking there would be difficulties: but when an aeroplane is about to crash you do not argue about the details of taking over the controls – someone has to do it – and how rare it was nowadays to find people not frightened of action! And so on – all with my father's flashing eyes going on and off like a lighthouse in a fog: and my sons listening to him so gravely; and the flashing being, what, a warning, or that of wreckers luring poor sailors to their doom. At one moment I found myself calling down the table – But Dad, things are more complex than that! And my sons turned to me still so gravely as if to say –

– Have you not talked about trust?

And indeed I need not have worried. My sons listened to the grave hooting in the fog; then went on their way.

The other strand that was weaving in and out of both my life at this time and the story of *Meeting Place* was to do with Mary of *The Rainbearers* – who indeed in life was the person from whom, with whom, more than anyone else I had learned about the interweaving of threads to make a pattern: about how good can sometimes come out of apparent evil; how the recognition of a connection between inner choice and outer event can give life wonder and meaning. At the time of my starting *Prism* we had had our reconciliation; and she had told me she was to be married. She had even come bounding into *Prism*'s tiny office one day like a Michelangelo sybil pressed against the ceiling; perhaps just to say – Look, there can after all be exuberance, joy, after such pain! Then later I had heard that she had again become ill, and I went to see her. And then in looking at the past there seemed again to be ghosts and accusations, recrimination and haunting. I wrote to her to say – I have done my best: what more can I do? I have tried to look at my responsibilities; have you looked at yours? But this produced a response that seemed to have nothing to do with what might really be going on: what on earth was it round some corner?

> I do not forget for one moment what you have done for me in this last year – nor how very much more you have probably done for others which it is not my business either to discuss or assess. But
> > (a) that which you have done for me might well not have been done by you as you are if I had not taken the initial step; and
> > (b) I do not know how much it is in terms of total effort, of total redirection of energy towards 'making amends'.
> You are caught most painfully it seems to me between an acknowledged sense of responsibility (in general I mean, not only to me) and an inability fully to act upon it.
> Don't again say – But *what* do you want me to do? The point is that what you should do is what you feel it necessary to do (again in general, not only in connection with me). And you will always know what this is if you give yourself a chance to consider the problem without saying at the outset that you are too weak, that it would be boring, or difficult, or socially embarrassing – or that it is not really up to you. Because then you are caught again in that circle of sense of responsibility and inaction.

I thought – God damn it, what on earth is it that she wants now?
 – She is married, isn't she?
 – But to a man much older than herself (as indeed I had foretold in *The Rainbearers*) –
 – You mean – It's true there is some loose strand that she may think it proper for us to tie in this bizarre interweaving between pain and pleasure?
After another year or so I wrote to congratulate Mary on the birth of her child. Here are extracts from her reply, and from her letters to me during the next two years. Bizarre interweaving indeed!

Of course it can be desirable to find a resolution for what indeed can be called a loose end; but also perhaps proper at the same time for this to remain as half-hidden as the answer to a riddle.

15.2.62

Thank you for your letter. I knew you would be glad about my baby. She really is a love; and enormously pretty.

Your letter made me laugh so much: great bubbles of inward laughter welling up – the funniness of life, my darling – the aweful (with an *e*) funniness. I hope you are well and the work goes, does it? Here is the letter I wrote you two years ago when *your* daughter was born. Too complicated to explain why I didn't post it then. But I would like you to know how much your practical help has affected things.

9.11.63

Notes on our search

1. Beloved – to be said once and not again – nothing to be gained by repeating it – It is true, has been true, through the worst years. We act as though the premise of love – the underlying cause of the explosion of energy – is proven. I think it is. We search through love, not through hate. But the reverse of the coin is there.

2. Our meeting was very fatiguing, very inadequate – but a step in the right direction. So much that cannot be said for social reasons; so much implicit in pain that I, at least, withdraw from. You know the classic Jungian diagram of this sort –

So cosy for them. Perhaps they only met last week for the first time. I still have almost no idea what each sees in the other, do you? Perhaps this is what needs to be found out. Whatever it is has always been there, and I see them both very much as children of the war.

1.8.64

I liked your phrase about the energy-producing thing we seek to touch. This, I suppose, is what our story has always been about, though perhaps we have not always known it. The treasure without price (the present from Fortnums!). Anything else that we can spare out of our committed lives must be incidental to the main search.

21.9.64

I should love a light lunch – either at the Hyde Park Hotel for a drink and then go out for sandwiches, or to the Berkeley, Piccadilly entrance, and go through to the Buttery for a scrambled egg?

?.9.64

Things to talk about – *Herbs*. I want to grow them on my roof. I so long to grow things. Will you tell me about this, or find me a book?

Twelve years – so long, so short. Jacob's seven years – gone in an eyeblink. The total familiarity – hence in one sense the relative unimportance. The need *not* to lose sight of the main issue – the finding and then the employing of the energy-producing thing.

The relative lack of tenderness – both our fears – can either of us learn to trust? Perhaps *this* is what our story is about – our inability to love and trust and accept that which is within us. Hence our search. Too complicated to write. Must talk to you about. Time time time time. Plans for this? And fatigue, oh dear! And oh the compliments on my looks in the next 2 days. Difficult.

Timetables. Cherishing.

I love our gaiety but I would hope for a little less – on both our parts it hides pain and untrusting – naturally, what else could we expect? But this is the problem – the working towards trusting each other in order to learn to trust oneself – in order to learn to love oneself. I am so sure of this.

I am sorry for some of the things I said. They were only a measure of my fear of betrayal. I believe this needn't happen again (betrayal I mean; the other will take time). *Do you*? or do you not think in these terms.

I lie here planning great Fortnums hampers for you. Do you remember when you sent me that one when I was ill once? Perhaps my happiest minute.

You started to say something about the symbols and how I handled them – then events intervened. I must ask you about this. I know much more than I did. Perhaps this is part of the search – the need to know *quite consciously* how to live with – no, flourish with – the symbols. Instead of being drawn down by them into murky depths. Herbs again.

Darling – even our choosing 'aggression needn't necessarily be hostile' seems to be reassuring.

You *were* clever. All that I must say I find most surprising.

So funny and odd too about hotel rooms. This I must say is something I had no idea about.

13

The novel that I began to write after *Meeting Place* was *Accident*. At the centre of this story there was the question of the relationship between the inner choice and the outer event, concerning which it is so difficult for anything to be said directly:

Stephen is a youngish-middle-aged Oxford philosophy don who has a wife and two small children to whom he feels committed. But his wife is pregnant again, and he has been married for seven years, and it is an Oxford summer with young women by the river like figures painted by Renoir. Stephen has two glamorously aristocratic pupils called William and Anna: he is charmed by the former and attracted to the latter; but he is faithful to his wife, and he finds himself acting as some sort of go-between for William and Anna. Stephen also has a great friend called Charley with whom in the old days he used to chase girls; Charley is a novelist and is now also married. Then Stephen learns that Charley is having an affair with Anna. So he feels – envy? disapproval? When the affair comes to a crisis, Stephen encourages Charley to make things up with his wife. This Charley does. Then Anna announces she will marry William – in some sort of revenge. Stephen says to her – Don't ruin your lives! Anna and William are on their way to Stephen's house outside Oxford to talk to him when the car, which Anna is driving, crashes and William is killed. Anna is drunk, and has no licence to drive. Stephen, however, is the first to come across the scene and he is the only one who knows that Anna was driving or indeed was in the car at all. So there is a moral question here – Should Stephen let it be known that Anna was driving, in which case her life will be greatly damaged but also his own, Stephen's, and Charley's (and the lives of their families) because the story of their involvement will come out; or should Stephen protect Anna by not letting on that she was driving even though (or because?) this will be protecting himself, on the grounds that this is the proper way to accept responsibility? Stephen takes Anna to his house; he telephones Charley in the middle of the night and Charley comes and they talk – about what to do, about the motives behind what they might do, about whether such decisions can be made on grounds of rationality – or if not, on what grounds can they be made? This scene is the centre of the story. In the end they decide – to do nothing except see Anna safely back to her college, and then to see what happens. They have tried to look honestly at the interweavings of responsibilities; beyond this, the outcome will be anyway out of their hands.

In the event the police never do find out that Anna was driving or indeed was in the car; so no one has to tell a direct lie. Anna goes back to her home in Austria; Charley and Stephen are with their families. William is dead, but Stephen has a new child. This child was born during the night when Stephen and Charley had been talking. For a time it had seemed that the child might die.

Accident became the best known of my novels up to this time. This was partly because of the good film that was made from it of the same name, though before this it had got the best reviews I had yet had. But it was with this novel that there began to occur what became more noticeable as time went on – that in spite of some people's praise, the way in which many people saw my novels was apt to be different in a central respect from the way in which I saw them myself – particularly in this matter of connection between inner attitude and outer event.

When I had submitted *Accident* to my publishers, Weidenfeld & Nicolson, who had done my last three novels and my travel book, they had turned it down on the grounds that they had had appalling reports about it from two 'very experienced and highly thought-of' readers. I was shown these reports, one of which said:

> This book seems to me a typical product of the kind of writer who thinks the novel ought to go somewhere without having any clear idea where or why. The whole story revolves around one incident; a middle-aged don hides from the police that a girl was driving a car in which someone got killed simply because he was attracted to her. Mosley himself says at one point in this book that novels should be about small things, which is fair enough if they are significant of something bigger, which the incident in this book is. But the trouble seems to me that the author is unable to bring the meaning of these events out, and tries to give his minor events a major significance by a pretentious and overloaded style... I found it mannered, pretentious, vacuous, and not even original. Publishers' offices are always full of books by people who write in this style presumably because it is so easy and sounds 'literary' almost as though it were full of some profound meaning which only the very perceptive reader will grasp, and who wants to be unperceptive?

Accident was written in much the same style as *Meeting Place* – the sentences and paragraphs were short and abrupt, as if by this there might be gaps, openings in a screen (language itself being a screen?) through which a reader might glimpse something beyond. There was the implication, hope, that some readers might thus find themselves glimpsing, reflecting upon, things in their own lives – this was the style in which my chief character, Stephen, tried to see himself, and by this he found that he might not quite be at the mercy of whatever it was that was happening, might even in some way affect it. So this was an attitude which a reader might see the point of and adopt: or on the other hand he might not! And as Weidenfeld's reader had put it – who wants to be unperceptive?

There is a scene in *Accident* in which all the main characters are having tea on Stephen's lawn and William asks Charley – Why can't modern novels just be stories about characters and action and society? And Charley says – We know too much about characters and actions and society. So William says – Then why write novels? And Charley says – This is the point, we can now write about people knowing.

However – What if people did not see the point of knowing?

And of course – What did I think I was up to, thinking I knew about knowing!

After Weidenfeld had turned down *Accident* it was read by my old friend Robin Denniston who had moved from the Faith Press and was now in charge of Hodder & Stoughton; he said he couldn't see what Weidenfeld's reader was on about, and of course he would publish it. And then there was a mysterious offer for an option on film rights; and then quite a lot of readers after all, yes, seemed to see the point about people knowing.

Then some time later (I am jumping ahead in time, but this is part of this particular story) I was rung up by someone who said 'This is Harold Pinter' and I thought this was a joke by one of my friends. But it really was Harold Pinter, and he said he was writing a screenplay of *Accident* for the director Joseph Losey, and didn't I know? I said – No. He said that the book had originally been taken up by Sam Spiegel as a possible 'vehicle' for Richard Burton and Elizabeth Taylor but this had not worked out (miracles can be too bizarre); so now he, Harold, and Joe Losey, were planning to set up the film themselves. This was just after their success as script-writer and director with *The Servant*. I felt – There could hardly be a more suitable miracle.

So Harold Pinter and I met for lunch and he was good about the book and he said he wanted the screenplay to stick as close to the book as possible. He asked me one or two questions such as – Was the girl, Anna, a victim or a bitch? And we agreed – Both. Then when he had finished the screenplay he sent it to me together with a letter which he asked me to open and read only after I had read the screenplay. So this I did, and it was a very good screenplay, but there were one or two important differences between it and the book. I opened Harold's letter:

> As you see, there's one major deviation, change – it might be said distortion – the fact that Stephen sleeps with Anna, and that Charley knows nothing about anything at the end.
>
> I must tell you that I worked very hard to follow your ending at all points to begin with and in fact finished a complete first draft following that course. But there was something *wrong*. This, of

course, could have been entirely my fault, my inadequacy, probably was, but the long debate between Stephen and Charley simply did not work, convince, sustain itself in dramatic terms. A novel is so different. You have so much more room. A dramatic structure makes its own unique demands. They're unavoidable. Anyway, the more the whole thing grew in me the more one fact sank in and finally clarified itself – that is, that Stephen, ultimately, must be alone in final complicity with Anna, or so it seemed to me. And, in many long discussions, to Losey. It seemed to follow; it seemed to be logical. Dramatically, it economised and compressed, and by narrowing the focus achieved a greater intensity. Or so we felt. So that Charley finds himself staring at a blank wall. And Stephen has to, will have to, carry his own can, alone, with whatever the can holds.

Possibly the main point, and the point you might consider an inexcusable distortion of your intentions, is that Anna and Stephen now sleep together. All I can say is that this, from what I've been saying, sprang into being as inevitable (their complicity, their closeness, etc.). And what do they gain from it? What is left in the morning, as it were? It's done, it happens, on they go – what meaning has been demonstrated by this?

Clearly there has been a certain switch of viewpoint in the passing of your work to me. Not too much, I very much hope, but one inevitable in that we're two different men, two different writers. I have willingly 'distorted' nothing – couldn't do that since I admire the book so much – but yes, there's been a change. But has there??!! We spoke once about the notion of 'correct' or 'incorrect' moral attitudes in Stephen at the end. But these are terms. I haven't attempted to work in these terms or stand as a judge. I have, I think, seen it as something that happens, that has happened, something that has taken place. But where possibly there is a shift of interpretation between us is that your view at the end is optimistic and I haven't felt it as such. But if I do not feel the end as optimistic, neither do I feel it as pessimistic. Something had taken place, something that will always live, on all levels.

If you feel the script fails to express the essence of your work I am very sorry. I don't feel this myself, and nor does Losey. We're very excited about doing it. All I can say is, this was the way for me, the way that found itself for me.

Thank you, anyway, for giving me the opportunity for doing this. It's meant a great deal to me.

Christ, I hope I've made myself understood – both in the script and in this.

Sincerely,

Because I thought that this was a very good letter, as well as the script being a very good script, I made not much more than formal objections to the changes from the book: we were different men, different writers, indeed; how could there not be changes? The scene between Stephen and Charley when they tried to talk straight – such a scene had never been part of Harold's style. The business of Stephen sleeping with Anna was perhaps of more importance: but this was one of the matters of importance to me about which other people were apt not to see the point.

The optimism of the book had depended on a recognition of connections. There had been the hint (though this could never quite be stated) that Stephen's and Charley's long and painstaking conversation might have an effect on the outcome of the predicament – and that it was necessary for Stephen not to take advantage of Anna by sleeping with her if anything was to be salvaged from the disaster. There was even a suggestion that the death of William might be balanced, if proper steps were taken, by the survival of the child. But such notions were somewhat mystical; how indeed if one tried to be responsible even belatedly for 'means' might this effect proper 'ends'? There had certainly been no sense of such attitudes in Harold Pinter's previous work that I had so much admired; how could there be in *Accident*? Harold's very great talent was in showing how people in a sense were indeed on their own with responsibilities tied like tin cans to their tails; their shows of communication were not much more than the playing of games. Perhaps what had drawn Harold to *Accident* was that much of the book was like this: Stephen and Charley were sophisticated people who recognised that of course much of human behaviour is to do with playing games. It was only in the crisis that they found the occasion to talk straight – and even then in the hope not so much of coming to decisions, but rather that by their efforts there might be a better chance of events occurring in one way rather than in another. About the matter of Stephen not sleeping with Anna – it had seemed to me important that Stephen should choose deliberately not to do this at a time when his wife was in hospital waiting for their new baby to be born.

I wrote to Harold making little mention, I think, of the omission of Stephen's and Charley's conversation, because the inclusion of this would indeed have upset the tone of the whole script; but I did say that I thought Stephen sleeping with Anna made Stephen too uncaring even in Harold's terms. Harold thanked me for my 'bloody marvellous letter' (I had told him how much I liked the script) and said he would look at the points raised. In the film I think the obviousness of Stephen's sleeping with Anna was slightly modified; but there was no ambiguity about the overall impression of people left staring at a blank wall.

At the back of the story of *Accident* was my friendship with Raymond Carr – my friend from just-post-war days when we had gone lurching through the undergrowth of Soho together; later we had often stayed with each other and gone on long holidays with our wives; recently we had braved the rigours of the week at Butlin's. At the time of my beginning to write *Accident* Raymond was a Fellow of New College, Oxford; I had gone to him and said – Can you help me to get material for my book? Raymond had invited me into the Senior Common Room; had introduced me to the currently most fashionable girl in Oxford. When I wrote the book I mixed characteristics of both Raymond and myself into both Stephen and Charley: I was somewhat like the don and Raymond was like the writer; or was it vice versa? I joked – Which would you rather be – the faithful one, or the one that gets the girl? All this should have remained a joke: there was nothing in real life like the story of the accident. But then when the book came out there were people who began to say – Ah yes, I was there at the night of the accident! I know the girl! – this with the wink of Oxford scandal. (There are sufficient motor accidents around Oxford.) And then I was told that some Oxford bookshops were refusing to have the book on display. The scandal was said to be (so the head of Magdalen College reported later to Losey at the time of discussions about the film) – 'it was all right for an undergraduate to sleep with one don, but two dons was one too many'. But Charley was not a don, and in the book Anna does not sleep with Stephen. I began to feel – Such a story would be acceptable if it were tragedy or farce; what is objected to is that it seems to suggest freedom of choice, and meaning.

This was a time when it was becoming the established literary convention that for serious literature optimism in any form was taboo (the chairman of the Committee for the Nobel Prize for Literature was soon to announce that 'pessimism is almost a qualification for the job' of being a serious writer). Optimism was taken to be a turning-away from the fashionable requirement that one had to face a one-dimensional view of bleakness. I wrote an article on 'The Contemporary Novel' in *Theology* in which I talked of the sort of picture presented by contemporary high-brow fiction:

> This, then, is the sort of picture that it produces. Man is an automaton, a machine for recording impressions. He is haunted by guilt for some crime he does not know if he committed or even remembers; his only means of protest against this is obscenity or blasphemy. He is a middle-aged child in a lunatic asylum, a scavenger for scraps of food in a prison, a drug-addict gripped in a nightmare. He has neither freedom nor responsibility.
>
> And this picture is being produced at a time when people in the countries from which these writers come have ostensibly more prosperity and freedom than ever before. I know of no way to make sense of this other than that suggested by Jung who would have had a field day in this confusion . . . believing as he did that consciousness (whether of an individual or a society) is always balanced by its opposite in the unconscious; and that truth, or what actually happens, lies within (or grows from) a tension between the two.

Of the novelists that I loved and revered at this time there was, still, William Faulkner: in his later works he was writing less of tragedy and more of humans' freedom to survive, endure, prevail. I wrote an article for *Time and Tide* in which I quoted from Faulkner's Nobel Prize acceptance speech of 1949:

> The young man or woman writing today has forgotten the problems of the human heart in conflict with itself, which alone can make good writing because only that is worth writing about, worth the agony and the sweat. He must learn them again, he must teach himself that the basis of all things is to be afraid, and teaching himself that, forget it for ever, leaving no room in the workshop for anything but the old verities and truths of the heart – the old universal truths lacking which any story is ephemeral and doomed – love and honour and pity and pride and compassion and sacrifice.

Until he does so he labours under a curse; he writes not of love but of lust, of defeats in which nobody loses anything of value, of victories without hope.

And I commented on this:

From the first he [Faulkner] has been a novelist who writes not only about sequences of events but about how people experience them, influence them, understand them. His complex style is an attempt to express this: from the first, too, he has gone beyond narrative description into a mingling, or juxtaposition, of things that are happening, people's thoughts about these happenings, and people talking about them. There is also this polarity, or writing in several dimensions, in the structure of each book as a whole; different parts of the book, sometimes describing slightly differently the same events, are told through the eyes of different characters . . . By these techniques he does achieve an extraordinary sense of the complexity and mystery of life as it is experienced, in contrast to a narrative style which remains outside.

He achieves also a sense of the 'verities' which he says are the only things worth writing about. If you want to describe honour and sacrifice you have to assume free will. If you want to assume this you have to have a dimensional space (in writing as in life as it were) to move within. The writers of a straight narrative style are often those who seem implicitly to deny free will. Faulkner's very technique is part of his belief about man and literature.

Another writer whom I had come at this time to love almost beyond all others was J.D. Salinger whose *The Catcher in the Rye* had made him famous in the fifties; but the book of his that I loved best was *Franny and Zooey*, published in 1961, in which a young girl, Franny, having been driven into a state of acute depression by the inanity of the world around her, is eventually lifted out of this depression by an intense imaginative effort by her younger brother Zooey. Critics had on the whole been witheringly dismissive of this book, and Salinger soon retreated into solitude, apparently vowing to publish nothing more. I recomended *Franny and Zooey* to *Prism* readers as an example of a truly Christian novel.

The importance of this story is that it is about free will and the way in which one person can touch another, profoundly, when that

169

person needs to be touched. Most clever novels nowadays are about determinism, and the way in which no one has a hope of touching anyone ever. It is thus easy for a non-religious critic to be understanding about a novel by, for instance, Evelyn Waugh or Graham Greene, because religious actions in this sort of novel are mostly abortive or depressing. But a novel in which a spiritual improvement is actually achieved by intense imaginative effort is something which, perhaps, imaginative people do not like to read.

The literary world seemed to have been taken over by a vast army of contemporary fashion in which freedom was denied and ideas of dignity and redemption mocked. Against this were a few lonely voices such as those of Faulkner and Salinger who were admired for what they had been once but whose recent messages were ignored: a growing posse of Faulkner scholars, for instance, chose to see him just as a gloomy chronicler of the Deep South. I comforted myself – What a grim life to be a soldier in the vast army of contemporary pessimism! of course it is far better to be a freedom fighter! But then – In what real sense was I a fighter for freedom? What in fact had been the point of my commitment to Christianity?

14

When I had read the Bible straight through just before setting off for South Africa, what had struck me was that the Bible (like so many books) ended just when an interesting bit might have begun – a bit, that is, about how to live in the world as it is, when it became evident that there was to be no foreseeable Second Coming. There was the Book of Revelations which was a sort of wild conjecture on what a Second Coming might entail; but about the coming of the Holy Spirit who, after Jesus had gone (so he said) would 'guide you into all truth' – well, the New Testament itself had been written in this Spirit, of course, and there was the story of Pentecost; but the later Catholic Church did not seem to have had much more to say about it.

Father Raynes's acknowledgement that he was to learn God's requirements 'through circumstance and the demands of other people' was in line with the information in St John's Gospel that the Spirit of Truth 'shall not speak of himself, but whatsoever he shall hear that shall he speak'. This gnomic utterance suggested – You watch, you listen, and by this you learn God's will. And such advice perhaps had to be somewhat gnomic: what virtue is there in understanding unless it is learned by and for oneself? For any more to be said on the subject of the Holy Spirit – this seemed to me to be the task of stories. In stories there could be described the patterns, connections – formed by circumstance and by the demands of other people, to be sure – through each person's observation of which there could be glimpsed (as in other works of art) the operation of life in this age of the Holy Spirit.

It was in some such light as this that I had begun to write novels again – in a style in which, I hoped, through whatever smokescreens were unavoidable, something beyond might be glimpsed or heard. But still, in a more didactic form, was there really nothing more to be said?

Every now and then I had a shot at saying what I believed about this to our children – in the evenings, perhaps, after wondering what on earth had been the point of prayers; on Sundays having come back from the cold slow church; in the garden like some old Adam in the intervals of chopping firewood – well, what indeed were humans up to? It did seem that there must be something more to say about all this: I could hardly say (now or ever!) just – Read my novels! For was there not a something-more-to-be-said required after all in the area of bringing up children – that about which things can be demonstrated indeed better than said, but does there not have to be some effort at saying, or how else can be demonstrated, learned, the essential point that one has to learn for oneself? It probably seems easiest for children if explanations make simple sense: but what in the end makes life viable may indeed not be that which seems easiest at the time.

So I thought – Of course I should have a shot at writing something straight (well not exactly straight) about all this.

The delay in the publication of *Accident* due to the switch from Weidenfeld to Hodder meant that once again I was discouraged about starting a new novel. So I embarked on a short book that was to be called *Experience and Religion* and sub-titled *A Lay Essay in Theology*. This was dedicated to 'My wife' together with a quotation from the book – 'We have got to say something to our children.' Once I started to write it I found it came quite quickly; it had been a long time, I suppose, in gestation. It was ready for publication at the same time as *Accident*: Hodder's thought it might be a good publishing idea to bring both the fiction and the non-fiction book out on the same day; one might be seen in some sort of parallel with the other. In the event no one saw much of a connection.

Experience and Religion was a shot at saying the things I had been finding I wanted to say ever since I had stopped editing *Prism* and finished my book about Father Raynes: as it turned out, it was some signing-off from my commitment to organised religion. The point at issue was – after one has struggled with and tried to learn about the business of dogmatic language and sacrifice, what can be said – or presented if it is impossible to talk too directly – about this age of the Holy Spirit?

I wrote:

> It is the point of this book to try to say something of religion in terms of what seems to be the way the world works rather than of what might be revealed; not because the latter might be untrue (whatever this means) but because there still has to be some reason for its acceptance. And there is so much known, and felt, now (as always) about the world in areas not covered by materialism, historicism, absurdity, and so on, that it seems odd not to talk about this, especially since these are areas in which men mostly live, and care, and try to organise themselves. They are areas in which theology once talked; but which now seem empty because things there are so difficult to define or prove.
>
> The areas in which things can't be proved but which men mostly care about and live by are to do with their loves, hopes, fears, commitments; their relationships, friendships, marriages, and so on; their children; what they try to fashion and create; what is their freedom and what their helplessness; what is the point of a person, of the world; what is happening, and what is its meaning.
>
> To talk about all this, in any form, has always been the business of religion.

There had been a time, I suggested, when it had been recognised that religious language was that of poems and parables and stories: however now:

> The common experience is that there is an enormous amount of joy, energy, order, significance in the world that does not get expressed by artists and thinkers of any subtlety now, and which gets hopelessly vulgarised by those with none. This can be dismissed as self-deception by anyone who wishes, but it is easier to deceive oneself into misery than into happiness . . . This confusion is partly due to what was noticed earlier – the lack of an intelligent language in which to discuss important things. What is required is a way of

thinking which will take account of both the hope and hopelessness, responsibility and helplessness, the good not in spite of but together with the evil. And this, at the moment, we have not got.

In *Experience and Religion* there were chapters on Marriage, Children, Language, Free Will: a chapter on Freud and Jung in which I claimed that such psychoanalysts were 'religious' in that they saw that through listening to what might be at the back of language there might be some power of healing. But they did not take the further step of looking at what this power might be.

> The whole validity of the description of this sort of process has depended on a peculiar mode of trust – trust that if one keeps on with these sorts of effort then in fact something will happen as is claimed; trust also, to make sense of this, that there is something apart from oneself working, if one lets it, for what one hopes to be achieved. For the point of this sort of understanding is that something happens apart from (though permitted by) the will of the person attempting it – while the person's will, though trustfully, is directed to something else. There has to be this faith, that is, in things apart from oneself being purposive – in something in a person's unconscious working for the person to be whole – requiring, as it were, the birth of the new Self. And because what a person has to face are instances in the outside world as well as in the unconscious, there has to be this sort of faith about the outside world too. A person has to trust, in fact, that there is a scheme of things both in the unconscious and in the material world that has within it what can be working towards his own proper functioning and health.

Connected to this was the question of free will: human freedom was not freedom directly to affect the outside world, but freedom to choose to be one sort of person rather than another. It was in the recognition of this ability to choose – and this being in effect the choice – that there were connections between the inside and the outside worlds.

> There are two factors necessary for a concept of freedom: the first is the idea of the thing, the will, at the centre, which is free; and the second is the idea of the surrounding order, connectedness, within which the free will or act can operate ... In all talk of freedom, morals, and so on, what is worth talking about is not what

a person ought to or can do but the sort of person he might or could be ... In order to achieve some confidence about how to do good a person has to be the sort of person who chooses to do good without knowing how he does it – not just by instinct, as in the past, but perhaps by trusting his knowledge of what makes him such a person.

What was required, that is, was some 'authority' or 'style': but such authority might be achieved 'not on a man's ability to make out a reasoned case to compel others', but rather 'on his courage in facing what might be his rationalisations and self-deceptions in himself, his freedom to be taken over and blinded'. One of the areas in which such disciplines might be practised was that of the family: 'for in marriage it is not only that one has to come to terms with the desires and compulsions of another but, which is more difficult, with one's own – marriage inevitably confronting one with these'. In marriage there are the paradoxes without confronting the demands of which there is no health – 'the commitment without clinging, the dedication with respect, the recognition of a unity within which there are separate identities'. And also in this area, of course, there are the demands on parents to confront the paradoxes regarding their proper relationship with children – the tightrope walk between modes of intrusion and allowing to be free.

> The sort of understanding that is being described is to do with a person's freedom to hold himself between opposites; of his belief both that this is possible and, if done, that there is a correlation between this and what works in the world: that these paradoxes are seen, and held, in the first place by a sort of commitment in the dark; and are continued by a process of facing whatever turns up, which is difficult but perhaps man's only freedom.

And indeed – in the trying in this way to be responsible for a generation of children, might there not literally here be the chance to alter what human beings are?

> The point of marriage, children, families, in this sense, is, as has been said, that these (and we know it) are man's chances to alter the world – in marriage perhaps himself, and with children the future. And it is in this that there is in fact a true religious movement

of our time; men and women working and talking in this way – not only families but counsellors, psychologists, workers in clinics, and so on – talking not in extremes but in paradoxes; looking at each case in terms of evidence and not of rules and projections; recognising that health, goodness, depend on a person learning something for and about himself, and not in accepting an imposed rigidity. These people are not talking about morals, they are talking about facts. They are saying – 'This is the way the world works; seems to work; we can tell you this but we cannot compel or even persuade you; we can just offer you knowledge to do as you like with.' They are saying – 'Evil is discernible from what people do, the results of this; it is not a matter of moral judgement: if people grow up in a certain way they do seem to hate, destroy, want to kill one another and themselves: if they grow up in another way they do not: so – make your choice.' The people who talk like this are the truly religious. And against them are all the people who think this sort of thing somewhat ludicrous – who think they need not learn anything of love and growth and death, who do not want to. The distinction between these two sorts of people is vital. And here the old apparent enemies, the cynics and bigots, are on the same side: together they depend on rigidity, separateness, man's helplessness; they even depend on each other for hate: they are against any concept of fluidity, relationship, change.

In all this there was the insistence that this is the proper way to talk about God; even that this is the way that has been suggested to Christians that they should talk about God, in this age of the Holy Spirit in which 'he shall not speak for himself, but whatsoever he shall hear, that shall he speak.' The Church will always be 'the guardian of the Spirit' but also because of the world's corruption it will 'in a sense be always perverting the Spirit' – was not the Church founded, after all, on the disciple who three times denied Christ? It is the individual who, it seems always, has the choice either to listen or to pervert; but now at least he can see clearly this responsibility.

In the penultimate chapter of the book I seem to be trying to say everything all at once again – a chorus into the wind; the song blowing on whatever might be its way.

What is implied by all this is, firstly, a faith in an underlying order of things – that there is an order, meaning, the effects (symptoms) of which we can observe even if we do not know what it is an order, meaning, of – and secondly, the knowledge that man's role in this is not just a passive one of analysing it, or trying to control it as it were impersonally, but of having control over what he recognises himself as part of and committed to. This is the religious understanding that implies not only the faith that if certain attitudes are held, certain actions done, then there will be good effects (though sometimes indiscernibly); not only the demand to find out everything possible about this order (functioning) by observation and imagination and action; but also the realisation that this sort of faith, understanding, control even, only comes alive and is effective as a result of what a man is – what he lives – not by what he does just by routine or necessity but as a result of the interaction of himself and the world in the heart. This is difficult in non-poetic language. But man does know that he has this sort of freedom, perhaps his only; that this is his chance, in a world of laws, to change the world; that he is (can be) that which controls the laws (fits in with them) and these are good. It is in this understanding that he sees how the absolutes which are the concern of religion – courage, integrity, and so on – are effective not only in himself but in the world outside him. It is one of the claims of this sort of understanding that at some level people do glimpse and recognise this; that this is what life is about, not just at moments of love and fear and death but centrally, every day, from the evidence of their unique experience. Religion is a sort of scientific way of knowing uniqueness; a matter of observation and action not in the mass (impossible when observing consciousness) but of oneself in relation to other people and things. And what is found here is this connection between faith, freedom, goodness. The way of thought that something religious has finally been revealed, something enshrined eternally in tradition, should be absurd for Christian people who say that they believe that this is the age of the Holy Spirit – of people being given the power to discover, act, know things for themselves. It is true there would be no Holy Spirit (as it were) if there were no God the Father (as it were) of the world's order, and no God the Son (as it were) of man's unique relationship to this. But here and now, and in the future, this is what we have been told for two thousand years but at last find ourselves landed with – man's responsibility; the bearing of it.

Experience and Religion did turn out to be for me a signing-off from the regular routines of organised religion; though I had not, I think, intended this at the time. The process had begun perhaps some four years earlier when I had read the Bible straight through and tried to pay attention to its story rather than to chopped-out bits and pieces: the story seemed so clearly to say – All right, after a suitable time of commitment and obedience, what you should have learned is to watch and to listen on your own. I regretted nothing of the commitment which had lasted some seven years (a traditional Old Testament stretch!); it might only be regretted, surely, if I had learned nothing from it. It so happened that *Prism* was coming to an end at this time (also after seven years) and this too seemed fitting: after Robin Denniston's editorship Timothy Beaumont had taken over and under his ownership as well as editorship *Prism* had expanded and flourished; he was now to expand it further by incorporating it into a new fortnightly called *The New Christian*. Towards the end of its life *Prism* had become involved in controversies concerning what was called 'the new theology': this seemed to advocate that the word 'God' might be dropped altogether from religious language and a phrase substituted such as 'the ground of our being'. This seemed to me to be turning away from, not confronting, the necessary paradoxes. In the last number of *Prism* I wrote – 'Perhaps it is a good time for this to be the last number of *Prism* when almost everyone is interested in God except the theologians.' (Again, what on earth did I mean by 'almost everyone'?)

One of the more worthwhile undertakings I had been involved in during these years was the befriending of people who arrived in this country from South Africa, often as refugees. I would get a telegram from my old friend the monk, Father Aelred, who was now the head of the Theological College for Africans in Cape Province, saying would I meet so-and-so at the airport and see that he got safely to wherever he wanted to go, or put him up for a while. In this way I met Desmond Tutu, later to become Archbishop of Cape Town, on his way to study at King's College, London; and Thabo Mbeki, now (1994) just appointed Vice-President of the new South Africa, whose father at that time was imprisoned in South Africa along with Nelson Mandela and who himself, Thabo, had had to be smuggled out of the country in order to avoid arrest.

Thabo stayed with us for several weeks at Lyminster and I helped him get into Sussex University. He was not more than twenty; he had the extraordinary faith and assurance of other African leaders of his kind, as if this were to do with a knowledge of fate being on their side.

This was a time when my books were becoming somewhat more known; *Meeting Place* was being published in France and there was an offer for *Accident* in America; there was even the mysterious option on the film rights for *Accident*, details of which were not yet known. I thought that for my next book I should try to write a thriller, to make money. And in the meantime I would visit America to make contact with publishers; and perhaps I would go on some great journey! Was I not at the sort of stage, religiously, at which people used to go on pilgrimages? to discover – with a vision of freedom, what happens next? I resigned from the positions I had held in the parish (I had imagined that people might miss me: I don't think they did); most of my friends in the Young Communicants' Fellowship had by this time anyway moved on.

I went with Rosemary to New York, where previously we had spent only one or two days on the way home from the West Indies. Here there was the extraordinary lightness in the air as if to do with some lessening of gravity; people seemed to float, untethered, talking, talking. This was the time when there were works by a new wave of artists in the galleries – Lichtenstein, Rivers, Johns, Rauschenberg, Rothko – works that seemed not so much to do with the creation and presentation of objects as an enquiry into what the processes of creation and presentation might be. It struck me – What is happening here, too, is a transition from old patterns; the splintering of things into bits and pieces like light. Rosemary and I dallied on the edge of this for a while; then she went home to be with the children and to do her own painting. My talk of marriage and the family in *Experience and Religion* had not, in fact, made it easier for Rosemary and me to spend much more time together: was this, paradoxically, part of what I had to be learning – the paradoxes between realising the nature of commitment and being free? There was this sort of feeling in the air – When you have achieved something, do you not move on? Of course there was danger! the seven devils wait in the wings. I wanted to hold to my marriage: but what are the terms for moving on?

I was walking across Central Park one day and I thought – All right, I have done my seven years or my twice-times seven years; what is the point of going on a pilgrimage if not that something new may turn up? I was on my way to a literary party; there I bumped into a woman who asked me what I was looking for, and I said – well indeed what did I say? There was a notorious underground pornographic film going the rounds of fashionable New York at this time, so I said I was looking for this film. The woman said – Well you've come to the right person! In fact we never did get to the pornographic film, but she introduced me into the strange and archetypal New York worlds of Andy Warhol and William Burroughs and so on; and such worlds were indeed like those of a pornographic film – systems of titillation which never quite came to a point; vacuums which remained vacuums however much they were filled. This woman, of whom I grew fond, had not been able to leave New York for several years because of the vacuum that seemed to hold her there (she would say, 'I get as far as Grand Central Station and then bang! I'm on a stretcher!'). So I suggested we travelled together across America to the West Coast: what better start to a pilgrimage than to free a maiden as it were from a psychological ogre's castle! We got to Chicago and from there embarked on a very slow train called the Santa Fe Special; at every station my friend announced that the time had come for her to throw herself under the wheels. Well, one or two devils had been expected, hadn't they? When we got to Los Angeles she said 'Please, now can I go home?' She did; and now lives happily in France.

I had planned to spend some time in Los Angeles but at first sight I disliked it so much that I flew on to Mexico City: it seemed I might dislike this too, but I loved the enormous murals of Rivera and Orozco and Siquieros; I pondered on the temples where there had been blood sacrifices at the rising or setting of the sun. In the evenings I sat on my own in cafés while men in huge hats strummed on guitars; I began to write in a notebook sentences which, it seemed to me, were the sort of thing I now wanted to write – not to do with the partly written thriller I had left behind in England:

not to do really, with anything I had written before – but something perhaps to do with people going on journeys, getting out of old routines, feeling partly and paradoxically free of old commitments not because they have failed, but because they have succeeded; saying – All right, we do now know all this, but what happens next?

I wrote: *You know how love flourishes in time of war, women standing on station platforms and waiting for the lines of faces to pull out, men's heads three deep in the carriage windows and arms raised like the front legs of horses in the Parthenon. The men do not want to go to war; they look forward to travel and the warmth of soldiers.*

I thought – Sometime, yes, this might be the start of a story about people knowing.

I went on to Yucatan and the Gulf Coast where there was a wind and the clashing of palm trees like that in Faulkner's *The Wild Palms* – the book which I had once loved beyond all other, in which the hero had chosen grief rather than nothing. I flew on to New Orleans which had been the setting for Faulkner's *Mosquitoes*, which I had also loved, and which had been about people being whimsical and happy; and there were small brass bands marching up and down the streets and playing the same exuberant music whether for a birth or a wedding or a funeral. I sat in bars and wrote in my notebook – *When you know that love flourishes in time of war – those kisses taken on street corners where you might be killed, barrel-organs outside pubs as meretricious as ballets – then, when there is no war, what do you do with these images? You have them from the beginning: are forced out of the tunnel into the football stadium; know the moment before the doors open when you are in the dark; then the roar, with the goalpost and the lion.* I thought – You mean, all this sort of thing might happen again; but now we would be knowing?

I returned from my travels; I worked again on the book that was supposed to be a thriller; I wrote an article introducing English readers to Andy Warhol. I thought – Yes, but what indeed would it be to live knowingly with the old images: not to put up smoke-screens; not to try to run away or kill them –

– something will turn up?

In the meantime I became involved in a daft imbroglio concerning a novel that my old friend Hugo Charteris had written in which, as was his wont, there were characters recognisably like people he knew – in this case Rosemary and myself and my father. I had read the book in typescript (it was called *The Riverwatcher*) and I had not at all minded the character that was supposed to be like me; this character was, of all things, an ex-Congo-mercenary, now some sort of gamekeeper ('riverwatcher') in Scotland. Hugo seemed surprised I did not mind: I wrote to him – All one cares about, surely, is that one should not appear wet. Rosemary had not read the typescript but had asked me if there was anything in it that she might object to: I had told her – There is one sentence about the character like you which says that in her eyes there is an expression 'as though she might be on parole from some other world – or a mental home'. Rosemary had said – Oh I don't mind that! But my father had taken violent objection to the character that was supposed to be like him and had set about suing Hugo for libel. So suddenly there were letters whizzing to and fro and outrage from Diana when I said that of course I would not join in the lawsuit against Hugo. My father had composed a dossier for his lawyer in which there was the remarkable sentence – 'And then there is the character who is like my son Nicholas, who in this book is portrayed as being not only a bugger but also impotent, whereas in fact he had a fine war record and won the 440 yards at Eton'. I found that I was touched by this. In fact the scenes in the book had little to do with Rosemary and me, but Diana wrote scathingly of my reluctance to care about whether people, especially my children, might think that they had. I replied that I thought my children were capable of distinguishing fact from fiction – 'for some a notoriously difficult accomplishment'. Diana replied that she did not think it a matter of my children being more grown-up than she was, but of my being 'one of those Anglo-Saxons' who pretend not to notice 'when they've been given a sharp kick'.

I thought – Oh but this is no proper sort of war! This is just an occupation for people who have to pass the time.

I had once before become involved personally in one of my father's libel actions; this was against my aunt Irene Ravensdale who, years ago, had published a book of memoirs to which my father had objected. I had then acted as a go-between, and had come under a certain fire from both sides. Now this to some extent happened again. Hugo wrote to me:

> Surely if you refuse to appear as a witness the whole thing will collapse, won't it? You hold both him and me in the palm of your hand, simply by our letters. Using them both you could reduce the whole thing to such a bath of mud that the judge would call for a decontamination unit and close the proceedings ...

At the back of both this libel action and the one against my aunt was the suggestion that my father (or in Hugo's book the character that was supposed to be like my father) had in some way on account of his infidelities been responsible for his first wife's death. It was true that this sort of things was sometimes said about my father: I had always thought it nonsense – husbands are often unfaithful; wives as a result of this don't usually die. But in Hugo's book the relevant passage had suggested only that this was the sort of thing people said; and in a story why should this matter? I wrote to Diana to say that to engage in a libel action would only encourage the sort of things that people said; and surely she and my father must be used to this sort of rubbish by now. Also was it not ludicrous in this context to suggest (as it seemed she did) that my father was fighting for the honour of the family. To this Diana replied that however much my father might make out that he did not care about the family, with regard to myself 'his intense love of you as a child and a young man' was markedly different in kind and in degree 'from anything I have known him feel about other young men'.

I was indeed grateful for this. And I was annoyed with Hugo for dragging up old gossip. I went back to writing my political thriller in which all the characters come to a bad or bewildered end.

My father after a time did drop the libel action, as he had done with the one against my Aunt Irene years ago.

I thought – But the novel I truly want to write is the one about how all true battles are in the mind; about how of course there is scandal, tragedy, absurdity – but so what? What matters is what can be learned from these.

I had my bits of prose about love flourishing in times of war: but not much of a storyline except – what will turn up?

Sometime later I wrote to Hugo that I was going back to New York for a while because since the collapse of the libel action I had been feeling somewhat self-righteous and – 'I always feel dispossessed in New York, very unrighteous.' Hugo replied – 'What are you doing in America? The mind boggles. Your third trip this year! Have you got a mistress there?'

PART III

The idea that to make sense of one's life one has to tell of the bad things as well as the good at least to oneself is at the back of much of this story: without a recognition of darkness as well as light there is no pattern; without pattern there is no chance of glimpsing a path through the maze. And without this what is the point of life; what is its wonder? Of course there is drama! But drama has little virtue if it cannot be looked at as well as suffered.

But then, what is this virtue?

It seems that creation, evolution, requires both darkness and light: life develops through the formation, breaking up, regeneration of pattern.

The idea that there is some demand upon humans to move on from systems in which they might be protected and thus moribund – move on, that is, in response to some call by what can be referred to as Spirit – this idea may be in tune with life but portends its own heavy dangers: it is in such a state of *hubris* that humans are apt to feel heroic, autonomous, sinless; and thus come to their own tragic or just dead ends. In *Experience and Religion* I had written of people 'being given the power to discover, act, know things for themselves'; in *Accident* there had been the talk of 'we can now write about people knowing'. I am not sure how much I felt of the dangers or even of the possibly farcical aspects of this at the time. But I did feel that I had to go off on some journey – to see what happened;

to discover, perhaps, what it is that is known if there is this knowing; to see (as in a maze) what are and are not dead-ends.

I had written in my notebook of the way in which love seems to flourish in time of war. I had assumed – We want love, don't we?

I had also written – All such battles are properly now in the mind. But, in any battle, as I must have known, there are humiliations as well as tragedies and triumphs: we can dream of being heroic; but what of being just silly?

(I had seen, of course, that there is a sense in which I was still a spoilt kid: but does one not have to make the best of what one is?)

A central question seemed to be – Does there have to be the risking of one sort of disaster or another for the chance of good emerging? Indeed there are disasters that are simply dead-ends. But what is the style in which there might be hope of good? Just that relevant possibilities should be borne in mind?

The idea that by telling the bad things as well as the good one makes patterns and thus that the act of telling itself might be 'good' on a higher level – this itself brings close the danger of *hubris*; any telling or indeed harbouring of the idea of 'goodness' being apt to send the situation immediately into its opposite. Any person, that is, who imagines himself heroic, autonomous, sinless, almost automatically is not: just as someone who feels himself protected and made effective by convention almost certainly is not. Perhaps that is why so many stories, even if about 'goodness', still have to be about absurdities and disasters – leaving the sense of goodness to emerge as a by-product of the telling. But what about stories about oneself? Can one really say – Of course there are these absurdities and disasters! – and hope that by the telling of these they will move (and be seen to move) into their opposites?

St Paul once asked God – Shall we continue in sin that grace may abound? And he answered himself – God forbid.

But then, he was talking to God.

He trusted, presumably, that if God so wished, He would forbid. And in the meantime the Spirit would go on operating through the ordinary daft human roundabout of humiliation and disaster and absurdity and love and joy.

I wondered – Can humans not come to accept this?

– We do wrong, we make fools of ourselves, we hurt others, we are hurt. We fall into the same old traps: we are like dogs that return to our vomit. We are also, if we recognise such fault, that through which grace may abound.

But how on earth can such opposites both be carried in mind and yet, if we are not to oscillate endlessly between darkness and light, also be not too much dwelt on? There has to be some giving up of consciousness in trust, it seems, if things are to move on. But would not such states of mind require some legerdemain like that of a clown?

Pulcinella hits Harlequin with a string of sausages. Columbine is abused by the wicked Scaramouche.

Oh we love the old favourites all right!

But you mean – one might trust that things might be seen as a bit more farcical the second time round?

A human being is only bearable, only makes patterns that are bearable, perhaps, if he sees himself (and lets others see him) as not only a hero and a victim but also as both – which is a clown.

You call that 'goodness'?

But you never quite know where grace (or deathliness?) may abound.

15

The so-called 'thriller' that I had begun to write after *Accident* was called *Assassins*; it was aimed at being popular, and perhaps being made into a film. The writing of it seemed representative of the hiatus in my life. The story is as follows:

The leader of an Eastern European country is on a visit to this country. There are Eastern European extremists who want to destroy the chances of a West/East *rapprochement*; they plan to assassinate their leader while he is on a visit to the British Foreign Secretary. The Foreign Secretary has a fourteen-year-old daughter who is abducted by the would-be assassin when she stumbles across him in the grounds of her father's country house. The girl comes to an understanding with her abductor, who is a boy with whom she seems to have more sympathy than with the people around her father. He agrees to let her go on condition that they both promise not to tell about, nor take advantage of, what has occurred. In order to safeguard this plan they concoct a story about how it is the boy himself who has rescued her from kidnappers. But by this ruse he is brought into the presence of the Foreign Secretary and the Eastern European leader in order to be thanked in front of television cameras for his part in the rescue; and so the girl wonders – is it after all she who has been tricked and will there now be an assassination attempt? And so, should she keep her promise not to talk? In the end (but the end of a thriller should not be divulged) there is darkness and not much light.

It seems to me now, looking back, that this was a good story; but lack of a heartfelt commitment to it resulted in some looseness of style. I have tried to correct this. But perhaps one part of me was saying to another – What on earth are you doing with these characters like balls on a pin-table when what you are trying to learn to portray are characters that are not?

I thought at least I could say – For once the central character in one of my novels is not like me! But a friend of mine said – The fourteen-year-old girl is exactly like you.

Assassins was not made into a film. The two novels on either side of it, which had been written with nothing of the sort in mind, were.

Surviving from my trip to Mexico – from my first or second trip to New York when I had felt: I am free! but what does it mean to be free? may I hope one day to look down on my life as if it were more than a pin-table or piece of junk-art in a gallery in New York – surviving from this sort of feeling of doubt or questioning or expectancy were the pieces that on my journey I had written in my notebook: *This was the spring when I had been married half my life and there was this drought, cherry and lilac, the crowds moving round the flower stalls and raising their straw hats and blazers. And when the call came they moved as one man and lined up on the platform.* And it was, indeed, as if life in our fine country house, that of Rosemary and myself, were in some sense running down; our sons were at boarding-schools; our daughter was suddenly too old to be playing games with me such as submarines under the bedclothes. Rosemary could now spend much of her time painting again: she went for a time to an art school in Paris; then to a beach by the Pyrenees where she might catch and portray people and horses as tiny figures against a distant sea. I had written in my notebook – *The trees I had planted through half my life were now growing; my house in its fields, my sons between nettles and hedgerow.* Rosemary and I still tried to do our best as a family: we bought a motor boat and trundled out to fish in a cold English sea; I got a tent and went camping with the older boys in the pouring rain on Skye. But what might be happening as it were round some corner?

I had written: *And God came down through the trees one day and scratched himself as if a man had walked over his grave or trod on excrement and said 'What are you going to do?' I looked round the garden and saw a father and a mother and three sons with bronze draperies over their knees and their heads pin-points. We sat in deck-chairs and ate from trolleys. I said 'I don't know.' I went to the attic where there was my paraphernalia of war, my uniform and moths, rats and sleeping-bag. My wife came to me: she said 'I don't want you to go,' I said 'I don't want to go.'*

So what was I meaning by all this: that we were coming to the end of a pattern that had once been life-blood to us but was now no longer, Rosemary and I?

I had been some sort of disciple of Father Raynes: but Father Raynes had had much of his insides cut out by the time he was fifty: this was what happened to people who were steadfast and obedient? And was I not right that it was suggested one might move on? Or was it simply that I had some itch; and hoped that if I sinned then grace might abound. Well indeed – God forbid! But it had seemed to me sometimes recently that there was part of myself coming after me to cut out my insides with knives.

All right! So you stand with your arms out, do you, and trust – what – a knife-thrower at a circus?

I had written: *My wife came with me to the station. There were the doors closing and the ghosts three deep in the carriage windows – the ones at the top innocent and the ones in the middle terrified and the ones at the bottom guillotined. They were smiling; afraid of feeling again. My wife said 'Take care of yourself.' I said 'I will.'*

There was an evening when there was to be a fancy-dress party at a neighbour's house in Sussex (you think that such things should not be seen as farce? of course farce is a way of dealing with shame) there was this fancy-dress party to which I had wanted to go and then at the last minute I did not want to go – might there not be a ghost lurking round some corner? I dressed up in fact as a sort of clown – in my father-in-law's white polo-breeches, a striped rugby-football jersey, a grey top hat. I thought – All right, in this dress I can still perhaps dream of another circus-act round some corner.

At the party there was a man whom I had known very briefly in the army; I had caught a glimpse of him just once in the intervening years when he had been with his newly-married wife who had struck me as someone so beautiful that the vision was indeed like being got at with knives. But this was when I had been editing *Prism*, and trying not to be interested in such things round a corner. Now it seemed – Oh good heavens, was this why I was suddenly reluctant to come to the party? But thank goodness I have come, as it were ready with my string of sausages; my ladder and buckets of paste.

There was this woman, girl, wife, sitting with her back to me at the party: she was dressed as a Pierrot. (I mean this literally!) And she was talking about Diderot. I knew nothing about Diderot. (Diderot who? Did he row on a dark lake with a sword?) I joined in the conversation. When the girl, woman, wife, turned to me I thought – Oh Lord, here indeed we go again! the bucket of cement over the head; the jug of boiling water down the inside of the trousers.

In my notebook I had written – *Nothing is more terrible than war; just the spring coming round again with bodies wrapped and the need to lance them like pins stuck in a wall-map.* And – *All battles are now in the mind; we must make our own war.*

But of course I knew – There are white crosses as well as daisies round the perimeter of a battlefield –

– She loves me, she loves me not –

– Petals, seeds, crosses –

God forbid!

How can one write about this? Perhaps by not separating too much what happened from what I tried to make of it even at the time in writing: life and the effort to find out about it, to fashion it, at last perhaps coming together.

At the fancy-dress party we danced. What need had there been for anything more.

A day or two later I had a letter:

I long to telephone you but I don't dare.

In my usual over-tentative way I sent you a copy of *Jacques le Fataliste* on Monday evening via your publishers but I have just discovered that they haven't even received it yet. If it ever does arrive you will discover my telephone number written just above the first chapter which I thought was a good place for it. I had resolved to do nothing further until it had arrived – but I must abandon this resolve.

I have thought of you continually since Saturday night. I hope this doesn't horrify you. I simply cannot forgive myself for my cowardice then.

If you would like me to put you out of my mind – or begin trying to do so, for it will take time – you must write and say so. Otherwise I shall not be able even to attempt it. Please don't worry how you say it or what effect it will have – I should understand your reasons only too well.

If on the other hand you would like to see me again and feel you will be able to manage it sometime please let me know. I shall be alone all weekend if you would like to telephone or write.

I have just got your book and am going to begin reading it this evening.

Oh yes, I have been here before. And it does not work, running away?

Jacques le Fataliste, I discovered, is a novel by Diderot. It arrived the next day. It seemed that Jacques was some sort of clown.

– Hullo –

– Hullo –

– I got your telephone number –

– Yes –

The book of mine that she had referred to was *Accident*. I learned later that at some point during the reading of it she rushed out into her garden and tore it to bits. It had, apparently, said nice things about marriage.

I thought – But surely the fault the last time round, when I first met Mary, was all the stuff about renunciation and self-immolation. Did we not learn – it might have been better to have simply got on with it? So –

Scene: the Palm Court Lounge of a London hotel. Lunch. Pulcinella, Jacques le Fataliste: attendant memories like ghosts.

I tried to speak the lines that seemed to have been given me – I

must tell you, this sort of thing has happened before. She said –
What do you mean this sort of thing has happened before? I said
– I mean, there was this, and then sickness and suffering and almost
death –

– You mean you don't want to –

– Of course I want to! –

– Well then! (with much scorn)

And afterwards she did seem to be saying – Well that was that
then, thank you.

(I've still got the bill: £3 5s. od., in those days, at the Grosvenor
Hotel.)

But did I not know – it's easier to begin, than to end, a war.

But to be sure I could write about this! in nothing of the old
style, of course.

The novel that I now began to write was one to which the
sentences and paragraphs I had written in my notebook seemed to
serve as a preamble. The novel was called *Impossible Object*, and
consisted of eight stories ostensibly separate but to be connected in
a reader's mind in as much as he or she became aware that they
were about the same people. The stories were told by different or
the same characters about different or the same incidents in their
or each other's lives. The point of this form was to make it clear –
humans are in fact not rational and all-of-a-piece; they are this facet
or that blown about in the wind; they are ridiculous and wonderful
and frightening all at once. The eight stories were interspersed with
more of the sort of passages that I had written in my notebook.
These latter, printed in italics, were some ironic commentary on
the sort of pantomimes – tragic or comic – that were going on in the
stories. At the back of all this was the idea – It has to be in the mind
(of a reader? of a creator?) that there are made connections: it is in
connections that there is the structuring of life.

By the end I had explained an impossible object as – *A staircase
climbing a spiral to come out where it started or a cube with a vertical
line at the back overlapping a horizontal one in front. These cannot exist
in three dimensions but can be drawn in two; by cutting out one dimension
a fourth is created. The object is that life is impossible; one cuts out*

fabrication and creates reality. A mirror is held to the back of the head and one's hand has to move the opposite way from what was intended.

The first story in *Impossible Object* is about a family which consists of a husband and a wife and three children on the occasion of the eldest son's first girlfriend coming to tea. She is a fifteen-year-old girl with a head like Cleopatra: she reminds the father of someone he has known before: he thinks – But I know all this! After tea they go down into the cellar to play a hide-and-seek game in the dark; the girl seems to be seeking out the father. So what does he do – if he thinks he knows all this! There is an accident, a sudden tragedy; the girl has, fatally, put her hand on a live light-socket in the dark. No one's fault of course. Or is it? The wife seems to be saying to the husband – You see: what are dreams; what is reality?

The second story concerns a different couple, a husband and a wife, who are lying in bed in the early morning; they have quarrelled the night before and are planning how to hurt one another again. They know – the best way to hurt people is to begin by appearing to be loving: then, when the other is vulnerable, love can be withdrawn. Their two young children come into the room: there is the question – Can children be used by parents to hurt one another? Or – Surely there must be some way out of these predicaments! For both husband and wife it seems there is a dream of a different style of relationship round some corner.

The third story is about the first couple again; they are on a holiday in Morocco without their children. The husband goes off on a journey into the desert; the wife, left on her own, becomes friendly with an Arab whom she meets on the beach. When her husband returns she tells him – I have made friends with this man on the beach; I would like you to be friendly with him too; do not be jealous! he is like a child; have you not often told me – What is the point of jealousy? we know about all this! So the husband makes a formal gesture of friendship to the man. But he thinks – All right: the cost (or the reward?) of such an acceptance can be some liberation from commitments for myself.

The fourth story, the central one of the book, is told by a narrator who comes to lunch each day in a London pub. He becomes aware that also having lunch each day in the pub are a couple, a man and a woman, who arrive separately but are obviously much in love. In the crush it is easy to overhear their conversation: it seems they are both married – not to each other. It becomes apparent to the reader that the man is the husband of the first and third stories and the woman is the wife of the second story: so they have broken out of their predicaments, their traps, have they? they have found some ecstasy round some corner! But it seems the woman is asking of the man something more – some commitment – and the man is saying – But we know about commitments, on their own, they don't work. The woman says – I don't believe that! The man says – You do, but you won't admit it. After a time they stop coming to the pub. The narrator thinks – They seemed to have been on the edge of what love might be: then to have lost it.

Sometime later the woman turns up in the pub; she seems to be looking for her lover. But she is followed by a man who is evidently her husband. He holds her; he says – Did you used to meet him here? She says – No. And then – I promise. The narrator thinks – Ah, what indeed is love!

Sometime later again the man comes into the pub with a woman who is evidently his wife. She says – Did you used to meet her here? He says – Yes. She says – Then why have you brought me here? He says – To exorcise it, ducky. The narrator thinks – Dear God, and I imagined those people might once have had the secret of what is possible!

Then some years later the narrator comes across the man once again; he is on a beach by a hotel in Morocco with his children. The narrator goes up to the man and says – There was a winter when I used to sit next to you at lunchtime in a pub. The man says – I remember you: I once wrote a story about a man who watched us in the pub! The narrator says – But I wrote a story about you! The man seems to be expecting someone to come out of the door of the hotel: the narrator thinks that of course it will be his wife. But out of the door comes the woman with whom he had seemed to be so much in love in the pub: she is a woman with dark hair like Cleopatra. She greets the narrator; then she goes down with the children to the sea. She seems to be like some goddess with her acolytes; or a victim. The narrator thinks – This after all is what love should be?

I began to write *Impossible Object* in a flat I took to be near the Pierrot girl (all right, woman) whom I had met at the fancy-dress party: oh yes, we had almost decided not to see each other again; then just one or two more times! then definitely no more; oh then of course this was impossible! Neither of us wished to break up our families. So like this we embarked on our ecstatic or our *commedia dell'arte* routines (take your pick) with our buckets and ladders on our tightrope. It transpired that shortly before the time of the fancy-dress party Natalie's husband had left her (I am going to call the Pierrot-girl Natalie after the title of the book I wrote following *Impossible Object* which was called *Natalie Natalia*) – Natalie's husband had left her and gone off with someone else but then had wanted to come back; she had said she would only have him back on condition that she too could have some sort of affair: he had agreed: then I had come along in my polo-breeches and grey top hat in the role of milkman or window-cleaner or indeed hero/victim in some avant-garde production of *Tristan and Isolde*. And Natalie had not taken too seriously the opening matinée performance as it were, so what was the harm in a second; and so on; but by then it was too late. So when I went away and Natalie was back with her husband and then her husband left her again ('I did not agree that you should fall in love!') I came back and then her husband came back so I went off again to my family – but Rosemary, most sensibly, was quite often away painting at this time. Oh this was a farce all right! But it was also a grand passion – and indeed like war, with its fears and triumphs and no one quite knowing what was happening. I would lie in the bath and ruminate on all this: This is really what love is like? a glory; a self-destruction; a miracle; despicable? How indeed can I find a way of writing about this! what on earth are people doing writing all-of-a-piece stories?

Soon Natalie was writing again:

> Darling – I came at 12 but you weren't there. If you come back before leaving for the country, please ring me. We have made the wrong decision again, and I can't bear it. I love you.

It was as if there was almost consciously an experiment going on. I had imagined that life might be like this: so you mean – Life really is like this? How amazing! Testing: testing.

Or – You make things like this in so far as you think things are like this? But even so (this was also what I had imagined) how can you make things like this unless in some sense that is what they are – and you have just learned to observe them. Some fifteen years ago Mary and I had tried to deny that things were like this and had failed; we had seen ourselves as tragic, all-of-a-piece; and so this for a time was what we had made of ourselves – nothing of the dashingness of clowns! But in so far as we had failed, we had also learned – perhaps in the sanity of 'knowing all this' there can after all be the ecstasy as well as the farce and tragedy of clowns.

Natalie wrote:

> Darling – Thank you for hanging my pictures. I came on Friday to look at them; it was already dark. I stayed and ate your last two eggs, which I hope you were not counting on for any morning's breakfast.
>
> I am being driven into a decision about the future and causing myself and everyone terrible suffering which seems unavoidable.
>
> Here are two more records of Bach Cello Suites, with the others. I have borrowed your copy of Pascal (in which I may never get any further than your name on the fly-leaf).

When I was back in my London flat I would lie in the bath there and wonder how to convey this sort of thing in my stories. Of course one needs stories – to say what life is like; for anyone to be able to glimpse what life is like. Oh indeed, most stories were about people like helpless pebbles on a beach being pushed around by the sea; and so people are; but people might see this; and so they might see the connection between themselves as observers and themselves as pebbles, and thus come alive; and so might readers see such connections within and between my stories and thus come alive – Eureka! I jumped out of the bath. I would sit in front of my typewriter dripping like some monster from the sea. I thought – You mean, I might indeed be able to say what it is impossible to say, in my impossible stories?

– When I leave Natalie, she wants to come back; when she is with me, she wants to go –

– You say one thing, then it is another –

– 'This is impossible' becomes possible –

– Eureka indeed! a current between poles –

– the basic stuff of the universe?

Or if that is one of the things one cannot say, then at least –

– Indeed we are like jugglers trying to keep our plates or balls or whatever up in the air at the same time.

Natalie and I managed to go abroad on a holiday together.

Rosemary came home.

I went to rejoin Rosemary.

Natalie went home: then left, to live on her own in my flat.

(Natalie was, of all things, also a painter. There was a lot of creative stuff going on –

So what were the strings of sausages then: one's own, or someone else's, insides?)

Natalie wrote:

> My darling – I have cleaned the flat, polished the furniture, turned the kitchen into a model of bourgeois efficiency and bought paint-ing-flowers and non-painting-flowers which are in one of your big white vases. I have re-hung Rosemary's lovely painting and brought in three of my own – a reconciliation less difficult than you have imagined. But mine will probably never be hung, as I have no idea how to go about it.
>
> —— wants me to come back, he has really wanted this since he saw me on Wednesday night and learned what my situation was. There was some talk of remaining apart for a while, of above all not coming together through weakness but through strength, but I knew that on his side this was not really serious. We spent the weekend together with the children in the country, which went well. Since then he has given up all pretence of wanting a further separation; he rings daily, is loving, and the only thing that is restraining him from applying real pressure is that he still has reservations about his commitment to —— and will have till he hears from her.
>
> Now perhaps I shall reveal my 'vacancy' – or what might not be vacancy but something different. I think I have felt everything one could feel about returning home – and the children. I felt, returning

on Saturday night, that this was reality – above all the children – and anything else was inconceivable. But I didn't stay. Yesterday, through a lot of the day, I was full of unhappiness, but by the evening I was exquisitely happy. I was alone here, I had painted during the day (terribly badly), I listened to the Bach record and the Neapolitan one, I drank your wine, ate fish-fingers, watched it grow dark behind the T'ang horse and felt more at home than I've ever felt anywhere. I cried a lot during the Neapolitan record, but that didn't matter. I remembered you and thought above all of our time in Capri.

I suppose I am back in a state of what —— condemned when we were living separately before as 'euphoric irresponsibility', the euphoria consisting by no means in one's joyful feelings, which may be rare, but in one's imagining of what is possible.

I have no desire to go back – no real constant desire. I feel a very real and constant desire to remain here, backed by two powerful feelings – my love for you and my love for solitude.

Whatever I said on the telephone, of course I shall always passion-ately hope to see you and to talk to you. You must ignore my pride. And yet, whatever you do, you will not succeed in divorcing me from you, because you cannot, but please don't try further. You need not see me, but if you want to I shall be here till I succumb to the pressures of responsibility and other pressures.

I am reading Goethe's *Wilhelm Meister* in Carlyle's translation. I think it is a magical book.

Wilhelm Meister is a story about people who go on various journeys in the course of which people tell stories about people on various journeys – and so on. There are no ends to the stories because there are no ends as it were to the people telling the stories so long as the people are alive.

Impossible Object is an effort to say – Of course this is what love is like, this is what life is like, this to and fro, being held between opposites. Of course there is pain (how can there be life without pain?); of course one of the poles – opposite to that of joy and suffering – is ludicrousness, the bucket of paste, the plank that swings round and hits the face of a clown. Humans cannot alter their predicament; they can balance it with this vision, this polarity; and they can do this because there is a force such as gravity in the outside world to help them – what a wonder! The temptation is to say – Love should be simple; truth should be all-of-a-piece. But if in fact they are not – then it is the temptation that causes delusion. Look round you: are not humans either tip-toeing along, or flat on the ground underneath, a tightrope?

Oh if we had all been different people, yes, we might each have found some simple commitment – what it is like to be a pebble on a beach?

Love is not only a striving for, but a breaking-up of, established commitment. You stand on ice; suddenly it melts; the clown tries to hold himself up by the seat of his own trousers.

All right, this is the style – of writing, of life. But what after all happens?

I am only half-way through *Impossible Object*!

16

All this was happening at the time when the film of *Accident* began to be made. I had attended the first reading of the script; I went to watch the filming in Oxford. There were all these expert actors – Dirk Bogarde, Stanley Baker, Vivienne Merchant, Delphine Seyrig, Alexander Knox – supposed to be bringing my characters to 'life'. But traditionally what actors aimed at, what they were good at, was presenting characters as consistent and all-of-a-piece: what else was the craft of acting? But had not I been saying that this effort is not to do with life, but with death –

– Life being a balancing between acting and realising when one is acting?

Years ago I had written in *Prism*:

> There is a sense in which the whole Christian life is a process of learning how *not* to be an actor – how to be most truly oneself. This is for obvious reasons an impossibility for professionals, for whom the concept of 'being truly oneself' can have progressively less meaning.

But then what did I mean by 'being truly oneself' – knowing that one is on a tightrope?

One day I was watching the filming in Oxford and Joe Losey asked me if I would like to be in the film: they were short of an actor to play the part of a don in an Oxford common room. I said – This is the sort of chance for which people wait all their lives, hanging about on street corners! So there I was, in a scene with Dirk Bogarde and Stanley Baker and Alexander Knox; and when the film came out it seemed – Oh dear, I am so evidently a non-actor knowing that he is acting!

Natalie had come down with me to watch the filming; Joe Losey asked me if she would like to be in the film too. I thought – And so our relationship will be exposed – non-actors being so pleased to be asked to do some acting! But Natalie had wandered off to look at some ancient buildings.

There was soon a time when I was indeed on the edge of catastrophe in my real-life high-wire juggling act – down on one knee on the rope; tea-cups and saucers flying in all directions. I moved out of both the flat in London where Natalie was now staying and my home in Sussex where my family (all honour to them) were getting increasingly fed up with my ludicrous gyrations. In order to get on with my writing I took refuge in a tiny top-floor room in a seedy boarding-house in Bloomsbury – the sort of place where travellers get a bed and a huge breakfast and no one talks to them and no one wants to know who they are. Here in a month or so I polished off, polished up, *Impossible Object* – this particular juggling act now spinning and sparkling like a Catherine-wheel at least in my head. I would work long hours sitting on the bed with my feet against a gas stove which was shaped curiously like an obelisk (I would think – Too narrow to get my head into?): two or three times a day I would go for a walk round a secluded cemetery that I have never again been able to find. I remember this as an exciting time, with apocalyptic things going on inside (goodness knows what outside) my head.

The fifth story of *Impossible Object* is about a man (the narrator of the fourth story?) who has got fed up with the sort of life he has become stuck in and goes off to look for a new girlfriend; he goes to Rome, and there finds a woman with whom he goes on a journey up through Italy. This journey was like the one I had gone on across America on the Sante Fe Special – though in fact it was with Natalie I had travelled from Naples up through Italy. At the end of the journey in the book the narrator comes across yet again, on the top of the leaning tower of Pisa, the very person whom he had been imagining he might have been getting away from at home: the dark-haired woman with a head like Cleopatra. This woman was like Natalie, yes; but in this story older now; she is with her husband again; and both her children are with her; they are older too; but where have we seen them, or not seen them, before? there might be some mystery here, not quite to be looked at yet. The narrator and the woman go off – to have at least one more lunch together. This story is called 'A Journey into the Mind'.

In the sixth story the man (the man of the first and third stories? the narrator? these are the same person? take your pick) has retired to a bed-sitting-room as it were in Bloomsbury; he has done this to be on his own, to be able to write. Sometimes he is visited by the woman like Natalie with whom he has been in love; sometimes he is visited by his wife and his children. He quite often thinks of cutting his wrists:

> I had the idea that all great lovers committed suicide – Romeo and Juliet, Tristan and Isolde, Othello and Desdemona. You put a penny in the slot and first Juliet did it and then Romeo and for your money's worth Juliet again. They gave value in the old days. And Tristan and Isolde – I could not quite remember – they had been on a beach – they had been inexperienced – and had managed it several times too. About Desdemona I was not so sure; she had been young, and had had to get someone to do it for her.

He does have a dab at cutting his wrists; but is prevented from doing this seriously by a plumber who has come to mend (but in fact breaks) the pipes.

In the seventh story the man is still in his bed-sitting-room; he has not been visited by his wife or the Natalie-like person for some time. He returns one night from walking round and round the town and he sees men waiting in a car outside the entrance to his building. They question him about the whereabouts of 'Natalie': he thinks they must be police – he has had the idea for some time that 'Natalie' might kill her husband or be killed by him: or her husband might kill himself – and the man has the impression that even now 'Natalie' might be in hiding upstairs in his room, to which she has a key. So he goes to elaborate lengths to get up to his room without being seen; and there he does find 'Natalie', and she gives no explanation for her presence; she seems to be under stress; they make love. Then it transpires that what has happened is that her husband has decided to sue for divorce: the men outside the building were there to obtain evidence for him to do this. So – All those dramatic dreams! this is the reality. 'Natalie' seems to be asking him – But you do want the reality? do you?

The eighth and final story is the only one told by a woman – the one who is like Natalie. She and the man and all their children are in the hotel by the sea in Morocco – this is where the narrator in the fourth story has come across them. She and the man are now separated from their spouses; they had gone abroad to wait for the birth of their child. This child had been conceived, it appears, during the night of drama in the seventh story. The child is now born, and the man and woman are in this hotel by the sea where his other children and her daughter have come to visit them. But now 'Natalie' – having got what it seems she has wanted – is still not at peace: she has wanted perfection: but how can there be perfection when her families are split and there are different fathers of her children? The man still seems able to do his juggling acts: he plays hide-and-seek games with his children amongst the trees: but was it not during some such game – 'Natalie' remembers he had told her – that some child got killed? Or was this just a story that he had written? Now, the man and the children plan to go out in a boat; this is sometimes a dangerous sea; the man says to 'Natalie' – But you and the baby need not come. She says – But I want to come! She does not like being left out – if she is, what is she doing here? What is all this splitting of families? When they are all out in the boat the wind gets up, and as they come into land the boat overturns and in the mêlée the baby is drowned. The man says to 'Natalie' – You had nothing to do except hold on to it! 'Natalie' thinks – There are some things for which one cannot be forgiven.

But then after all – is not this a story? Is 'in fact' the baby drowned?

In this last story the woman has her daughter and her baby; in the second and fifth stories she has what might seem to be the same

206

two children – but these stories are later in time. So – can it be that indeed the last story was just a 'story', and the child who was said to be drowned is in the other stories in fact alive?

Interspersed with the stories in *Impossible Object* are the bits of commentary as it were in the style of those I had begun to write in Mexico. Now after the end of the last story there was a piece in which I seemed to be speaking directly to the real Natalie:

> *You used to dislike happy ends, feeling it is better to have your heart cut out like an Aztec rather than suffer the prevarications of Spaniards. So I have given you an unhappy end like those of your favourite films – the girl shot over and over in the snow like a rabbit, the car drowned in a few inches of water. There is also a happy end, though this is less explicit. But you always read books more for form than for content.*

The so-called 'happy end' – that 'in fact' the baby might not have been drowned – might be seen, that is, by anyone who wished to make the imaginative effort to see it: but any reader could choose to do this or not; to choose what he wished to see. My narrator had given Natalie 'an unhappy end' in the last story because this was the way in which she was accustomed to seeing things: and indeed this is the sort of way in which people are apt to see things. With unhappy ends they feel at home; perhaps guilt about other things thus seems easier to bear. And indeed happy ends may have to remain somewhat secret – or people who like unhappy ends might come after them with knives.

The last image in the book is that of the hero and heroine as dancers after the end of a ballet – *They came in front of the curtain and held hands. They were very tired. They poured with sweat. From the roof there fluttered eggs and roses.*

It seems to me now some lack of courage that I did not make the chance of a happy end more explicit: it had remained so hidden! But at the time – there I was holed up in my bed-sitting-room in Bloomsbury: childrens' lives all around me seemed in danger of being dashed on rocks. I had my own guilt; it seemed some insurance, I suppose, clearly to say – Oh yes I know there might be a terrible price to pay for playing around on rocks!

But I was also indeed quietly trying to say – Up to a point we can choose our way of seeing things: and by this we may even affect (though it is this that is difficult to say!) whether this happens or that –

– things die, things come alive –

– liveliness might depend on recognising some choice between the two?

Few people saw the possible happy end to my story. But then – I hadn't expected them to, had I?

But what on earth was I to do when I had finished writing *Impossible Object*? The writing itself had been my tightrope – or rather the pole that had kept me upright on my tightrope. When I emerged from my bolt-hole in Bloomsbury – what? – no rope-ladder to the ground? the audience – family and mistress – have all gone home?

There was always the story of the man who had cut his wrists, I supposed.

Just then I had a letter from an old girlfriend whom I had not heard from for some time who said she was in Paris and why did I not come over and visit her? So I went, and we set off on a walking-trip over the Vosges mountains in the depths of winter and we finished up at Colmar in front of Grünewald's *Crucifixion*. And it was all rather like the journey in the fifth story in the book, in which if you want to deal with absurdities you pile up more absurdities; and then, with luck, things have been going on unnoticed and are alive.

When in fact I got home people did indeed seem hardly to have noticed that I had been away.

So – Hoopla! Upsadaisy! Give us a leg-up, will you? Ready with that bucket?

On with the motley, or whatever it is called.

I was able to have another shot at trying to demonstrate what I meant about the dead/live child (crucifixion/resurrection?) when after the publication of *Impossible Object* the film rights were taken up by a producer who approached Joseph Losey to make the film. I had remained on friendly terms with Joe since the filming of *Accident*. He wrote to me to say how much he liked *Impossible Object*, and about a film:

I'd like nothing better than to be part of such an undertaking, excepting I wonder what film can do in any way to extend or supplement what you have already written down? Of course – with luck – films have bigger audiences, but a film of this book would require the discovery of the visual, impossible fourth dimension. But that's what we've been trying to do.

I worked on and off for a year writing a script of *Impossible Object* for Joe Losey. I liked trying to get it right – especially the business of how to show the happy/unhappy end. (In the end a film was made from my script not by Joe Losey, but by John Frankenheimer; the story of this will be told later.) Joe Losey wanted me to incorporate in the script the sense of ironic commentary contained in the interludes to the stories: by the use of images there might be a sense of timelessness and thus in some sense be a 'happy end'. No one seemed to be much interested in the issue of the live/dead child: it seemed to be thought – The impact of the last scene where the child is drowned will be too great for an audience to accept that it was just a story. I would say – But so long as the chance of seeing it like this is just there, it will not matter if an audience will or will not accept it. At the very end of the script the man/narrator comes across the woman like Natalie once more in the Piazza Navona in Rome. He says – You seemed to want an unhappy end: but you do see this, don't you? She says – See what? In the background there is a glimpse of her husband playing with her and his (the man/narrator's) two-year-old child.

The book *Impossible Object* was on the shortlist for the first Booker Prize in 1969, but its ambiguities seemed to give the judges a hard time.

The chairman reported:

Nicholas Mosley's *Impossible Object* caused most trouble and took most time. Again and again the discussion turned to this complex (or complicated) telling of a love-affair whose phases are reflected in eight independent stories linked by short densely allusive commentaries. In some ways and places everyone thought it strained, miscalculated, even absurdly pretentious; but three at least of the stories were separately effective, and everyone found too that the author's method could produce resonances so strange and fine that the novel was not to be set aside.

I thought – Well, I couldn't hope for much more than that, could I?

By this time liveliness was indeed coming to an end in our beautiful house in Sussex. In *Impossible Object* I had written – *There was this time when we looked out and saw the icecap coming down from the pole; saw that we had been in our cave too long with our ancestors' bones and drawings like tooth-decay; that we should move out through forest and plain till we came to the desert, and should camp there without food and water until we were saved from being preserved for a million years.* This was what I had chosen to write; this sort of thing that seemed to be happening in life. But to what did all the talk of desert and famine refer – that I had fallen in love with a Pierrot-girl at a fancy-dress party? But in such an event – this was what I had been saying – there is indeed an interweaving of grand archetypal images and farce.

I had intended not to write too much about Rosemary in the present book: believing (as with the children) that she would prefer any such story to be written by herself. But it seems now that I will be writing more of Rosemary in the proper place – she who started out on a long journey with me, whom I loved, and who taught me that of course when once two people have been truly joined together, even when they go their different ways, there is something in them that in a sense is never wholly apart.

In the meantime there tumbled into my lap one or two other events that I supposed could be seen as either portentous or farce. In 1966 my aunt Irene Ravensdale died; she had been a baroness in her own right, and the peerage passed to me. This title of Baron Ravensdale had been given to my grandfather, George Curzon, in 1911 in such a way that for just one generation it could pass through the female line – he having three daughters and no son. George Curzon was also an earl and a viscount, but on his death the former title would become extinct and the latter would have to pass through the male line of a younger brother. This Ravensdale title, however, could pass for just one generation through the female line and thus to his eldest daughter my aunt Irene, and then if on her death she had had no children it would pass to her sister, my mother, and then on her death to me, her eldest son. My mother had died in 1933 and my aunt Irene never married and had no children; so there I was in 1966 suddenly landed with the title of Lord Ravensdale. I thought for a time of giving it up (I had six months in which to be able to do so): would it be anything but a handicap for a novelist to be a Lord? But I could carry on writing under my old name of course; and had I not made a point of saying that one should accept whatever windfalls turned up? Also just at this time I was beginning to write another novel partly about politics – *Assassins* had been about politics but from as child's-eye view – and what a chance there would be now, from the House of Lords, to get some sort of parliamentary worm's-eye view!

In order to make sense of my entering the House of Lords I thought I should join some party, or how on earth would I know what was going on? In the past I had once or twice voted Liberal – and at least once Labour, and once Tory. (I had thought – Of course it is floating voters who have power in democracy!) Now I did not want to be Tory or Labour, so I joined the Liberals: when I took my seat in the House of Lords I was sponsored by my godmother, Violet Bonham-Carter, and my old friend from *Prism* days, Timothy Beaumont, both of whom had recently been made Liberal life-peers. I realised almost immediately that I would make a very bad peer: it was not that I thought there was anything wrong, or useless, about the House of Lords: on the contrary it seemed to be a hive of dedicated men and women doing painstaking and necessary work on details of bills that the House of Commons had no time for. But the atmosphere was indeed that of a hive into which one had to fit if one was to be operative at all. One might make a speech, to be sure, to which no one listened; but the serious work went buzzing in corridors and committees. And this I knew I was no good at. I was in fact for a short time made the chairman of a Liberal Committee which was to consider the question of state funding for the arts: as a chairman I was pathetic: what on earth, I felt, could be said about funding for the arts – except that money obviously just had to be poured into Opera Houses and National

Theatres and Galleries and Museums, but if we were going to talk about creativity in art, what could state funding possibly have to do with this? But still, politicians have to talk about things like this. So all right, I was not a politician; I was getting material for my book. Writers have to observe, to listen: politicians have to come down on this side or that. But for how long could I stay honourably on this particular tightrope? After a while I applied for Leave of Absence from the House of Lords, which is what peers do who have no aptitude for the job.

Another chance event that happened at this time was the break-up of the family trust in America from which, ever since the death of my mother, I had been getting a good income. This suddenly came to an end on the death of my great-grandfather's last surviving child. In theory his descendants should now have been able to get their hands on their share of the capital, but in practice this prospect was in jeopardy because of a threat of litigation between various branches of the family – there was some ambiguity in the wording of my great-grandfather's will about the terms of the break-up of the trust. So one side of the family were threatening a lawsuit if the will were interpreted in one way, and another side of the family were threatening a lawsuit if it were interpreted in another; and the trustees were saying – Unless you can all agree on some compromise then the entire capital of the trust will be frozen while the case disappears for years into the jaws of the Chicago law-courts; so that instead of the question being whether one side of the family will get a slightly higher percentage of the assets than the other – which is all that is in dispute – it will be a question of no one getting anything at all except the lawyers. This prospect had so startled myself and my sister that we had gone on a mission a few years previously to try to reason with our American cousins: but we had found them for the most part entrenched behind war-like slogans – Ruin rather than dishonour! Better dead than settle! And so –

– Good heavens, might I really have to begin to earn my own living?

(not half a bad thing, did someone [myself even?] say?)

– What me, with my sort of novels?

– And with a wife and a mistress to support? Oh well, it is quite funny, as I kept on saying: one does what one can, and sees what happens.

The outgoing trustees called for a meeting in Chicago of all the beneficiaries of the trust – some twenty or so descendants of my great-grandfather. This was to be the last chance of compromise before the capital assets went into a possibly terminal entombment. Such was the bizarre (but commonplace?) attitude to battle on the part of the family that everyone, except the Curzon branch, chose to send their lawyers to this meeting rather than go themselves; the Curzon branch allowed themselves to be represented (as well as by their lawyers) by me. So indeed I began to have fantasies about some role here for a battle-hardened (oh!) high-wire artist doing his tricks on his one-wheel bicycle: might I not whirl through enemy lines upsetting barricades like applecarts? Such were my fantasies: but a convention of Chicago lawyers?

When I got to Chicago it did seem to be the case, yes, that I was to be the only direct family descendant at the meeting; so might this not in fact give me some power? On the night before the meeting I was asked out to dinner by a member-by-marriage of the family who was one of the most implacable opponents of a compromise; he seemed to wish to break my own resolve; he said he would show me something of the night-life of Chicago. We went to ever more cavernous bars and night-clubs until we ended in some sort of brothel; here in some despair I lit a small cigar (fantasying myself as Clint Eastwood perhaps? what is the point of films, if in such circumstances fantasies are not useful?) and in so doing I inadvertently set fire to the dress of the 'hostess' beside me. The dress (but not the hostess) went up in flames. The dress was said to have cost several hundred dollars; there was a great uproar; suddenly there were people acting like Edward G. Robinson and Robert de Niro holding people by the lapels of their jackets and pressing these up under their chins. But now my cousin-by-marriage had to defend me as his guest – and so we were in some buddy-buddy movie after all! and eventually out on the streets, dishevelled, but with our arms round one another's shoulders. And by the next morning it was my companion who had flown home.

At the meeting the lawyers were saying that they had instructions not to budge from their entrenched positions. But when I stood up I was able to say (as James Stewart? Gary Cooper? the lone innocent) – Gentlemen, it is no longer a question of one side of the family or the other getting this or that money: unless we come to a compromise it will be you, gentlemen, who will get the lot. So it is up to you. And so on. (You do not think that things can work like this? Well, try it.) Oh yes, I had one great advantage over James Stewart or Gary Cooper – which was that I stammered. (I have not said much about my stammer in this book? Often nowadays it does not seem to matter – but then, yes, indeed it did.) There I was reeling and lurching as if whatever high wire I was on were drawn precisely between my head and my throat; oh I was a clown all right! the pot of glue solidifying over my face. In later life it was suggested to me that the hidden point of a stammer is to disarm people's aggression against oneself; also to disarm the idea of one's own aggression against others. (I did not know of this explanation at the time.) Anyway – perhaps it is the case that a stammerer becomes so embarrassing to an audience that it begins to feel it will do almost anything to get him to stop – in this case settle for something like sixty-seven-point-six-two-five per cent of ten per cent or whatever – and this sort of compromise was, in the end, agreed by the meeting. And I was able to go home and think – Well at least I have done something to earn my unearned money.

So after a time there was capital for me to be able to put down a deposit on a house in Hampstead: this was at the time when I was working on the film script with Joe Losey; when Natalie was still in my London flat. And just at this time Rosemary's family handed over to her some property in the Isle of Man which had been bought originally as a hedge against death-duties – but when Rosemary went to visit her property she fell in love with the Isle of Man, she said she wanted to live there, to paint what she had always loved to paint – the changing shapes and colours of the landscape and the sea and the sky. And this was just at the time when most of our children were away at school; and so indeed there seemed not much more sense in keeping our lovely family house at Lyminster. When the children had been young we had had some shot at seeing it as some bourgeois Garden of Eden: how lucky, I suppose, that I had not been chucked out before for gobbling the fruit of trees! But neither Rosemary nor I, I think, yet saw the sadness of this: there was a lot going on elsewhere in both our lives: we still imagined we might be together and be free.

But with angels with terrible flaming swords of course blocking the way back.

17

The book that I began to write after *Impossible Object* was called *Natalie Natalia*. The title referred to the heroine: Natalie was the ravenous side of her and Natalia the angelic. The situation described was similar to that of the love story in *Impossible Object*. The narrative – at the beginning at least – was more straightforward.

I had thought – The idea that liveliness depends on an activity like that of a juggler on a one-wheel bicycle, is describable not only in the form of a network of impossible/possible stories; it might be portrayed as a state of mind in which complexities are faced and thus perhaps new forces liberated. The state of mind is a style of observing the paradoxes with which life confronts one: the experience is that if one does this, one becomes aware of being part of a pattern infinitely larger than oneself. For instance – love breaks you up but then from time to time you need to be broken up; so this is a chance of contact with processes of learning.

The hero of *Natalie Natalia* is a member of the House of Commons called Anthony Greville. He has become an MP because he has had the talent to be something of a juggler; he has been both gratified by and contemptuous of power. But now he wants to get out. Politicians, it seems to him, are people who, in order to function, have to be largely unaware of the style of their antics. This is how he sees his fellow members of the House of Commons:

Politicians are active and predatory people who have little to prey on now except each other. They place themselves in circumstances in which dreams of conquest are still possible – these carpeted and stone-flagged corridors are clearings in the jungle; here the elders gather and rave against their enemies. Their enemies are amongst themselves: but their sanity is still that of hunters. Around them are heroic mosaics of kings and rebels of their past: once there were panoplies to killing, now their descendants have their dreams. In the marble halls where the populace makes demands on them they can still feel martyred: not at the stake, but in listening to triviality when dreams are so grandiose. Politicians are like sleepwalkers: they do not want to wake or the shock might put them to bed. They are large-scale men forced into such proximity that they have no room for expansion: when they put a hand on your shoulder it is as if they are touching wood; you are a platform, or a bead in a rosary. In the central sanctum where on green leather benches the initiates come apparently to sleep they feel most at home; but they do not sleep, they remember their origins: the whoop and gurgle of hippos, the rustle of leopards in the grass. The gathering of elders has turned inwards, but it echoes its old sounds to remember its identity. Afterwards the elders go out to the quiet world and dinner.

Greville is getting out of politics but he wants to do something useful before he goes. He has been involved in the affairs of a colony in Central Africa which is about to become independent. Here an African leader called Ndoula has been imprisoned; he is thought to be a revolutionary. Greville becomes one of a fact-finding mission due to go out to Central Africa; he will have a chance to visit Ndoula in prison. Shortly before setting out he is approached by a white priest from Africa who asks him if he will pass on a message to Ndoula: this appears to be a coded message probably to do with a possible rescue-attempt to free Ndoula. Greville says to the priest – But you cannot expect me, on official business, to pass on such a message! Then he thinks – But what a way for me to get out of politics!

Greville has a wife called Elizabeth and three children; also a mistress, Natalia, who is like the woman in *Impossible Object*. But unlike the man in *Impossible Object* Greville does not seem all that battered by the impossibilities of the situation; he has settled on his tightrope (as it were) with a chair and table and pot of tea; he might even (the cad!) show some pleasure in this accomplishment. But he knows that if tightrope-tricks are to be pleasant it would be better of course not to admit this – not even, almost, to himself. Natalia has a husband called Edward who is also an MP; he too seems to have a mistress; so they are all (Elizabeth is preparing somewhat thankfully to go her own way) engaged in acrobatics – forming a complex impossible object – one of those circus-groups perhaps whose flashing knives or torches go whirling in a network across a stage. There seems to be no reason why, with luck and endurance, they should not be able to keep this act up in the air for some time. But when you are occupied, exposed, like this, there does seem to be, often, together with the flashing of knives, the claws of some great bird overhead; one slip of the wrist and – there is the bird with its talons around your head.

Greville goes on his mission to Central Africa and there he is taken to the prison camp in the desert where he talks to Ndoula. He does pass to Ndoula the coded message; but because he has some shame about the betrayal involved in this, he finds himself in a state of mind in which he is wanting consciously not to let the left side of his brain as it were quite know what the right side is doing. There is a party for colonial dignitaries at the Governor's residence and Greville gets spectacularly drunk; he rides a child's bicycle into a swimming-pool. And so, literally, what a good trick! he will now be labelled as unstable or a drunk, and will have to get out of politics. The story is put out that he is having some nervous breakdown; he goes to a rest-home in the hills to recuperate – and to ruminate on questions concerning the virtue of existence on a tightrope; the virtue, if any, of one's right hand not quite knowing what one's left hand is doing.

At this point in the book I did not quite have the courage, it seems to me now (just as in *Impossible Object* I had not had the courage to make explicit the possible non-death of the child), to make explicit the fact that Greville had passed on a message to Ndoula that might be instrumental in effecting his escape. But there was a real problem here: Greville doubted the propriety of his action; he nevertheless felt he should do it: it seemed that it was necessary for there to be some ambiguity, secrecy, in the writing, just as there was ambiguity and the need for cover-up in Greville's mind. But then – in the way the story came out it was difficult for a reader to catch the incident at all; and yet this was such an important point of the story! And with regard to Greville's so-called breakdown – this might either be genuine, or part of his trick to get out of politics – or indeed, both! But how could there be a style of writing in which this was both ambiguous and yet quite clear? The problem here was similar to that about the things that one cannot quite say, perhaps even to oneself, or they turn into their opposite. Greville, for sanity, had to be sad and anxious about passing the message on to Ndoula and yet to feel he was right; both to believe and not to believe he was having a nervous breakdown. (Indeed this might be the sign of a nervous breakdown? but still – how sane!) These are not just tricks: they are mechanisms by which reality is balanced in the mind.

It might have been necessary for Greville to confuse himself if he was genuinely to confuse the outside world: but what of the reader? Could it be justified to be found saying to a reader – Well, you have a choice: you either see this or you don't –

– But if you want to get any handle on life, this is what life is like.

Greville goes off to recuperate in the rest-home in the hills of Central Africa; from here he writes long, somewhat feverish letters to his wife and to Natalia. He finds that he is near the place where the earliest traces of human life have been found; he ruminates – What is it to be a human rather than an animal? What is the consciousness of humans, if it can properly hardly be described? To these questions he does not have much of an answer – nor did I, I suppose, at this time. But I had, like Greville, some passionate commitment to the journey – to the writing; to the effort to discover whatever it was that was happening.

Towards the end of his time in Africa Greville writes in his notebook a passage that gets as close as he can to what he has been trying to say:

> Events that are supposed to be important – pain, infidelity, all forms of political manoeuvre – are seen as peripheral to a central effort of which they are symptoms, like sweat. This effort is the construction

of a certain style in which a man can trust what is happening and thus can affect it when reasonably he is dead. What happens is the quiet walk in the garden; his meetings with one or two women. This is living. His own part in it would be tiny; but he would not imagine it anything else.

But when Greville does come home, he himself does not do much more than try to climb back – refreshed perhaps – on to his one-wheel bicycle. He goes off to pick up his threads again with Natalie; but he finds that his wife and son are themselves off to do good works in Africa – about which he is pleased because they at least will be freed from the routines of his bicycling acts. But for himself – is this the best he can do: to be brushing up on his acts?

In real life Natalie and I were in fact doing not much more than continuing with our somewhat farcical, sometimes ecstatic, sometimes near-tragic, juggling. Natalie would go back to her husband and I would go home; Natalie's husband would leave her and Natalie would move to my flat; then after a time it was as if I had no home, I would be on my own, or Natalie and I would go off on a journey abroad together. But was this really a journey to find what life is like? or was this idea a fabrication of someone blown by the wind. (Or, oh yes, both!) There came a time when the situation I had imagined in the seventh story of *Impossible Object* actually came about (as time went on, several situations I had written about in *Impossible Object* seemed to come about); Natalie's husband began to petition for divorce. In the book there had been the two men waiting like gangsters outside the flat: in reality – oh there is not much of a joke, nor indeed of excitement, in processes of divorce! Suddenly, after all the tricks and the exuberance, there were the plates and balls crashing to the ground. And what in truth had we been playing with – people's guts, livers, heart-beats. Somewhere perhaps there was the chance of it being funny. But in the meantime – what a terrible tawdry air of dismemberment, as if a real bomb had gone off on a stage:

In the High Court of Justice Probate Divorce and Admiralty Division (Divorce) I, the Petitioner, herein make oath and say as follows –

1. I refer to my petition herein dated 17th May 1968 whereby I allege that the Respondent committed adultery with the Co-respondent from about July or August 1965 to December 1965, on further occasions in 1966, in August 1967 and from February 1968 to the date of the Petition. The said Petition contains a prayer for damages of £10,000 and costs against the Co-respondent . . .

I felt – I am so sorry, my children, and my children's children: shall I lie down and die?

But wait: – 'a prayer for damages of £10,000'? Was there not absurdity in this after all?

And then –

– 'further occasions in 1966' – was this not the time when Natalie and I had driven up through Italy getting material for the fifth story of *Impossible Object*? when we had visited Etruscan tombs and the frescoes at Orvieto and the street corner in Turin where Nietzsche had gone mad (there had been the plaque saying that he had 'triumphed in the fullness of the human spirit'). And 'August 1967' – what was that? Oh yes, we had gone to Talloires on Lake Annecy and had eaten dinner under pine trees at one of the best restaurants in France; and the passing moment had been so perfect that Natalie had felt, like Faust, that she might have to say Stop! and so be claimed by Mephistopheles; and so – (this scene went into *Natalie Natalia*). And then 'February 1968' – ah, that was the journey to Vienna and Budapest and Prague and Dresden and there had been once more such beautiful things to see! Natalie and I had not been speaking to each other much; but then – is it not proper to be silent in the face of so much beauty? And of course there is always likely to be darkness at the back of or beyond beauty –

– even in the form of a notice from the High Court of Justice, Probate Divorce and Admiralty Division.

So – how to answer this?

– In something of its own bizarre style it seemed: with a pig's bladder and a string of sausages:

Before I knew the Respondent the Petitioner had left her and was living with a Miss ——. In February 1965 I learned that the Petitioner had again left his wife and was having a relationship with, and had proposed marriage to, a Mrs ——. In June 1967 the Petitioner confessed to having committed adultery with a Mrs —— and also that he was having a relationship with, and was considering marriage to, a Miss ——.

I thought – Let us hope that they all had as nice a time as we did, my Natalia!

In *Natalie Natalia* I wrote:

> One of the happiest times Natalia and I ever had was a summer when Edward brought proceedings for divorce: we were summoned by Potterton, my lawyer, and Dangerfield, Natalia's: we had an audience at last to whom we could talk about each other. They asked – Has intercourse occurred? I thought – We are like gods being interviewed by the clergy. They asked – How many times?
>
> Potterton told us we should not see each other in private – in any place, that is, where intercourse might occur. I wanted to ask – Then what is public? It was explained – A restaurant; a bandstand. I wanted to ask – You mean, there intercourse might not occur?
>
> In Kensington Gardens we became one of the couples that lay on the grass; there were toys in the bandstand playing. I thought – Perhaps intercourse, if we had faith, might yet occur. We were the generation of children blessed with nowhere to go. Foxes had holes: I lay my head on Natalia. The sun always shone. Ghosts were around us like detectives.

Looking back on it, what on earth did one make of this old style of divorce – lawyers behaving like nannies when faced with children's shit? Society has to protect its citizens from the terrifying effects of sexuality? All right. But then – how little is learned from protection –

But what indeed is learned from sexuality?

I sometimes seemed to have faith in an Old Testament sort of God, ready to bash people into shape in spite of, or by, any old mayhem. Then perhaps I wanted to trust some New Testament sort of God who said that one might love but of course be ready to die; and without death, no resurrection. And often then – Just watch, listen. But what were any of these processes about except the taking out of hearts, taking them to bits, and seeing whether or not they could be put back slightly differently –

– wine and roses as it were on the altar of that temple in the sand-dunes by the sea –

– the one in which old hags had been dismembering a child: the one in the presence of which serene people walked on the beach –

– but who was the child: and who is made serene?

Natalie and her children came to live with me in my large new house in Hampstead; Natalie and her children went back to the flat where we had begun; Natalie and her children went back to her husband. Natalie's husband put out his petition, withdrew it; put out a new petition, withdrew it; Natalie and her children returned to Hampstead. Natalie when I first knew her had been a painter; now she was taking piano lessons from a teacher who trained concert pianists; she owned a grand piano that had to go with her every-where she went. In order to get it in and out of my Hampstead house a crane had to be hired which could reach from the street to the first-floor window: the man in charge of the crane used to watch the operations and once he said – 'This piano goes up and down like a yo-yo.' Sometimes, when Natalie and her piano had gone, Rosemary would come to stay; I would hurry from room to room taking down Natalie's paintings and hanging up Rosemary's. In the holidays the children would spend some of the time with me; then I would go to stay with Rosemary and them in the Isle of Man. There was a wild derelict cottage on Rosemary's land where, under a roaring wind, I wrote the obscurest bit of *Natalie Natalia*. For this I had had the idea – Our minds form the myths by which we live: why not write a myth about the way our minds make myths?

I thought that by my explorations I might get down from my tightrope? Stay up a bit longer? Find that it was indeed a rope around my neck.

Children are said to be those who suffer from the break-up of a marriage. And one cannot say about children – They might learn through suffering.

Sometimes I was upbraided by my sister Vivien for my lunatic behaviour and I would say – Perhaps I am doing it all for the kiddies so that they will not be hooked on such a father! My sister would say – No, you cannot say that!

My eldest son, aged eighteen, set off for Timbuktu on a motor-cycle; he got there, nearly died, bravely rode his motorcycle back.

My second son, aged eighteen, hitch-hiked round the world: in Japan he learned how to make beautiful pottery.

My third son and my daughter would sometimes come on holiday with me and Natalie and her children – like the last story in *Impossible Object*.

When I could not sleep at night I would go for long walks round Hampstead Heath. Once there was an old man silhouetted against the sky and shaking his fist and shouting – Why? I thought I might shout back – Why not?

At one of the worst moments of this time when the divorce petition was going ahead and there were gossip-column reporters popping up here and there like the ghouls on a Ghost Train journey, I had a letter from my old friend Mary of *The Rainbearers* whom I had told of my present circumstances and had added – I cannot bear it that it is something in me that seems to make life like this.

Darling –
I am sorry, sorry, sorry. Oh love – it is only I in the world in quite this position to say how sorry I am.

Love = electrical torture machine = leading to infinite pain – so great that even the remembrance of it made me cry the last time I saw you. But also – leading to something most steadfast. *I know.* Admit about the net which you know is so strong and important! And my daughter – both due directly and indirectly to the pain you inflicted. I think you *do* bring grief: I think you also bring something enormously vital and positive. I don't think it is appropriate, rele-vant, to feel guilty about either of these, since they interact. *Please* don't.

You say – 'We will never be quite certain what we ought to do.' My love, I think this is exactly the muddle we got into before because I (you) believed you meant 'ought' and actually you meant 'can'. *This is very important.* You left me because you *could* not leave Lyminster (shorthand) not because you *ought* not. There were oughts due to both R. and myself, but in the end 'can't' settled it. And I think this is true again. And yes, now is too late to hop it.

But, as we learned, practicalities do help – even minutely – and how else does one exist in grief except from minute to minute?

I suggest – but remember I don't know the whole story – that

[Natalie] should go on a combination of pills; they do numb pain and help distress. Or why not my dear little hotel in France?

Know only that our 22-year set-up is a miracle. It is *strange* – do you know how strange? – to be in this position. You are not *only* an electrical torture machine to have produced this miracle!

I will ring you next week – or you can always ring me – it would be lovely to see you. I understand about your being shadowy.

Take care of yourself, love. Ask me if there is anything I can do.

And I would think – Well, in spite of all these terrible acrobatics and miseries there are still such nudges as if from a cloud to put you together again, as well as knock you down, like Humpty-Dumpty.

Then it happened that almost immediately after coming to the end of some near-final draft of *Natalie Natalia* (yet how could I finish it? I did not know the end myself), at a time when those concerned were beginning to seem to be not so much on tightropes as on endless treadmills – and not for the first time indeed I had had a terrible quarrel with Natalie and she had walked out of my Hampstead house –

– and I had thought: Good riddance! and then almost at once – Help! I cannot bear this –

– just after this, I was driving with my second son and his girlfriend to a pop concert near Bath – I had been commissioned to write a filmscript around a pop concert of all things! – and I was thinking – It will soon be time for me to ride my own damned trick-cycle or indeed car not just like Greville into a swimming-pool but over a cliff –

– just then, on a quiet country road, a car pulled out from the slow-moving line of traffic coming in the opposite direction and like some avenging juggernaut headed fast straight at me, seemed to try to brake, lost control, then rammed the offside of my car hard as I tried to pull off the road. Most of my bones were broken on my right side, and I became unconscious; my son and his girl-friend, on the near side, mercifully had only minor injuries. (My son remembers coming to and seeing me holding my right wrist with my left hand and the broken bone of my right arm moving within the skin like a trapped animal: he relapsed into unconsciousness.) Ambulancemen arrived and gave me a lot of morphia; I remember weird exhilaration alternating with the pain: so the retribution that I had thought fitting had come about, had it: good heavens! The ambulancemen were having difficulty in releasing my foot from the wreckage; it seemed witty to say – See if you can get it out at the same time as the rest of me, will you? But then when the pain came in – Let me die.

When I became fully conscious I was in a ward of Nissen huts in a country hospital near Bath. I was on my back with my right leg and arm suspended by pulleys and wires. My thigh-bone could not be set for another week, and each time I moved it was as if razors were cutting into the ends of nerves. I thought – Under torture I would say anything! I was with a group of elderly men with broken thigh-bones at one end of the ward: when the nurses came to wash us, we would each yell in turn. At the other end of the ward were motor-cycle boys who had crashed and had the lower part of their legs in plaster. When the old men cried out the boys would mock them. I once shouted – They are in pain! and the boys made whooping noises – Pain! Pain! I thought – If I survive, I will kill you. Then – But it is not simple, to try to deal with pain.

There was one old man who, when the nurses came to move him, would shout – Oh you buggers! A clergyman in the next bed would say – That is one thing they are not.

There was a very old man in the bed next to me who at the same time each evening would start to haul himself out of bed by his pulleys and wires; and then, to get more leverage, he would stretch across towards mine. I would shout – Help! Murder! A nurse explained – You see, he was used to going out to the pub each evening for his Guinness.

Rosemary came down from the Isle of Man to stay near the hospital and visit me each day: for this alone may there be angels for her all the way to heaven. In great and genuine gratitude I told her that I would from now on be eternally faithful to her: I would never see Natalie again. But it seemed, understandably, that she hardly wanted me hanging round her neck now when with such painstaking effort she had become for the most part free: and anyway, why should she believe me? As for Natalie – she was off for the summer to St Tropez. I wondered – Are there no tricks to stop me thinking about Natalie in St Tropez?

Sometime later the driver of the car that had run into me was had up in court charged with dangerous driving. The magistrate said to him – Can you tell us what happened? The man, a robust Somerset farmer, said – An uncontrollable force took hold of my wheel and hurled me into the oncoming car. The magistrate said – Come come, you mean your steering broke? The man said – No, an uncontrollable force . . . and the police confirmed that his steering was in order. I liked the idea of this: had it not seemed proper that I might be smashed up by some juggernaut?

I lay on my back with my limbs in the air like a beetle. I would think – How is it that when one is not in pain one does not remember it: should one not give up one's life to the alleviation of pain?

Can it be that one is like that terrible God that knows it is not the point to take away human suffering?

18

My involvement with Natalie lasted another two or three years; but after the accident it was never quite the same. The change was from high-wire to something more mundane. I was, in fact, learning to walk on crutches. This passed the time.

I recuperated with Rosemary on the Isle of Man. I went back to my large, now almost empty, house in London.

I was rescued from sombre thoughts by Joe Losey, with whom I had remained on close terms although the projected film of *Imposs-ible Object* had not yet found financial backing. Joe had written to me that the script was 'an extraordinary extension of what I have tried to do in film'; that Catherine Deneuve was 'actively interested'. But the would-be producer wrote that he had submitted it 'to at least two major stars for the male lead; the reaction of both was that they just didn't understand the script and so couldn't really know whether or not it interested them'.

Now suddenly Joe telephoned to say that he had another idea. For years he had been trying to get under way a film about the assassination of Trotsky, but always the scripts had been bedevilled by Marxist jargon which actors found it impossible to make sound not ridiculous; yet how could one make a film about Trotsky without the jargon? Joe said to me – But you are the most non-political writer that I know; perhaps you could write an actable script about Trotsky? There was one stipulation – the first draft of a new script would have to be ready in three weeks because this was the timing required for a real chance for money for the film to be available; Alain Delon had become interested in the project and would like to play the part of the assassin, but he would have to see a suitable script very soon or he would have to become involved with other commitments. With Alain Delon's name, there would be the money. Joe said to me – Do you know anything about Trotsky? I said that I had admired his autobiography. I thought – But of course I can do this script! What a fine new tightrope!

I got hold of Isaac Deutscher's three-volume biography of Trotsky and I read this at night and I wrote my script during the day: I still, as a result of the accident, had to spend much of the time in bed. Two or three times a week the producer's huge chauffeur-driven car would come to my Hampstead house (I was being looked after by my loyal housekeeper, June, who had once helped us daily at Lyminster) and the chauffeur would pick up the pages of the script I had done: each morning I would think – But this is impossible! each evening it would seem – But I am very lucky. Suddenly it appeared that the whole project was off the ground: Alain Delon had seen enough of the script to say he would be committed (he is reputed to have said 'This writer understands the mind of an assassin!'); the money-men were saying that they would thus be committed. There began to be a bandying-about of big names for who might play the part of Trotsky: Laurence Olivier? Dirk Bogarde? Richard Burton? In the wake of all this, money for the *Impossible Object* film seemed now to be available. Joe Losey asked me – Will you mind if *Impossible Object* is postponed? I thought – How should I mind any of this? I have lain for months like an upturned beetle: I am getting better: I am out of a treadmill and into films.

Through most of 1971 I was involved with the film of *The Assassination of Trotsky*. Although I had written the screenplay for *Impossible Object*, I had yet to see any lines I had written spoken by actors in a film. I was soon whizzing about on my crutches like a spider on his web; down to the London Library; on to have talks with Joe Losey in Chelsea in the evenings. Joe was in the last stages of putting together his film *The Go-Between*. We would go out to have dinner: Joe's wife Patricia was away – as indeed were both

Rosemary and Natalie. Joe and I would talk about Trotsky, about politics, about ourselves; we would drink a lot of whisky. Joe had been a fellow-traveller and Communist sympathiser at the time of the Second World War: he had been one of the Hollywood people blacklisted and driven from America by the McCarthy witch-hunts of the 1950s. He had come to work in England and had recently had great successes in the films he had made from scripts by Harold Pinter. He would talk about his past – about his contacts with mysterious Russians and Eastern Europeans in New York in the 1940s. He seemed to agree – The art of politics is that your left hand should never quite know what your right hand is doing. I would talk about my father – who had been in the same style of business as Trotsky, after all. In fact in many ways my father had been like Trotsky – they were both people who had had a chance of large-scale power but had thrown it away for the sake of – what? – the purity of their legend? I suggested a phrase – A Stalinist is a Communist in power: a Trotskyite is a Communist out of power. Late at night, after a lot of whisky, Joe and I would agree surreptitiously that if one was to be a Communist at all it would be better to be a Stalinist: what was the point of being a politician who could not face the machinations of power? Then in the morning I would shamefacedly see – But of course it would be better to be almost anything but a Stalinist! Liveliness is in the effort, even hopelessly, to get the best of both worlds – to be a politician and to recognise the squalors of power.

In the first draft of my script Trotsky was an old man living in the outskirts of Mexico City; there did not need to be much about Trotskyite politics in this script because at that time – the spring of 1940 – Europe was being overrun by German armies and Trotsky seemed to be reconciling himself to the postponement of his dream: indeed he looked down on this, and on his history, with some irony. Also there was little political sense in the desire of his great enemy, Stalin, to kill him: Trotsky had almost no power. But Stalin sent an assassin all the way to Mexico City for this purpose – it was as if what was necessary to both Stalin and Trotsky was the pursuit of some legend. I had thought – Indeed this is like my father: I can write about this! But I realised that in further workings on the script I would have to explain Trotsky's place in political history, so I tried to do this in flashbacks – to Trotsky's years as a revolutionary, as the head of the Red Army, as Lenin's right-hand man, as Stalin's rival, then to his defeat by Stalin and exile. This could be done, I thought, either by archive film or the simulation of such film; there need be no jargon. I was also putting in flashes of what was going on in other parts of the world, and of what might be in Trotsky's mind. Joe Losey was encouraging me in this – he wanted the film to be in the style of the *Impossible Object* script. And as for the life of an old man in Mexico City – well, there had always been a part of Trotsky that had seen himself not only as a politician but as a solitary writer and artist. Joe Losey and I worked at putting as much politics as seemed necessary into the script.

As it progressed, the script seemed to be going down well. Joe began to say things like – Beware, or you will be one of those writers gobbled up and ruined by Hollywood!

I would think – Gobble me up first! worry about indigestion later.

A time came when we all – Losey, myself, production manager, art director, and so on – set off for Rome where on the outskirts was being built a replica of Trotsky's house on the outskirts of Mexico City. The Loseys had the use of a beautiful apartment just off the Piazza Navona; during the day I would work on the script while the others went about their businesses; in the evenings we would gather at one of the restaurants in the amazing square where the Bernini fountains played and floodlights lit up the façade of the baroque church and real and toy pigeons fluttered round the heads of wandering crowds. Then after dinner we would go back to the Loseys' flat and have a script conference. I was no good at this: writing to me was something to be done on my own – listening, waiting, scratching away as if at some almost impossibly fragile mosaic buried in sand. After a magnificent dinner in the Piazza Navona people at the conference would ask – But why is this character saying that? where is the consistency? what is the motivation? I would want to say – You think people are consistent? You know your motivations? These characters are Communists and assassins! I began to think – Oh dear, perhaps Hollywood will not gobble me up after all.

I did not mind much if my script was altered here and there. I had done my job: it was up to the people actually making the film, surely, to see that it worked. I had once dreamed of becoming a film director myself: this dream had not got beyond *The Policeman's Mother*.

Joe Losey and the production manager and the art director all had their wives or girlfriends with them: these played some passive but apparently vital role in the business of keeping the bits and pieces of the film-making team together; they would sit around in the square, in hotels, in apartments, like queen bees waiting to be fed by, and to feed, returning workers. I had said to Rosemary – Why not come to Rome? and Joe Losey had pressed the invitation. But Rosemary had said, with truth goodness knows – But I could not bear just sitting around in Rome! Then suddenly it happened that Natalie and her children had nowhere to go for their summer holiday; and so – could they not come to Rome? I thought – But Natalie will not just sit around in Rome! Then – But film people must be used to drama.

Joe Losey had met Natalie once or twice before: we had coincided, by chance, on a trip to Venice – and this meeting had been a disaster. Joe had in some way insulted Natalie and we had had to walk out of a projected lunch. But then, what about the *Impossible Object* script? (Joe had written to me – I hope this doesn't influence my view of the character in the script. I had written – But Joe, surely we know about all this!) I had been warned by a scriptwriter who had been a previous favourite of Joe's – Beware! he charms his scriptwriters, then turns on them. I had thought – Oh but I know about film directors being prima donnas; they have to be, if they are to hold all the other would-be prima donnas of film-making together.

When Natalie arrived in Rome she was willing enough to keep away from the film people: I left the Grand Hotel where I was being put up free and we got a room in a beautiful small hotel near the Piazza Navona which had a balcony which opened on to the terraces and domes of a baroque church. Natalie would go out sightseeing each day; Joe Losey would say to me – You know she's no good for you, don't you? I would say – But you like *Impossible Object*!

There was a day when Richard Burton and Elizabeth Taylor were due to arrive at the port of Rome: they had been touring in their yacht in the Mediterranean; it seemed that Richard Burton was ready to be signed up to play the part of Trotsky in the film. Myself and others in Losey's entourage were put on call; we had to stay by the telephone all day ready to go on a reception committee to the sea. It was a very hot day. Natalie said – But you promised that as soon as you had a day off you'd spend it with me! I said – But this is like being on call to meet King Solomon and the Queen of Sheba! Natalie said – I thought you said it was Richard Burton and Elizabeth Taylor.

So Natalie and I went off to look at San Paolo Fuori le Muro which was a Romanesque church with beautiful pillars. I hoped – The yacht may yet be delayed. Then – But, anyway, what is duty, and what is obsequiousness? When we got back to our hotel we found that the yacht had indeed arrived and the deputation had done its stuff and Richard Burton had stayed just long enough to sign a contract and drink champagne and then the yacht had sailed away again into the blue. I was thus in somewhat bad odour with the film people; and I regretted – I will never now be able to say that I met Elizabeth Taylor.

But when Natalie's children arrived they of course wanted to meet the film people so Natalie and I quarrelled and I was able to take them to see Joe Losey. Then I drove Natalie and the children over the mountains to a hotel by the eastern sea, and here there were young men hanging about on the beach like crabs, waiting to be attentive to Natalie. When I was back in Rome it was hotter than ever and I found that this was a weekend when almost everyone, even the film people, was away at the sea. In the Piazza Navona there were children playing in the Bernini fountains; no one stopped them; I sat with my feet in the water and then turned and lay back and floated off – beneath and between the legs of huge gods and horses rearing – this fountain is called The Source of the Nile. I thought – Oh well, this odd journey I am going on, perhaps it is like a mad but wondrous journey to the source of the Nile.

I heard that Rosemary was ill in London. I flew back to be with her. Joe Losey had agreed – There's not much more work for you here. Natalie said – But you will always in the end go back to Rosemary! I thought – But I will never be as good to Rosemary as she was to me when I was ill. In London Rosemary had to have an operation and I tried to look after her; but there were such cataracts going on in my head! With all that was happening at that time indeed I was not much good with Rosemary; and she had been angry for some time anyway with my cavortings up my imagined Nile.

After a while the film entourage moved from Rome to Mexico City, where the first scenes on location were to be shot. By now it was obvious that I was no longer needed on the job, but I wanted to see the first shootings and Joe Losey said I might come in useful. Also perhaps once more it might make sense for me to go on a journey on my own. So I flew to Mexico City where I had been some six years before and where I had begun to write the first sentences of *Impossible Object*: I had said that life was impossible, and by this I had thought I might make life possible – but always in war? I went to look again at the enormous murals I had so much loved – by Rivera, Orozco, Siquieros. I thought – These people had a vision of death round the corner: of how life resides in the recognition of struggle, of it being against deathliness that there can be war. At one moment it appeared that I might indeed be of some use to the film people: local Trotskyites in Mexico City had seen my script and had been making objections: they said there was not enough about Trotskyite policy in the script; they were threatening to picket the filming. Joe Losey said – Someone should go and talk to them. I said – I will go! Joe said – But you don't care about politics! I said – That is why I should go. I set off in a film-company car to a house in the suburb where the Trotskyites were gathered; this was near to where Trotsky had been murdered – Trotsky's house was still kept as a museum by his grandson, a man of great probity and dignity. The Trotskyites were seated round a table like a group of Marxist–Leninists in a social-realist painting: I asked them what exactly about Trotskyite policy they thought I had left out of my script. They conferred for a time and then said – Equal pay for blue-collar and white-collar workers. I said – You really think I should get Trotsky, in exile in Mexico City in 1940, to stand up and say – Equal pay for blue-collar and white-collar workers? After a time they laughed. Then they produced a bottle of brandy. Then we got rather drunk. After a time they said – You understand we have to make a political stand about these things. I said – Yes, I understand that. When in the middle of the night I got back to my hotel I found Joe waiting up for me like an anxious parent. He said – We thought you might have been murdered! I said – I like to think I might have been murdered.

Alain Delon and Romy Schneider were staying in a neighbouring hotel; they had once been lovers; Alain Delon now had a new girlfriend and Romy Schneider was said to be unhappy. So I thought I would ask her out to dinner. I took her to a small restaurant that I thought was suitably primitive and out-of-the-way where old men in huge hats strummed on guitars; after dinner Romy said to me – Now I will show you the real Mexico City! She took me to a club run by a man of such palpable villainy that it seemed impossible that we were not in a film. He sat at our table and said to Romy, 'Who is this boy you are with? Get rid of him!' (I was forty-eight.) As a reward perhaps for my sticking it out, when we got back to Romy's hotel she asked me up for coffee. She said, 'If Alain comes down and finds you, of course he may kill you.'

I had a good time in Mexico City. Joe wondered about offering me a part in the film as a Stalinist agent, but I did not have enough confidence for this. I thought – Stalinist agents would not act as if they knew they were acting?

When I got back to England – but I do not remember much about this time – Natalie was with someone she had met in Italy; Rosemary was in the Isle of Man –

I thought – Something will never be right about this absurd script from which I myself am acting: I need to be re-written!

When the film people had done their stuff in Mexico City and were back in Rome I heard that Joe Losey was having difficulties with my Trotsky script – with the flashes that were supposed to explain Trotsky's political past and Stalin's obsession about killing him. Joe, I was told, was intending to leave these flashes out. And it seemed that there were new figures now in the entourage round Joe – Trotskyites or Stalinists or whatever – who were influencing him to alter other bits of my script. I thought – This means that a lot of Marxist-Leninist verbiage will be put in! I telephoned Joe who said it was true he was having difficulties with the flashes: about the rest, he was elusive. I went to see Josef Shaftel, the producer and financer of the film; he explained that neither he nor I had any rights over the script – Joe Losey had artistic control. I said – But there'll be no sense in the film if they cut out all the flashes and put in jargon in their place! Josef Shaftel said – If you're so anxious to put over your ideas, why don't you write the book of the film? He added that in fact he'd commission me to write such a book now, since he already had an arrangement with a publisher; the only stipulation was that it would have to be done in a hurry – it would have to be ready for the publishers in eight or ten weeks to be in time for the opening of the film. I said – Write a book about Trotsky in eight or ten weeks? He said – But Nicholas, you haven't asked me about the money. I was beginning to say that I didn't have to worry too much about such things: then I said – How much? And when he told me I said – So what sort of book should it be? He said – But Nicholas, it doesn't matter what sort of book it should be; I've signed a contract with the publishers.

When Joe Losey heard that I was doing a book of the film he wrote to me from Rome to try to put me off. He said that it was true that he had had to do a certain 'kaleidoscoping' of the script; that he had been anxious about the question – 'What political statement will the picture make?' And:

> I must confess that I myself am still baffled about the answer. I don't think it will be either pro or con either Trotsky or the Soviet Union as such. Of course, it is inescapably anti-Stalinist in a sense. What I am afraid of, and what I would regret very much, is that it may turn out to be no statement at all or, even worse, an essentially nihilistic one.
>
> I think the actors' work, and my work, and the camera work, and all the other contributing creative work – including your fictional scenes – are very good . . .

But then he came to his concern about my book:

> Forgive me for bringing this up: you have sprung from the loins of whom you have, and it is one thing for you as such to write a screenplay, and quite another to write a book on such a controversial figure . . . I feel very strongly as the film has developed that neither you nor I have begun to do the work necessary to produce a definitive work . . .

I wrote to Joe to say that I did not see why the son of a Fascist should not write a book about Trotsky, and that of course the work would not be definitive. And as to what sort of political statement the film would make, I hoped it would make an artistic statement, which was different. I said I would be coming to Rome both to talk about this and, for the purpose of my book, to look at some documents in the files that he and I had collected together.

In Rome I found that indeed there was a different atmosphere about the entourage around Joe. There was a Marxist or two; somewhere in the background a couple from Paris who claimed to have the authentic behind-the-scenes view of Trotsky. Joe told me that he had even been telephoned by his old Stalinist contact from his Communist days in New York, who was now in Eastern Europe and had said something like – We will be very interested, Joe, to see what you make of Trotsky! The people round Joe now all seemed to be talking and waving their arms: no one seemed to be listening. Joe gave me the files we had collected and I took them back to my hotel and in one of them, quite out of context, was a letter from Joe to the Paris couple apologising for the shortcomings of my original script; these were due, he suggested, to the scriptwriter's lack of political experience and commitment. When I handed the files back to Joe, he looked sad. I said again something like – But Joe, you and I are supposed to know about all this!

Back in London I heard from Joe:

> I gather there must have been words in my letters about the script to the Paris executors which offended you. I don't think that there is much point in rehashing. You gave me a very good skeleton and some excellent scenes. I did think the film needed more politics, and I do think it might have been a better film with the flashes, but

we never got the material, and we never really had time to think them out ... Flashes only work when they are as carefully considered and as integral as they were in *Impossible Object* and *Accident* and *The Go-Between*.

I thought – But of course the flashes were carefully considered! They were the politics: they were also the art.

I set about writing my book about Trotsky in eight or nine weeks. I got it done; I put in what I wanted to put in of politics and of Trotsky's past. And I said what I had wanted to say from the beginning – that for large parts of Trotsky's life he was up to his neck in politics of a kind that was squalid – a dim farrago of deceit and lies and murder and betrayal in which words and commitments could mean anything or nothing and attitudes were histrionic. However, there had always been a part of Trotsky that had recognised this and had not wanted to be totally immersed; in fact he had said as much when he had tried to explain why he had not made more effort to succeed Lenin in the 1920s. He had wished, he said, to maintain a certain detachment from the day-to-day tawdriness of politics. As a frontispiece to my book I had put quotations from Trotsky – 'There is an irony deep laid in the very relations of life: it is the duty of the historian as of the artist to bring it to the surface.' And – 'It is certainly victims that move humanity forward.'

When I delivered my typescript to the publishers it was their turn, I suppose, to feel that I was not quite the right person to have taken on the job – they seemed to have expected some 'faction' thriller. One of the publishers, an old friend, remarked rather gloomily that my book might make 'quite a good introduction for students to Marxist politics.' I was pleased about this. I sent a copy to Joe Losey, who wrote to Josef Shaftel that the attitude of the book would do the film harm.

I went to see a private showing of the film in Paris. It turned out that Joe had in fact left out all the flashes except, literally, one – of Stalin's head floating ghost-like in some water; this was effective. But he had put in not much jargon in the flashes' place! So the omission of the whole dimension of memory and imagination and even much mention of the past gave the film itself a curiously ghost-

238

like quality; it was as if none of the characters quite knew what on earth they were there for. (I wondered – Perhaps this indeed gives an eerie feeling of the real-life characters at the time?) The film in fact was a fairly faithful rendering of my very first tentative script, with none of the later additional substance and nuances. It appeared gutted. I thought – Politicians may be people who appear gutted? But film-goers will not recognise this.

However, there was also something odd about the way the actors spoke my lines – or perhaps they were just bad lines. Anyway, the actors did not seem quite to know what to do with them; they seemed to be trying to make them 'sincere': and of course politicians do try to make their statements sound sincere, but of course they fail; but what these actors seemed to be failing to do was to act this interplay between sincerity and failure. Was this something that actors could not do? Or was it my responsibility for not having made something of this more clear. But might it not in fact be possible for actors to act the absurdity of politicians not quite aware of the absurdity of their language, but still of course knowing they are not quite sincere –

– Oh yes, there had been something of this in the style of *Impossible Object*.

Shortly before this time it became apparent that Joe Losey would not be making the film of *Impossible Object*; he had fallen out not only with me but with the would-be producer. But my agent wrote to me to say that as a result of pre-presentation publicity about the *Trotsky* film there were now several people interested in the *Imposs-ible Object* script – in particular the Hollywood director John Frank-enheimer. This was the zenith of my career in films – with no one yet having seen a finished product of one of my scripts.

Just before this time Natalie and her children arrived back at my Hampstead house and so life continued on its old not-quite-so-tight rope. But now there were so many other flying acts, tumbling acts, whirling around my head – ideas about what could be acted and what could not; questions about whether actors could act the impression of what could not be acted (I mean, could actors act reality? and if not, how could reality be shown?) – so many ideas, enquiries, that it seemed that soon I would have to have another shot at giving expression to them on my own.

19

The film director John Frankenheimer had recently left Hollywood and had moved to Paris and was looking for a script different from those for the political thrillers with which he had made a success in the past. He was looking, it seemed, for something with which he might enter the European art-movie market – so my agent sent him *Impossible Object*. I was summoned to meet Frankenheimer for breakfast at the Connaught Hotel.

John was a tall, athletic-looking man; he paced up and down his sitting-room in the Connaught Hotel. He wanted me to tell him, he said, why I had written the script the way I had; not the basic story, which he understood; but why I had written it in different pieces and from different angles that seemed almost but not quite to fit together; and what were the flashes here and there – real events, or in people's minds?

So I embarked on my party-piece about impossible objects – it is life itself that does not seem quite to fit together; but in so far as you can look down on the ways in which you seem to be in pieces then perhaps you are not; and by virtue of this, things fit together. One cannot avoid the tragedies and absurdities of life; but by seeing them, there can be seen, or made, a pattern. In the script, in the acting, there had to be seen a distinction between the times when the characters know they are acting and those when they do not; in so far as they know they are acting then they are watching themselves, and with this part of them they are not acting. And so on. John Frankenheimer paced up and down, every now and then turning to me like a caged tiger and baring his teeth. I said – For most of the time we are all of us actors – in social-life, in love-affairs; we act to try to protect ourselves; to get what we want. But there are moments when we stop acting – or in so far as we know we are actors we have stopped acting – and then there is the impression of being in touch with some reality – which perhaps, we realise, is what we really want. This is what I have tried to give expression to in the script.

Breakfast was wheeled in, wheeled out again. When I had finished John Frankenheimer said – I'll do it! – and went off to set about raising four or five million dollars.

So this was still a magical time for me in films: no one had yet seen *The Assassination of Trotsky*. For *Impossible Object* Alan Bates and Dominique Sanda were lined up to play the leading parts. The money was suddenly available; it came largely from France or from French Canada, so it would have to be a joint Anglo-French production. I had to move some of the scenes from London to Paris, but this was not difficult. Everyone concerned said – Yes, yes, they understood the business of acting and not acting; even of acting not acting! indeed, for actors this would be a lively challenge.

John Frankenheimer got on well with the real-life Natalie so there were no conflicts here as there had been with Joe Losey. John and his wife had an apartment in Paris on the Ile Saint Louis overlooking Notre-Dame; Natalie and I were put up in a hotel on the Quai Voltaire. John asked Natalie to help with the music for the film; she and I prowled round Paris looking for records of flute music – Bach flute sonatas that might merge into Berber flute music for the scenes in Morocco. John said that if we would stay in Paris and be part of the filming all summer (1972) he would find a flat for us on the Ile Saint Louis. This might have seemed a magical prospect, yes.

But there is always a problem for a scriptwriter when once his script has been accepted; so much time has to be spent waiting around; and I had already worked for so many years on this script! There were certain aspects that I could go on tinkering with for ever – the question of whether the 'narrator' was to be played by the same actor as the 'man'; the old question of whether, and how, it was to be even hinted that the drowned baby of the last story was only part of a story and was in fact alive. There were script conferences again: the demand for answers to questions – Is this or that really happening or is it in the mind? What is the reasoning here, what is the motivation? Then suddenly – How will this be understood by an audience in some small town in the American midwest? In the script there were flashes that held it together as there should have been flashes to hold together the *Trotsky* script – memories, premonitions, resonances; some archetypal, sometimes realistic. I would say – But it need not be differentiated too clearly what is inside or outside the mind: an audience needs to become involved, not to be made to understand. I began to feel, as before, that these questions were not the business of a conference; the task of dealing with them belonged to the unifying vision of the person making the film. I began to long to get away and to work on some new unifying version of my own – not go on picking at the bones of what I had already made. I wanted to write something about the difficulty and yet the necessity of seeing things in the way that I had not quite yet successfully, it seemed, been able to portray. In the afternoons in my hotel I began to look again at the draft of a play I had sketched out some years ago. This had been sparked off by my *Good Samaritans* play in which an assortment of characters had been stuck at an airport; I had thought – I will write a sort of parallel play, in which actors wonder what on earth they are doing stuck not so much at an airport as in a script on a stage. Meanwhile, in the *Impossible Object* script conferences, people were saying – But look here, Nicholas, when all is said and done, what we have here is just a good straightforward love story! I would say – But what we have not got here is just a good straightforward love story! I began to be obsessed – It is myself who has become stuck in this script! I must get out.

In the spring of 1972 Natalie and I with her two children and my two youngest children set off for a walking-tour in the mountains of the Black Forest. It was very cold and there was still snow on the ground; I joked to John Frankenheimer – You see, we are behaving like that family in the last story of *Impossible Object* who went out in a boat; we are likely to be caught in a blizzard; then we may find out what is reality and what is the fiction of the child that is drowned! I do not think anyone except myself thought this funny. As it happened, on our first day in the Black Forest there was a blizzard and we had to walk through it for twelve miles with our rucksacks on our backs – finding out, I suppose, what is fact or fiction; funny or not funny.

On returning it did not seem possible to hang about in Paris through the summer. I wanted to do my own work; Natalie's children were at day-school in England. We gave up the idea of Paris. I told John Frankenheimer that we would come over if ever he wanted us; but I suppose this was the beginning of the end of the impression of things being magical.

Then just at this time the film of *The Assassination of Trotsky* opened in Paris, and received on the whole not good reviews. The point was made – This is a film about just an old man in Mexico City; where is the history? where are the politics? of what was the scriptwriter thinking? I comforted myself – Well, there is my book. When my book of the same name came out in London it got some minor reviews; then suddenly there was a half-page hatchet-job from Philip Toynbee in the *Observer*:

> English intellectuals are still the most protected and insulated in the world. Some have fought in wars; some have been, by chance and intention, the witnesses of grim events in foreign parts; some have been connected with left-wing international politics. But most of us know about the worst realities of the twentieth century only by reading about them or, at best, by hearing about them from those who have played a real part in them. We are, indeed, the spoiled children of the century, and though this is nothing to be ashamed of, it is also something that we should never forget.
>
> This is the book of a spoiled and protected intellectual child who seems to have quite forgotten the kind of temptations and limitations which this status imposes on him.
>
> I am sure that what lies at the heart of Mr Mosley's lapse – he has, after all, written some highly skilful novels – is the English intellectual's hankering for kicks: his urge to associate himself, however vicariously, with the 'great dramas' – so he sees it – of the twentieth century. He regrets – perhaps even resents – the fact that

he was never chased by the GPU; was never put in a concentration camp; has never starved in an Asian famine; has never even been involved in some major campus demonstration in any country where such demonstrations have some conceivable effect on what happens in the world . . .

I thought – But Philip Toynbee is talking about himself! It is he who did no fighting in the war!

But still, such reviews hurt.

When the *Trotsky* film came out in London it was picketed by Trotskyites carrying placards saying that it was unfair to Trotsky; when my book came out it was ignored by the Trotskyite press. But then mysteriously I was taken up by the Trotskyite Workers' Revolutionary Party; I was sent their literature and asked to their meetings; I was given the ultimate accolade of an invitation to a party at Vanessa Redgrave's house. She said to me, 'Oh you are the author of that marvellous book!' I said, 'Why do you not review it or stock it in your bookshops?' But I suppose I knew enough about politics not to need an answer to that question.

When my sister and my brother saw the *Trotsky* film they said to me – How did you manage to get Richard Burton to act just like our father? I said – I never even managed to meet Richard Burton!

There were other endings to euphoria at this time. My novels had been having some critical success: it had been reported that *Natalie Natalia* was a front-runner for the latest Booker Prize. But the publishers had described it in the blurb as a novel by an important British writer, so Auberon Waugh girded himself up for another hatchet-job:

> Plainly no publisher could single out Mr Mosley for his import or meaning, even when stupefied by food and drink. Three-quarters of the book is without any coherent meaning of any sort, and though occasional vivid impressions may be created by words and images which Mr Mosley throws together with such reckless disregard they cannot, with the best will in the world, be said to have any meaning.
>
> In what other way can any writer – let alone a novelist – be described as important? If Mr Mosley will open his Roget at the reference to 'novel' he will find it entered thus: 'a work of fiction, novel, romance, penny dreadful, shilling shocker, Minerva press;

fairy nursery tale; fable, parable, apologue.' Importance does not seem a usual connotation of the novel. Perhaps they mean Mr Mosley will influence other novelists to write like him. I only hope and pray that he doesn't.

Although there can be nothing less important than novels, those who, like myself, have an affection for them, can only be saddened by the shriek of delight from chicken-brained, trendy reviewers which greets every pathetic lurch into the literary cul-de-sac which has already been exhaustively explored by Joyce, Woolf, Durrell and every witless, inarticulate trendy ever since. Mosley's *Impossible Object* was hailed by Vernon Scannell of the *New Statesman* as 'really trying to make language behave in a way it has not behaved before'. It afforded the *Sunday Telegraph* 'a most powerful and extraordinary experience . . .'

I thought – Dear God, it doesn't really help to say that such people are talking of problems to do with themselves.

These two hatchet-job notices together with the not-good press I was getting for my script for the Trotsky film – combined with rumours that in my absence alterations and simplifications were being made to the *Impossible Object* script – also the latest disappearance of Natalie who, after yet another row, had once more removed herself and her children and her grand piano out of my Hampstead house – all this signalled the end not only of euphoria but of my involvement with films. When I enquired about the *Impossible Object* script I was told by John Frankenheimer that my concern would no longer be required. I remained on the best of terms with Alan Bates and his wife Victoria, so I was able once or twice to visit the filming in France as a guest of theirs; but I could not make out what was happening to the script. When the film was done I had to get a lawyer to insist that I had a right to see it. I wondered (as I had wondered with the Trotsky film) if I should have to ask for my name to be taken off the credits. My agent Anthony Jones and I sat in a tiny cinema in Paris and watched the film; the experience was not unlike that of watching *The Assassination of Trotsky* but more harrowing because there was so much of my own life-blood involved. The skeleton of my script was there: but not the style, the knowingness, the irony of acting/not acting, whatever resonances might have made sense of all this. Actors acted as if they were either joking or sincere: but the point had been the passionate struggle to find, or create, what sincerity or non-sincerity might be. The film was like a TV advertisement: but for what? Not for knowing. For the impossibility of acting knowing? But I felt John Frankenheimer had been brave in trying to stick even to the skeleton of the script, and I was sad that I had not myself been able to stay to give the bones more flesh.

The film *Impossible Object* was never distributed commercially in Britain or America; it had some success on the Continent, and even won the *Palme D'Or* at a film festival in Atlanta, Georgia. It sometimes turns up on British television late at night under the title, *Story of a Love Story*. I watch it with embarrassment, and some fascination.

Central to this time of the ending of euphoria was the fact that Rosemary, who over the years had put up so remarkably with my grotesque lurchings on what I liked to call a tightrope, had reached a pitch at which she announced she would be part of this circus-act no longer. I could not blame her. I hoped that she might not too much blame me. I wrote to her to say that I had made what efforts I could, at various times, to re-establish our marriage. But now I seemed in danger of losing everything. She wrote to me:

Dear Nick,   20/10/71
I do not talk to the children and allow them to think their father is a beast. This is horrible of you. I want their GOOD, not my JUSTIFICATION. I said 'We had an argument and I moved out and thought a change would do me good.' I leave all the non-communicatory shit to you: all your wonderful offers 'turned down by Mum': how many times have I accepted them, and how many times they had built-in time-bombs, you can work out.

For God's sake with the children cut out the 'I said to her she said to me' bit: say we are going forward to new lives – for better or worse, for happiness or sadness: that we *both* love them and they have two homes and we do not resent each other. What they want is reassurance about their lives and what it means for *them*: and then answer their questions.

I am not interested in making you out a beast (conventionally it possibly would be easy). Don't you know me at all? It seems not.

247

There is a great violence in you against me that you have not faced, in my opinion.

Darling Nick,   31/01/71

Thank you for your letter, the first that I feel has been written by you. Perhaps we will never understand each other, or only years later. Can anyone possibly think I am sailing ahead determined to be a painter? I don't think they do; perhaps you misunderstand.

I think you are right to wake up in thumping anxiety for me in the night, because over the past few weeks I have hit some bottom, from which I hope I will now go upwards.

I saw my escape as a matter of life or death; I did think if I had stayed on and we had more scenes I might really die or have a complete mental collapse; I am sorry but I can't see it as my wanting to be 'a painter' and your being hurt. I think you hurt me as much as it is possible to hurt anyone so ill, by that first scene when you thumped and told me to leave – who could stay after that? And how strongly you must have felt it to do it to anyone so ill; and I did think afterwards when I was so hysterical there was a terrible déjà-vu feeling to your reactions – it had all been done before – I could not bear your depersonalised attitudes. Then a week later you disappeared without a word. I think it would have been the equivalent if for 2 days at the Bath Hospital I had not turned up: I know you would have minded; you used to know it was me without even seeing me among the crowds who went in.

I think your attitude about me being a painter and you being hurt is really untrue – and you say it only because you can only face up to yourself if you think and say this to the world at large. I think this is dangerous and very close to your left hand not knowing what your right hand does.

Darling Nick,   2/11/71

Thank you for your letter, of course I hurt you back, you have in a sense dismantled me over the years. In Bath what I said was you must mean this (what you offered) when you were better – you have so many times said things and then the opposite, hardly pausing for breath – and I have stopped trusting your words (your feelings are so unstable), and so often your words mean nothing, never get into life, and I feel are often never even meant to. I am sorry if I hurt you in Bath, but all I can say is there is not much gap between my words and intentions, and I did care for you for about three months with the *whole of myself* (and not one distraught bit). Yes, it is true something in me has died, this also must have been true and applicable to your feelings about me years and years ago – how otherwise

The Rainbearers, etc. – a paean to your love for another (I was a clown in mauve). I felt you somehow make out you are fighting back against injuries done to you by me. I can't help feeling from the beginning it was the other way round. I do feel you bluff yourself about your actions and intentions, and there is a sort of void in you that you know nothing of, and it lays all kinds of destroying tricks on whoever is closest to you. In a sense this is what you cherish, for your work.

I never saw my relationship with you as a battle till the [Natalie] thing and then I did feel at a certain stage that I gave up. So what? If we do not see our future together, what do we do?

The only real grumble that I have (I think this is really what I feel) is that you grumble about things that you must have known were going to happen and in fact caused (not in moments of dottiness) but deliberately and over months and years, and indeed also in your work as an artist. When you have said you want us to be together I have never felt that you wanted to take me on hurt and all – but that you had weighed up that it would be the best of depressing alternatives for you.

With regard to my saying I was free, of course it is a big change when your youngest child leaves home for boarding-school. I do feel the second half of my life has to be different – I think you too do about yours – otherwise your actions make no possible sense. I don't feel bitterness as far as I know and of course I will have times of longing for you, but I think we have to try separation and see how we sort ourselves out.

Is it true that my leaving was a relief? (apart from your concern and our closeness over the years). Please try to be honest about this. Honesty in the end hurts less.

It seems to be that you don't acknowledge cause and effect. Once the bull enters the ring it goes out dead (has to); seeing this in the ring resulted in my understanding this for the first time – the nature of inevitability. This sequence can be changed only by a miracle, an act of grace, or an enormous natural occurrence (an earthquake or something similar). Children can't grasp this (as applying to themselves). They think they can jump and avoid the bullet.

Our chain of events has brought us to where we are now, there has been a lot of good and a lot that has been achievement, and the children mercifully seem all right. But we have both nearly died in the last two years, and we are being pushed to change if we are to live.

I thought – I am so sorry; but what is being sorry, yes.

– I know about the ways in which people seem appallingly helpless; about the business of writing which is like a journey in a troika in which people are thrown to pursuing wolves.

I was trying to go on with the play about the group of characters who find themselves as if trapped on a stage; they are trapped as it were by their scripts – by their inheritance, their conditioning: in what sense can they get out? This play – the spin-off from *The Good Samaritans* – was to be called, simply, *Aerodrome*. I became obsessed by this play. Of course we are stuck with our terrible drives and deceits and fears as in some conventional melodrama; but is it not possible to become aware of something quite different going on as it were off-stage? But how are we to recognise this? or to get in touch with it? There seems to be some deathliness either in staying wholly within one's script or making desperate and futile efforts wholly to get out; one has to recognise that one is on a stage; but just by this recognition, perhaps, to be in touch with what is outside.

I tried to say to Rosemary something like – We are all in one sense bulls in a bull-ring, yes; we are pursued by archetypal figures with spears and darts and knives; we face the inevitability of death. But are we not also, in some sense, surely, in your other metaphor, children who can jump and avoid bullets? We feel trapped and helpless within hurtings, ragings, resentments, despair. But also – Look; listen: is not the very fact that we can see and say this a symptom of what you call a miracle, an act of grace? And what you call the enormous nature occurrence, the earthquake – might it not be this that is going on off-stage?

Rosemary wrote:

Dear Nick   7/11/71
    Part of what I feel is that you can never be pinned down, you always jump, slide sideways, and often disappear both in talk and in action – no matter what previous assurance has been given – so where should I stand, live or act? You will say anything to win the person round; tonight you said 'I will be able to write if only I can be alone'; but you usually say you can't be alone. If I say – 'Well now you say "I can write if only I can be alone" and usually you say "I can't go on being alone" so nothing is right' – you become angry and say we cannot communicate; so all your wife can do is to

listen or play the games that most people play with each other, which you both scorn and demand. I often feel all you want is for everyone to be won round, and then for you to be able to continue your often (in my opinion) fairly sad antics, while the spotlight always has to remain on you.

You are like people in the war who always said to anyone in hospital 'You are lucky dear, don't you know there's a war on?' My sufferings are more internal and less spectacular, partly because I am not so much of a play-actor, but it is at these moments (of suffering) that I feel you cannot help me because you live in your fantasy and if I touch this with ME you collapse – so you have your own built-in trip system (as far as I am concerned).

I have written to a solicitor as I do think, if you and I think we have no future together, some kind of action must be taken. So do you want a divorce or separation?

Darling Nick,
I don't want to go on writing blaming letters, I didn't mean humans were like bulls, but something about the nature of inevitability. One will never get a clear picture from anyone else (the task of a go-between is also a thankless one); they always get it wrong. All I think I know is that you must *not* feel guilt, as it has all been part of the life force within us, and one is not irrevocably hurt if one keeps in this stream, and indeed one can never get into it without being hurt. Of course it was 'joint' – even *The Rainbearers* – it was essential to you as a writer, it was essential for you 'to be a writer' for your very survival, and I would never have stopped it – how could I? (You remember the film *Elvira Madigan*?) You have asked me before why I married you and I have answered before – we both wanted it. But I would say – why did you? Yes, I have walked out.

I do truthfully want you to be well, and to go on strongly. Maybe there are things which you could be helped to unravel, and you would be less often on the brink of horrors. I am sorry, and hate to think of you on the brink of horrors. You have done so much from a difficult start.

Now don't worry about me, I feel full of hope each morning, tired and low by evening, but I *am* going to get well.

For the summer holidays of 1972 I had rented a large house in Cala D'Or in Majorca, imagining that it might be filled with some or others of my shifting family-circuses of tumblers, banderilleros, loved-ones, children, phantasms. As things turned out it seemed for a time that I might be there on my own: Natalie remained away. In the end I settled in with my two younger children, Robert and Clare, aged sixteen and twelve; we each carried a mountain of books. Mine were chosen with an eye to trying to discover whether anyone else had the slightest idea about all the stuff that was going on in my mind.

We lay out and read in the sun each day, Robert and Clare and myself, in separate compartments of a large flat roof. It seemed that what I wanted to discover was – in what way might it be possible to look at the patterns, the programming, of our own minds; does not the very fact that we can have this notion mean that it is possible? I read Husserl, Popper, Suzanne Langer, Gregory Bateson. The latter above all seemed to know something of what I was trying to find out: also how difficult it was in words to pin this down. I handed on to Clare, my twelve-year-old daughter, a book by R.D. Laing on the subject of impossibilities in family relationships: she said – 'I did not know other people knew that families are like this!' I thought that perhaps I should write another play, besides the one called *Aerodrome*, to be acted by the same actors: by this it might be shown that in a sense of course one is never off-stage, but it might be by becoming aware of one's different roles, of moving between them, that one becomes aware of what is off-stage. By being aware of one's own programming, that is, one might also be apart from it. And this might be the miracle; the act of grace.

Sometime during our long summer holiday Rosemary came to stay and we were all rather formal and composed, sunbathing in our separate compartments on the connecting roof. Perhaps we had at last in some sense stopped acting: or stopped caring whether or not we were acting – this was what we had wanted to find? Or perhaps we were like those denizens of Plato's cave who at last had become aware, even though it was at the back of them, of the sun. Afterwards we might have to go back into our caves. But even then we might be able to say – You see, those are shadows: that is the sun.

PART IV

As this story comes closer to the present it becomes more difficult to write. This is not only because of what might be hurtful to others, but also because in so far as this has been a story about learning from bad things as well as from good, then, when the bad things continue (which they do, since one is human), in as much as there has been any learning, it may result in things being liable to appear in an ever more garish light. Perhaps this is what is meant about the seven devils that come in the place of one that has been cast out: a person does not get rid of devils; he or she has to come to terms with recognising and living with devils; to learn to say – Do your worst; now you are out in the open we can not only learn from you but take you on; of course there will be fearful battles along the way.

In Thomas Mann's story of beautiful people who walk hand-in-hand on a beach it is suggested that they owe their serenity to the recognition of what is going on in a temple where hags are dismembering a child. But it is not the human task simply to achieve serenity: humans are in partnership in the business of redemption, not of peace. Regarding the image of the temple this is what one learns – that humans are not only the beautiful people but also the hags and the child.

The idea that by recognising this sort of complexity one is not only looking at life but affecting it should not be too difficult when there is so much evidence that at the heart of things there is some partnership between observation and what occurs. If humans want to change, it is this that they have to observe – themselves as possibly beautiful people aware of themselves also as hags and child. Thus they may reach a state of grace the nature of which, like that of an art-work, however, may be just beyond words.

Life contains absurdities, tragedies, cruelties: humans either see parts of themselves in these, or turn away in blindness or despair. If they see themselves as part of a pattern then they are in the business of creating pattern; people who see themselves as only serene are as helpless as those who see themselves as only in darkness.

There remains the hurt that one does, has done, to other people. One can talk of patterns formed by recognising the darkness in oneself; can one talk of patterns as a result of one's hurting others? This indeed might be a denial of one's own darkness – and thus of the chance of light.

I suppose one can say that for others too there is always a choice.

I have said that I did not intend to say much about Rosemary in this book; but just as I was finishing the first draft, Rosemary died. So she will be able to tell no story herself.

Rosemary was a beautiful and rare being who grew up with an ability to be sufficient to herself. Perhaps she had to have this in order to survive: she achieved it with great elegance. Her family was one in which people had learned to be self-sufficient: but such a style of survival is both a consequence of, and leaves, wounds.

Rosemary and I loved, and married, because we felt we could help to bear and to heal each other's wounds; but also inescapably, perhaps, we felt we had to try to learn to be sufficient to ourselves. We achieved something of this. It seems to me now that the bad hurt I did to Rosemary was in the early days of our marriage: someone wounded uses (abuses?) the trust of those closest: we were both of us children fighting for our lives. After this perhaps our love became set in its pattern. Rosemary's upbringing had given her the idea that she had no right to make claims on others. I suppose I tried to make few claims on her.

She had always wanted to be a painter: at the end of her life she was painting pictures, it seemed to me, like no others in the world. She said in her letters to me that it might not have been of the greatest importance to her to be a painter; but in the way things turned out it was, and she had moments of choice. It is always difficult for a mother with children to be a painter: this requires a more vertiginous tightrope-act than that of a father and writer.

I sometimes think that Rosemary was perhaps too upright, too particular: if she had leaned more heavily first now on one side then on the other she might have found it more possible to balance on her rope. But with such lurchings and gyrations going on around her – what a virtue to be upright!

In her later years Rosemary lived on her own in the Isle of Man – in her windswept, four-square, stone-built farmhouse on the edge of the northernmost moorland by sand-dunes and the sea. In winters she would travel – to Israel, to Australia, to America – always with her easel and box of paints and stack of canvases. One winter in Los Angeles she went into hospital for a minor operation and came out with a major injury to her back; after this she walked only with difficulty and spent much time in a wheelchair or in bed. She continued to paint – her landscapes and seascapes with changing patterns of sun and cloud; strange mythical scenes in which humans spring or hang like seeds from trees, or swirl upwards like smoke or sparks from flames. In these last years I went to visit her quite often: there was the impression that in some proper way we had done what we could for each other: she and the children had come to be on good terms with my second wife.

When Rosemary died, of a stroke at the age of sixty-two, I was at her bedside, with Shaun and Ivo and Robert and Clare. There had been dramas and sadnesses in our lives, but Rosemary had perhaps achieved something more lasting than serenity. There were her hundreds of paintings stacked neatly in every room of her house; for years she had said she had not wanted an exhibition (she had had three or four in London when she was young); but recently it seemed she had been preparing many of her pictures for show. Her last paintings were two series on mythological themes – Alice in Wonderland, and Little Red Riding Hood and the Wolf. In one the child ventures into a magical world just off-stage; in the other the child goes on a journey and at the end is eaten by a wolf. In the image of the temple in the sand-dunes by the sea perhaps my lovely Rosemary was never quite enough of a hag; did not often see herself thus (do not painters and writers at times have to be hags?); she was all too much the beautiful person or the child.

20

When I got home from my long summer holiday with my pile of books which I had hoped would be something like the stone tablets with which Moses came down from Mount Sinai – well, what had I learned? That human dramas, repetitions, indeed go on and on: that it may be possible to stand apart from these and look down? But people still suffer, die. So what is it that may be lifted to another level?

The writers whom I had been reading seemed to be saying – The human species as it stands is no longer quite viable. The contradictions within it that have helped it to survive – the ruthlessness combined with the instinct for being part of a team – may yet, with modern technology, blow it up; what is required is for some new human type to evolve. This type with part of itself will be able to look down on the old antics with which its other parts are involved – the loyalties and the ruthlessness; the confrontations of 'Us' versus 'Them'. And at this level humans might be able to signal to others on the same level of looking – and discover and share some style of dealing with the other parts of themselves.

In the autumn and winter after this long summer holiday there were still the long-running performances on my particular stage – Rosemary was planning one of her trips abroad; Natalie's piano was now on some up-beat of its yo-yo string – so what might it mean, that if you looked down on all this, things might change? In the course of my reading I had been struck by how the claims of psychoanalysis were in tune with whatever I thought I was discovering: just by the effort to look at the haunted and haunting patterns of one's past and of one's mind there might be healing; this did not expunge the old patterns, but made them bearable and thus to some extent impotent. Natalie, however, had been going to one or another psychoanalyst for years and this did not seem to have affected the style of dramas that went on around her. But then – how could one tell what might be happening as it were off-stage?

Once or twice in perturbation I myself got in touch with Natalie's current analyst: I said – But look, nothing seems to change! Natalie's analyst said – What you are saying is that with yourself nothing seems to change. I said – You mean, I might need analysis?

Natalie's analyst gave me the name and address of a colleague: she even made an appointment for me. I thought – Damn it, am I not committed to the idea that one has to take a look at whatever turns up?

So I went to see the analyst with whom Natalie's analyst had so oddly made an appointment. He was a kindly-looking grey-haired man who sat in a chair while I sat opposite him. I told him of the latest circus-acts in my life – the grand pianos bouncing up and down, the high-wire acts that ever more frequently turned as it were into the spilling of tea-trays over people's heads. Even as I spoke I suppose I began to hear my own words and to wonder – Well why indeed have I been for so long in thrall to these performances? At the end of my recitation the analyst said – You're a greedy baby. I was much struck by this: such a bold thing to say! I wondered – Should I not be insulted? But then – Had I not myself so often used the image of myself as someone keeping a whole load of plates in the air –

So I said – Ah! Then – What's wrong with a greedy baby?

He said – Have I said there is anything wrong with a greedy baby?

So I thought again – Ah! And then it did seem to me that there might be something interesting here: not just about this description of myself, but about what might be the vices and virtues of greedy babies.

So I began to go to this analyst three or four times a week:

getting off a high wire onto this particular treadmill; to learn how on treadmills one might feel at home?

For all I had read, and listened to people's stories, about psychoanalysis, I had never had much of a picture of how the game was actually played. I had imagined that the patient talked and the analyst gave his interpretations: but in my case it seemed more a matter of myself talking and the analyst listening and then just by this myself coming to listen for what might be the hidden import behind my words – for what might be behind bombardments and smokescreens. I had on my own been playing with this sort of imagery for some time (and this indeed had been the style of my talks with Father Raynes), so it was not difficult for me to feel at ease with the style of it here. Indeed there was a comfort in the circumstance of finding that the game could be played once more with someone else – not an adversary, but someone who might every now and then as I talked make a remark like an umpire signalling a wide or blowing a whistle. I wondered – Indeed thus one might pick one's way through minefields. To what end? But this was not the point. It was oneself who might change: not the score in a game, but the player.

Anyhow, here were the mists and smokescreens of my memory and verbiage – and here were figures looming up out of the fog.

At first, I suppose, there was my father. But he was such an obvious bogey-figure: what on earth had ever been hidden, screened, about my father? He had always been like some lighthouse visible for miles – his eyes flashing on and off to guide sailors or perhaps lure them to their doom. He had made all too little use of smokescreens for himself – seeming intent on publicising his own propensity to grandeur or doom. But in private life, in my childhood, he had often seemed to me to be the one grown-up who was willing to look at, to try to shed light upon, things around him; he had sometimes thus seemed to be the one grown-up I knew who was sane. And what more can be asked of a father? Whatever terrors my father had had for me had been clear: there had hardly been the need for them to be driven into the unconscious. Or so I said it seemed to me. And what struck me now was that my analyst seemed to agree. Psychoanalytically speaking, someone so un-devi-ous as my father seemed not to have been a bad parent.

But then – my mother? My poor so-called victim mother?

My mother had died when I was nine – of peritonitis, after an appendix operation. It was sometimes said – it had been said to me by the time I was eleven – that she had lacked the will to live out of despair at my father's latest infidelity. This had not seemed to me to make sense: people do not often die because of their spouse's infidelities. Was it not rather the pattern here that people liked to say such things about my father?

I had been told – Everyone so adored your mother!

In analysis whatever journeys there are back to the formative influences of one's past have properly to be done as it were on foot: there are few lifts, few plane-hops, provided by one's analyst; this is the point – there have to be time and space on the journey for processes of learning for oneself. Change happens as a result of the action of the pilgrimage; healing comes almost inadvertently. The analyst sits like some sort of lodestone to offer direction; some sounding-board to give back resonances or echoes: the patient floats and paddles in a fairy-story sea. Sometimes the analyst makes noises like a hooter or a bell; sometimes he makes noises like a mermaid on a rock; sometimes he appears to be asleep. Oh yes, and sometimes he does throw a bit of jargon into the works – a crash-bang per-cussion-spanner. But then soon all is calm again: what were we talking about? Oh yes, my mother.

– You mean my mother, dying when I was nine, might have left me as a hungry baby?

My analyst would sit like one of those statues on the banks of the Nile.

– Or you mean before that, just after I was born, when my mother went off on a summer holiday to Venice and left me with a Nanny and a wet-nurse who was a drunk; and I was sick much of the time and nearly died –

My analyst would sometimes make a mewing noise like a cat.

– You mean, it might have been then that I formed the ravenous need to scrabble for love like cats under dustbin-lids in alleys?

Sometimes it was as if we, my analyst and I, had been moving against a backdrop of a dark and thunderous sky. Then suddenly it was as if a bright light came down! and it seemed there might be nothing left for an audience to do except to get up and leave the theatre.

But then there might be bits of my analyst's percussion-jargon coming in: so I would try to see –

– You mean, when a child's mother disappears, it is not only that the child is hungry, but that it is liable to feel that itself is responsible for its hunger and even its mother's death? By this it clings vainly to a sense of its own need for reparation and control –

– But how do you know these things: is it your experience that people commonly feel like this?

Sometimes my analyst would seem to be guiding me into what might seem a fairy story. But it was a story that often enough rang bells.

– What you are saying is, that in later life such a child is drawn to damaged women in order to save them from the chance of the sort of death suffered by the mother? clings to them so as not to experience again his own murderousness and fear of death –

Damaged women indeed! Sometimes it was as if not only a white light were coming down, but a bemused sort of smiling.

My analyst would say – Why are you laughing?

I would say – Don't you think it's funny?

– That you nearly died? That your mother died when you were nine?

– I am protecting myself by laughing! Haven't you said that it might not be a bad thing to protect oneself?

Sometimes, of course, my analyst was smiling.

There came a time when I had been going on about my continuing high-wire act with Natalie – about how we could not settle together and yet I did not seem capable of getting away: so what was at the back of this pattern, my alley-cat hunger, my need to cling to women whose own needs were self-destructive? And these ideas were wandering somewhat ghostly, in a fog: there was nothing lasting in the white light coming down. Then one day I happened to be talking coincidentally about my old Nanny – my Nanny who in my childhood in all practical ways had been a mother to myself and my sister – and I was saying how of course I had been dependent on Nanny; she had saved our lives; but at the same time there could be something adamant about Nanny – when she was angry she would refuse to speak to me and I would trail round the house after her as if begging her for – what – a word? a bowl of milk? a dustbin in an alley? And then it suddenly struck me – and this was, yes, like a great white spear of light coming down – that it was a description of just this sort of scene that I had been giving shortly before when talking about one of the facets of my life with Natalie – the way in which when something went wrong she would refuse to speak to me, and I was left trailing round the house in some rage and misery after her. And so – You mean, do you, good heavens! somewhere in my mind, in my heart, my beautiful and apparently oh-so-vulnerable Natalie is indistinguishable from my tight-lipped but oh-so-indispensable Nanny? And that is why I am hooked? why my grown-up life seems so impossible both without and with Natalie? Oh there are times when the white light coming down raises more than a smile: indeed, what an exuberant joke! These are the times, I suppose, when there is some liberation.

What is seen in a flash, of course, takes time to filter through to any change of need or habit. I would say to my analyst – But what shall I do? He would say – Go on coming to analysis.

Before I had started going to analysis I had been working on the play to do with actors who find themselves trapped on a stage: I had embarked on the second play to be acted by the same actors but in another drama and in different roles: the point of this was – of course in life we are persons who play different roles: but this does not mean that there are no such things as ourselves; our sense of ourselves depends on how we are aware of how we play different roles – on the bit of us, that is, that remains as it were off-stage. With parts of us perhaps we are never off-stage; yet just through knowing this we can listen to, learn from, what we know is off-stage; we can get into relation to this; and so in this sense it is part of us. But in the actual writing of these plays I was plunging about on ground that still seemed for the most part impenetrably bound by fog. I thought – All right, I'd better concentrate on my analysis.

Just then – by one of those coincidences that seem to crop up when one is perhaps putting oneself in the way of them – Rosemary's mother died and left Rosemary all her papers; amongst these were letters and papers to do with Rosemary's mother's elder brother, Julian Grenfell. I had for long thought I might like to write a book about Julian Grenfell; he had been the eldest son of an aristocratic family and had been killed in the early years of the First World War; he had written one very good poem 'Into Battle'. As a young man he had seemed to have everything – good looks, intelligence, privilege, money – and yet he was one of those of his generation who seemed to welcome the First World War, apparently as a means of escape from the dead-ends in which he found himself at home. From the trenches he had written 'I adore war' and 'It is like a big picnic.' This attitude had made him seem a hero to an older generation but something of a monster to a later one; I wondered what papers concerning him had survived, and hoped there might be enough for me to write about him. The Grenfell family themselves had seemed to me to be ambivalent about Julian: he was a hero to them because he had been a hero in war, but still – there had always been this 'but still'. It seemed to refer to something about which I might have sympathy with Julian. When Rosemary's mother died Rosemary handed on to me all the papers.

This was just after I had embarked on my analysis. The crates and trunks of the Grenfell family letters filled a large studio room in my otherwise now often somewhat empty house. I delved about in these papers. I thought – Indeed there are parallels here with the delving about in my own mind.

Julian Grenfell had been a product of his class and culture; he had also rebelled against these. At school he had been good at work and good at games; at home he had had an adored and adoring mother who had taught him the virtues of excellence and conquest. But then when he had left school he began to question every tenet of the society in which he had been brought up and in which his mother was a totem; these tenets were centred on the assumption that people like he and she should enjoy the exercise of power while making out that this was some self-sacrificial duty – and that such a contradiction should never be mentioned nor even noticed. When he was twenty-one Julian had written a short book that was his polemic against conventional society – a plea for individuals to be honest with themselves and by this to influence the world. It was an astonishing book for an upper-class young man in 1910 to have written. His family had hated it, and it was never published. Then Julian had had some sort of breakdown which was called a 'brainstorm' by his family; he would lie for hours with a loaded shot-gun by his side. Then he recovered, joined the regular army, and dutifully fitted in. When the war came indeed it might have seemed like one of his childhood family picnics. It was not long before he was killed.

There were superficial parallels between Julian's background and my own; in other ways there were not. His mother had survived him; she had both adored and fought him; she had rejected him, and then had waited for him to come back. The hardest traps to escape from are perhaps those with as it were a double row of teeth – that bite alternately hot and cold. Whatever troubles I had had, they had not been so devouring as Julian's. And he had not had the chance of going to an analyst.

So long as I was writing my book about Julian Grenfell things seemed to trundle along helpfully in my analysis. There were times when I would say – Oh well, perhaps after all what I am learning is how to settle down peaceably with Natalie. Then my analyst would sit upright as if an alarm bell had gone off and he would begin – Now look here! From the start, it had seemed that my analyst was trying to wean me from Natalie.

This was a time when we were all in our separate compartments – Natalie and her children now in the flat I had taken years ago to be close to her; Rosemary back in the Isle of Man; I on my own in Hampstead; Natalie's husband on his own at what had once been a family home –

– then Natalie's husband suddenly died. Oh I had feared this, yes! Had I not written about the chance of it in the seventh story of *Impossible Object*? But when it came, indeed, there was some fear –

Death is final: no longer the chance of anything being possible on a tightrope. What would he say about this, my analyst?

– I suppose you are all now going to have guilt –

– Yes of course I am going to have guilt –

– What happens is the responsibility of the person to whom it happens. There was always the possibility that this might happen.

Yes. But no one quite knows how to handle death. Is it right or wrong to feel oneself in some way responsible?

It might seem that this occurrence would have made things more easy for Natalie and me. Of course it made things more difficult.

At a death, does not the whole intricate circus troupe have to disband?

I tried to look after things with Natalie as well as I could for a time. But the purpose of psychoanalysis seemed to have been anyway to get us all off the high wire.

– If only this or that had happened or not happened!

– But it did. Very sorry.

– And what now? (One learns to talk to oneself.)

Natalie herself seemed to be demonstrating that nothing now was possible.

There are times indeed in analysis when nothing seems to be happening; it is then I suppose that the analyst drags out his wilder bits of jargon – those for instance about breasts and anuses and penises – some form of these existing, it is suggested, in the head. This is supposed to be getting to the heart of things, but I never made much sense of it: was one talking of the inside or the outside world? Or do you really mean, what is the difference? And then perhaps again the question – Why am I laughing?

My analyst never seemed to be much interested in my relationship with Rosemary. I do not know if he was right or wrong about this. Perhaps analysts, like novelists, like to see what is emerging as their own original work.

About the children he would say – Whatever harm you have done to them has been done already; let them go: what you become yourself, now, may be what they will be able to hand on –

I would think – But something must happen other than my endlessly coming to analysis –

– Something will turn up? This is what I have put my faith in.

What turned up, after a time, was my second wife Verity.

Verity, in her early thirties, had separated from her first husband and had set up in her own house with her two-year-old son Jonathan. She too was going to analysis. She had got as far as learning to be on her own; was wondering perhaps whether anything new would turn up.

What unimaginable coincidences and manoeuvrings must have gone on off-stage!

I have written of the following scene in my novel *Serpent*.

Verity and I had been asked separately to the theatre by mutual friends: this was the result of other friends dropping out. The show was *The Rocky Horror Show*: I hated it; Verity loved it. When I explained later why I hated it she said – I have never heard so much rubbish in all my life! Oh yes, this rang bells! Things out in the open: the message across Verity's desirable kitchen/dining-room – You do see, don't you, that to be open is the point?

On Verity's table was a photograph of her small son Jonathan: I said – Ah, that makes one want to start again! (I was a cunning operator: I wanted to get Verity: Verity seemed to be knowing as well as so pretty.) When Verity's analyst heard the story about the photograph he said – At that moment Nicholas's goose was cooked!

The next day Verity came to have dinner in my house. There was a cuckoo-clock that I had picked up on my walking-tour with Natalie through the Black Forest. While Verity and I were on the sofa – discussing, what, those psycho-sexual appurtenances in our heads? – the clock went – Cuckoo! Cuckoo! Verity said – That clock'll have to go. I thought – You do mean, don't you, that my old circus tricks will have to go.

My analyst said – You have now found your good breast.

I thought – For once the jargon does not sound too absurd.

Verity's and my analysts, *in loco parentis*, seemed to smile on our plans to get married without much more ado. I had not wanted a divorce until then –

– But Rosemary and I, having got as far as we could, might be whatever each was to the other more profitably apart.

And with Verity I might have a chance of going hand-in-hand through whatever strange landscapes would now turn up: Verity being someone who might not be surprised at what such landscapes might contain –

– Dwarfs and ogres as well as gardens of delight –

268

– Consciousness (and thus unconsciousness?) keeping an eye on things like caring parents with semi-autistic children –

All right!

Anyway, this was the curtain coming down on my tightrope act with Natalie.

My analysis was thus indeed trundling along to good effect so long as Verity and I were settling in together and I was doing my biography of Julian Grenfell. Julian's story was one in the telling of which psychoanalysis could help. But then Julian died, and I came to the end of my story. So I thought I would go back to the plays that a year or so ago I had abandoned.

The second of these plays had figures in it that were obviously drawn from my own conscious or unconscious. There were a millionaire and his wife living in a house on the top of a mountain; a young girl whom the millionaire is trying to seduce; a grandson who breaks in; a black-haired woman who seems to have come striding on to the stage by mistake; a man – her lover? myself? – who comes to find her (or is it to mend the electric light?). All these figures seemed to have chosen to act on a stage, but in order to demonstrate something quite different – different, that is, from what an audience might expect to be appropriate on a stage. It was as if the actors were saying to an audience – Look: we have come on a stage in order to show you that the archetypal drama stuff does not really matter; it can be a fog, a smokescreen; what matters is what might be going on elsewhere: you do see this? Do you?

When I tried to talk of this to my analyst he would say – You mean, you are trying to do some sort of self-analysis?

I would say – I think I am trying to describe what might be results of analysis: I mean, what it might be like if one is able to look at the patternings in one's own mind –

My analyst would say – Well, what is it like?

I would say – I'm trying to find a way of putting it. I can't put it easily into words here, or my being able to write it may stop.

My analyst would say – If you can't put it into words here, what is the point of your analysis?

I would say – But you can't talk about the doing of any work of art; you have to let it happen –

He would say – It seems to me you like mysteries; you like tying yourself in knots. All your life, you have liked tying yourself in knots –

I would say – But it is you who are now tying me in knots! And I am trying to find a way of living with the unravelling.

There came a time when it seemed to me clear that my analyst was saying that if there were things at the centre of my work that I could not talk about, then my analysis should stop. So I wrote to him to say that I accepted this.

He seemed put out. I wondered – But did he not know what he was up to?

Verity wondered – What will become of us now!

I thought – You mean, myself as one babe in the wood will now take out all my troubles on you, the other?

Then – But sooner or later we will each have to go through this predicament, will we not?

– Until such times as we learn, like my actors are learning and hoping to help others to learn, to hear for ourselves what might be going on just behind our words, off-stage.

So I went on with my plays: with sitting and staring at the words of my plays instead of lying on a couch and staring at the ceiling. It was as if I were saying to Verity – Indeed no more high-wire acts! and no more treadmills now: we have to grow up. Here I am trying to look at people looking at the patterns of their own minds –

I suppose Verity thought – Heaven help us; you think you can do that?

21

This second play which I had started, which was in fact to be the first play in the structural scheme I now planned, was called *Skylight* – this title referring both to the bright sky at the top of a mountain, and a window in the ceiling of the space in which my characters seemed trapped. This was the play that began like a conventional play of the thirties – the scene is the terrace of a rich man's house on a mountain. Off-stage are the sounds of a party in progress. The elderly millionaire comes on with his arm round the young girl; the girl is drunk or doped or perhaps just suicidal. The young man who breaks in has apparently climbed the mountain: he says he is the grandson of the millionaire: he might also be – a gate-crasher, a member of a revolutionary group come to bomb the millionaire's house. And one of their number might be the girl? The millionaire is at a loss: he calls for help to his wife. When she comes on she treats him like a baby. (Oh yes, all these might indeed be archetypal representations of the playwright's earlier life.) But there does seem to be some revolutionary violence going on off-stage – in the valley? in the streets outside the theatre? But in fact – there would be a difference! The actors now seem to be at a loss; to ad-lib; stage mechanisms seem to be breaking down. People come in from out-side: are they stage technicians? more actors? people from the streets? Who knows! Well, what would be the difference! People in the audience are not so half-witted – or is it that they are clever? This is quite like life.

In the second act the actors seem to have stopped acting; they are hanging about, listening; indeed there might be a battle going on in the streets outside: but where else have actors to go, except on a stage? We are all, after all, trapped within our minds. So we have in a sense to go on acting – whatever the reality is outside. But now it seems there is an actual bomb in the theatre and it might go off – or is this still acting? There are scuffles on the stage; lights go on and off (in the set? in the mind?), the stage-set seems to be being dismantled. One of the actors climbs down into the auditorium. He seems to say – But you do see what is happening: don't you?

In the last act the revolution seems to have taken place; the women have taken over the scene. A man has fallen over the edge of the mountain (the edge of the stage?); his body is brought back by other men on a stretcher. The people carrying the stretcher are people who – have come in from outside? were members of the audience? have come to help the people on the stage? They place the stretcher within a circle of dismantled stones. Oh you mean, this is now symbolic! the circle of stones is – a tomb? a womb? the nucleus of a cell? Even – Is not everything we do symbolic – of whatever it is that might be going on off-stage. And of our struggle to see this? The actors come to the front of the stage: they seem to be looking amongst the audience again – You? Is it you? They are separated from the audience by a screen – the invisible fourth wall of the stage. So all this is like the mind! If you don't see it – how can you get through? The actors seem to have been carrying out some experiment: not just – What is reality, what is not: but also – What is dead, what is alive. So – What is asking this: a way of seeing things, waiting to be born? It does seem that the actors, watching the audience, are saying – You create things by your way of seeing things: you create – This is fantasy, this is reality. Such can be a seed, an idea, in the mind of someone watching (you? you?); or indeed like a child waiting to be born.

After a time the actors seem to have done all they can. Perhaps we can all go home: to another stage? Either something has lodged within the mind, or it has not.

But there will be another attempt, another night, won't there?

You mean – All this might be an effort at understanding: at some new state of mind being evolved?

This was the sort of thing I had been failing to say to my analyst; when he had been saying to me (oh with some justification, yes!) – You like tying yourself in knots.

I had tried to say to him – You call these knots, all right, but what is reality? Here I am on my back on this terrible couch and you are sitting beside me and we are trying to look at these dramas in my mind: it is not I who tie myself in knots, we are all tied in knots; it is by looking at them we hope to get out. So we watch, listen, for what seeds might be growing off-stage –

My analyst used to say – You and your horticultural metaphors!

And I had thought – I must get on to a different play.

The play that came after *Skylight* in the structure that seemed to be growing was the play that I had originally called *Aerodrome* and now I called *Landfall* – a landfall being both a fall of rock that entraps, and the first sight of land when one has been a long time at sea. This was the play that years ago had started the whole pattern – the pattern of trying to be able to look at patterns – the characters acting the experience of being trapped not on an aerodrome but on a stage. They each seem to have come on from some quite different story; but, since they are here, their stories are connected? They are the same actors as those in *Skylight*, to be sure; here they are just playing different roles; you see? So in what sense might be their reality? You mean, off-stage? But does this mean something more than – they know they are actors? They do seem in some despair; they have to carry on acting in their trap; but do they? They stop; start; what else is there to do? Some people come on from outside: are they from a different play: do they know they are actors? Oh we are all people stuck as if by a landfall in Plato's cave! some are haunted by their pasts; some are trying to look at the ways in which they seem trapped in their present; some do not seem to see that by seeing this they might get out; but some do. Occasionally they seem to recognise each other (they have been together in other plays? there is some network?); but often of course it seems they have just to get on with the play. A man has lost his child (or is it his wife?); others are involved in some conspiracy. They talk to themselves, they talk to each other; every now and then they talk to the audience (is it you? is it you?). Again – is this not like life? But look – what are the connections between their stories and what they are there for? They are demonstrating more than being trapped on a stage. They are here for some purpose: they are saying – You see? If you do, one or two get through.

Oh indeed – beyond the walls of the stage or cave which are like glass screens there might be some sort of bomb going off, or sun –

The difference is – you choose?

–This is death: this is life –

This is handed on.

Or would you rather continue in your melodramatic plays?

But the curtain has come down.

Time to leave the theatre. Time for a cup of tea.

We can always have yet one more try, can't we?

All this was going on in my head; on the bits of paper like blank stone tablets in front of myself as a madman hanging on half-way up Mount Sinai – at a time when Verity was settling in to my Hampstead house, when our sad divorces were going through, when Verity and I were able to believe – Sad things do happen; lights go on and off on a stage; but something new will grow?

We had hoped to be the children of self-knowledge, Verity and I – not browbeaten by that frosty old God in Eden. But as children of psychoanalysis, what guidance in fact did we have about growth? Freud had suggested that the best that people might hope for was a change from neurotic to ordinary human misery: this was hardly what we wanted to listen for off-stage. Jung, to be sure, had talked about change: but he had gone out of his way to say that what was likely to grow were battles with new and unexpectedly liberated devils. The more one withdrew projections back into oneself, that is, the more vulnerable one was to undiverted hauntings from one's past – or even from the universal human situation. Perhaps what was wanted to deal with these was something born out of the confrontation with ordinary human misery –

We wanted a child, Verity and I. We thought – Even if we ourselves are too haunted by conditioning to become much more than people who know that they are haunted by conditioning –

Perhaps we can be parents to that which will be able to see this so clearly that it will have been conditioned more into the vision than the ghosts.

We married. We did not start a child straight away. So either you go to a doctor who does something to your insides or tells you what to do to yourself with cold water –

– Or –

We happened to go on a camping holiday that summer, Verity and Jonathan and I, and we passed near Assisi –

And at Assisi there was a fresco by Giotto, reproductions of which we had both much loved; it was of the Virgin Mary and St Joseph and the Child going across the desert with a donkey –

So we all lit candles at Assisi.

And nine months later our son Marius was born.

(I thought you said you cannot talk like this!)

(Yes I have said I cannot talk like this.)

During these months it seemed that what I was writing about was the birth of a child.

It seemed that I would have to write a third play to go with *Skylight* and *Landfall*, so that the actors could form some circuit; so that there could be some structure within which, from which, whatever new liveliness there might be might take root and grow.

In the mind, of course, in the mind.

This third play was to be called *Cell* – something in which you are locked up; also that within and from which new life may break out.

In *Cell* the actual stage-set is structured as if it might represent a brain: there is a lower level which occupies most of the width of the stage; it is a cellar, or junk-room – or what might be the unconscious part of a mind. On an upper level there are two compartments separated by a central back-to-front partition; these could be the left and right hemispheres of a brain. In the lower level a young man is seated on a bed; he is the actor who acted a young man in the first two plays; he is engaged in some sort of phone-tapping, with probes, trying to make contact with – what? – the outside world? the upper two parts of the brain? He succeeds in this only intermittently and obscurely; lights come on briefly here and there. In one of the upper compartments of the stage there is glimpsed an old man like God the Father or Karl Marx; he is reclining on a bed (or a cloud?) of books. In the other compartment is a wild man with his arms in a straitjacket who nevertheless appears, by the sounds he makes in the dark, to be able to play a flute. (This man is called, in the cast-list, Dionysus: you know the resonances of this? Do you?) The young man downstairs perseveres with his experiments. Above the roof of the upper structure – at street-level as it were – a young woman appears: she is dressed like a hiker on a journey: she seems to be in flight from pursuers. The experiments that the young man is doing result in a manhole being opened at street-level; the woman is thus able to climb down a ventilation shaft that runs vertically at one side of the structure, down to the outside of the lower level. By a series of experiments, mimes, coincidences and small explosions (no one after all quite understands the operations of the brain) the woman manages to get through into the downstairs level of the cell: there she joins the young man and together they try to make contact with the higher levels. There is a stove-pipe up into the upper room on the left; they push a probe up; this transfixes the old man who is sitting on what seems to be a lavatory; nevertheless he can seize the probe and use it to get through to the room on the right. This in turn releases the arms of the man in the straitjacket: he looks up to a skylight high in the wall of his cell. (Skylight? do you see? Do you?) It is this that has been making music – of the flute? There are connections! The whole structure, as if it were some organ, or mechanism that has been pent up but is now freed by the probing, begins to shudder and boom and shake –

Well, what indeed do people know about the workings of a brain –

They depend on the relationship of the parts and the whole –

So there has been some explosion, some breakthrough –

Some illumination, oh yes –

(Organ, organism, orgasm –)

For God's sake, isn't there an interval?

After a time the characters begin to see that the partitions on the stage might be on hinges: that is, there might be opened up

276

the barriers that have hitherto prevented the proper working of the brain. Two more women have appeared from outside; all the characters that appear from outside are women. (You mean they are catalysts? What can words tell.) They watch; listen. Well, what is it that women seem to be able to care about just as it were off-stage? There is some sort of nest formed by things fallen from the upper level. Something might be being born? The men are occupied with the dismantling of the partition on the stage.

The central partition on the upper floor swings on a central hinge: what were two compartments now are one. Hullo, hullo, do you remember me?

– Off-stage, you mean? In a different play? –

The mid-height horizontal floor partition moves on a central back-to-front hinge; this is hindered by the upper-floor partition which is now at an angle and thus getting stuck against the ceiling. Hold it! Back! Forward! You mean, there have to be coincidences of more than one hindrance moving at the same time?

– You are the only person I have ever loved, you see –

– Oh yes, I have loved other people in my life –

– Who are you talking to: yourself? to me?

Both.

So that's all right!

There is one partition it appears that they have not yet taken down: this is the legendary fourth wall that separates the actors from the audience at the front of the stage. But if it is not there, how can it be taken down? But of course it is what is not there that can imprison the mind! The barrier, you mean, between acting and not acting? between knowing what is acting and not knowing? the barrier that guards the path right round the world to the entrance to the garden again by the back way –

So the actors, God help them, turn to the front of the stage. There is the audience – the outside world – the journeys perhaps that they have to go on. Or you mean, they may be like seeds, and there may be journeys that one or two members of the audience will have to go on –

The actors seem to lean on what might be the partition between themselves and their audience at the front of the stage. There is a noise like that of gunfire (the revolution, the bomb, at last coming or going off?). It is as if the whole stage has become freed with a bang and is beginning to tip up and forwards on a hinge along its front; and thus the whole auditorium may be going down – some break-up of ground indeed! – down both to disintegration and a possible seed-bed for birth – with a seed-pod bursting over it. It is as if the actors, that is, were about to be projected over, on to, the audience's either fallow or stony ground. Take your pick. I mean – you: you. Well, one never quite knows, does one, what is or is not being born. Or perhaps – how else does one know?

We go out anyway into the world, don't we; my children and my children's children –

So stop to see –

– It is alive? it is dead?

– In the head, in the outside world –

In the outside world things do indeed die and come alive.

I thought that I would call these plays *Plays For Not Acting*.

(Oh we can all act! we have our scripts given us by birth, by circumstance. We have to learn how to stop acting. And what happens then? Oh I see.)

But then – did I think I had learned not to act?

Testing. Listening.

Here were Verity and I intending to be model spouses and parents in some psychoanalytically re-cycled Garden of Eden. Oh dear!

But better such a hope, I suppose, than just an acceptance of Freud's ordinary human miseries.

But what of Jung's strange new devils?

People who cling to unconscious delusion and projection have some built-in balances: inability to see can preserve an illusion of sanity. But when he or she has to some extent taken projections back – oh then indeed there can be terrible rumblings and explosions as if indeed a whole stage, a structure of mind is exploding –

– Like an organ or an orgasm to be sure –

– But also there were these plays like hungry children crying in my head.

How can one put one's arms round one's own mind; hold it?

Verity would say – I thought you said we would share every-thing –

– And now you are putting your arms round these plays in your head!

It was somewhere about this time that our son Marius was born. As the time approached he was said to have a huge head: there might be a danger to the mother or the child. We had planned to have the child at home with soft lights and sweet music: but now here we were having to be in a hospital in one of those rooms in which someone might well be in a straitjacket. I was taken aside by the gynaecologist who said – We may have to do a caesarian oper-ation; if we delay too long it may even have to be a choice between the mother and the child. Verity said – But we can carry the possibilities as long as we can, can't we? And in the end Marius was born naturally with his huge head.

Watching, I thought – Indeed all birth is a breakthrough: the sun coming through the walls of a cave.

It seemed that as a corollary to my plays there should still be some story of who my six characters might be as it were in reality, off-stage: of course this would be just one more story! But still – what is reality except the recognition of a complexity: the structur-ing, the imagination, of a dimension that you know is there just because you know the boundaries of a stage.

The story, or short novel, that I wrote to put at the end of the plays, was called *Cypher* – a cypher being both a communication in code and also (potentially) the key to such a code.

In *Cypher* the scene is a university town. There is student rioting and a laboratory building has been set on fire; it is possible that some radioactive substance may have been loosed into the atmosphere. So this is what might have been happening in the streets outside the theatre! My characters from the plays are now identified as – Eleanor and Max, Jason and Lilia, Judith and Bert: two elderly, two in their thirties and forties, two young. They know each other: they feel themselves akin in a way of seeing things. In the situation in which they find themselves they are not particularly surprised by the threat of catastrophe: we all live, do we not, on the edge of the Bomb: of the hole knocked in the skull of the atmosphere. These people are also aware of the propensity to catastrophe in themselves: how else might they be represented in the plays; they know themselves as often dramatic actors and clowns and babies. They also know that it may also be only by catastrophe, by break-up, that there might be the chance of some sort of change – for something new to emerge – like a seed, the denizens of some Noah's ark, indeed some kind of baby!

At the centre of *Cypher* there is, in fact, Lilia's baby; it is a few months old; Jason is the father; or it is possible that Max might be the father – but what does this matter, what matters is that it shall survive, as if carried through a desert on a donkey. And so all six persons conspire – no not conspire! everything of importance happens by coincidence, by so-called chance – it so happens that all six form some network to protect and carry the baby: well there have been some bizarre coincidences in the protection and evolution of human life, have there not! Here for instance – Lilia's husband Jason hopes to have an affair with the girl called Judith; because of this Lilia removes her baby from the house where, shortly after, jagged glass is blown by an explosion over the cot where the baby would have been lying – you think that one cannot talk about things like this? All right, but you can just put one thing after another: just say – Listen; watch; don't you think things like this happen? Good can come out of – . But you can't plan things like this, no!

Also – with the possible escape of radioactive substance into the atmosphere thousands may die: but then are there not too many people bumping around in the world anyway? Oh indeed one cannot say this! (Apart from any other consideration, Noah might find his ark sabotaged.) You can talk in biblical fairy-stories, yes; you can say – God is responsible. And this has been a good way of putting it. But now these people do not want to talk of God: they say – God knows, God is saying it is time we were responsible. So – Look to the proper means, and the proper ends will be what happens.

– You mean, for instance, a married man, the father of a young child, is having an affair with a girl –

– But he didn't! he knew he wanted to –

– And because of this it happened that the child –

– The man was both himself and the God that forbade. Watch; listen –

You mean, such a god is one that can still come across in mysterious ways –

Don't you think so?

One or two of these people are scientists: they know – Reality is determined by the experimental condition. And so –

At least they manage to safeguard the child.

And the radioactive substance in the atmosphere? Well, what in fact are people doing about this? Testing; watching –

It might be useful for people at least to have the vision.

Around and between the three *Plays For Not Acting* and *Cypher* I placed essays that I had written as a result of my reading during the long summer holiday which now seemed such a time ago; the writing of all this had taken – four, five years? The writers I had then read had all seemed concerned with the question – granted that for the human race to survive some new attitude, some new style of understanding, may have to evolve (if it does not then old systems of antagonism may simply blow us all up) then, having said this, what can be done or said from within the old systems is just to prepare the ground for such a new attitude to occur – in the knowledge that such an occurrence would depend on a coincidence of environment and chance. But then (some suggested) what is chance? Is it not simply a word for that which cannot be explained rationally: and thus might be – anything? These essays circled round Bateson, Popper, Langer, Nietzsche – even the so-called 'early' Karl Marx before his head seemed to have got jammed down on his shoulders as if by a rationalist hammer. There was also the playwright Brecht who had said that what was required on a stage was for actors to let it be known that they knew that they were acting; also – 'What matters most is that a new human type should be evolving and the entire interest of the world should be concentrated on his development.' In his politics Brecht had been a trickster: in his plays he seems to have seen that it is the opposite of a trick to recognise that actors are doing tricks upon a stage.

Sometime after I had come to the end of all this (but have I ever come to an end? What am I doing now except going back, going round and round, like the plays and the story and the essays themselves, to try to understand, to demonstrate again, to make tiny amendments so this or that might better fall through the sieve, or remain lodged in the mind?) – shortly after I had reached a state of not quite such obsessive tinkering with all this I came across an article in a scientific magazine which spoke of something called Catastrophe Theory; this was a mathematical theory which explained (so far as I understood it) how sometimes in both biology and physics there were what appeared to be steady states that took a sudden jump – flipped over on to a different level as it were – and this was the 'catastrophe' in the content of which there might be decisive change. This idea struck me with as much force as, years ago, that of an Impossible Object had done: by one's being prepared as it were for catastrophe might one not even be an agent in the mechanisms of change? It seemed that of course I should call my plays and my novel and my essays – not much to do with theory after all, but – *Catastrophe Practice*! I mean – my stumbling across this title was the sort of coincidence that happened: this was the sort of event for which my characters were practising – some style, some attitude to do with watching and listening, that might be ready for a chance, a flip-over, that might occur in the outside world – or indeed in the brain. And my characters, by their alertness, might even encourage this or that occurrence; and thus they themselves land as it were in liveliness rather than in death. Of course this is difficult to talk about. What is simple is often a lie, because there seems no need to interpret: but without recognising that you always interpret there is no truth. It does seem that this sort of situation is what humanity is facing now – There will either be some flip-over into a more embracing form of consciousness, or there will be increasing odds on a simple, antagonistic blowing-up. A matter of luck – all right – but can we not brush up our attitudes so that this piece of luck rather than that might be encouraged and even emerge? And in experience – does it not seem that some people rather than others have a greater propensity for luck? And so – for luck for the world? Sh! One can indeed hardly say this. Leave it then. Let the curtain come down. Let the audience go home. And then whatever goes on can go on secretly; in a cell, a cellar; in the mind, in the dark: which is what it does anyway –

And in the meantime –

One foot over the coal-hole –

Catastrophe practice might involve a few broken bones?

Seeds might have to hope to flourish on somewhat stony ground.

22

When I had finished *Catastrophe Practice* I imagined it was the best thing I had ever done or ever would do: I parcelled copies up in large box-files and sent them off to publisher, agent, one or two friends. It soon became apparent that the work was flipping over down a man-hole of almost limitless depth; I listened in vain for some faint ping! from the bottom. No one seemed to be interested in, let alone see, what I was up to; it seemed I had been writing in code all right, but had not provided a key.

And it was all very well for me to say – But you are looking under a lamp-post: it has to be in each person's journey in the dark, that there might be a key!

Verity and I gave a large party in the garden of our Hampstead house for 'catastrophe practice'. It was a night that blew hot and cold: people danced round braziers on the lawn.

I found it possible not to mind non-recognition all that much: what on earth had I been writing about except that new life had to lodge and to grow secretly?

Verity and I had long ago, I suppose, awoken from our dream of being fully wised-up members of some analysands' Garden of Eden: however, we still hoped to settle on a level rather better than that of Freud's ordinary human miseries. But in fact we were in the very ordinary situation of a couple with two small children – Verity's son Jonathan was now seven; our own son Marius was three – but we still hoped to see ourselves on some pilgrimage as if with a donkey:

we would find when we got there where we had wanted to go. Of course there would be pursuers – in the mind; in human nature. We had few illusions about the chances of self-protection.

My older children were now for the most part away: we let the large house in Hampstead, and lived in two fairy-tale studio-cottages at the bottom of the garden which had been derelict but which now we did up. We bought an old ruined farmhouse in the hills of Majorca and set about doing this up too and making a garden; we got a small boat in which we rowed out to sea.

These were good times: what is there to write about good times? They are to do with stillness; and further possibilities growing secretly.

The chief devil that did pursue us as we trundled along as it were with our donkey was the old archetypal one to do with a writer being torn between his family and his work. Verity and I had forsworn anything like the old high-wire romantic infidelities of which we had both been once such handy practitioners: but now as a family we were like old tumblers somewhat on top of one another in the two studios at the bottom of the garden – in one we slept; in the other life went on; but where could I write? Oh we were a lucky, if spoilt, couple all right: but Verity was eighteen years younger than me and she needed companionship and help with the children that I did not always give. This was the time when I was trying to be still and to listen for the murmurings off-stage for *Plays For Not Acting*. To allow space for us all I got a room in a basement a quarter of a mile away and there I felt I could work: could listen to – what? – myself? the murmurings of a road-mender's drill? Of course there were times when in the writing of these plays I thought I was mad – the only person in step in an army of those who, if they had understood me, still might have thought I was mad; waiting for echoes to come from the caverns of my own head. And it did seem that I was spending more and more time with this ghostly family in my head rather than with my proper goodly family up the hill – to whom I had indeed once offered hopes that I would try to be a model father. Verity began to say – I could deal with the threat of real-life mistresses! what I cannot deal with are these mistresses in your head.

Oh a common enough predicament. What can you do about it? You can try to learn to live with it – of course, in your head.

The disappearance of *Catastrophe Practice* into what seemed like a publisher's limbo or septic tank had not made me regret or abandon what I was trying to do: every time I thought of abandonment, and then looked at my plays and my experience again, I thought – Of course these are journeys into the dark; but what lightning flashes on strangely living landscapes! At the end of *Cell* there were the seeds being thrown to the audience: I thought – I must not give up; I must do more to bring these seeds to fruition. I wrote to my agent, Michael Sissons:

> I see *Plays For Not Acting* and *Cypher* as the nucleus of what in the future will be a much larger structure – a series of novels about each of the characters in *Plays* and *Cypher* separately; about their backgrounds, who they are, the turning-points in their lives, etc. These stories will for the most part be straight narrative stories; much easier for the reader than *Plays* and *Cypher*. I can do this without too much difficulty once the nucleus is there: it is the nucleus that has to be a bit mysterious because after all what I'm trying to do (as in the Essays) is to show the feel of a new way of looking at things, and I can hardly be expected to be doing this if the language of the nucleus is just something expected. But once this is done, the further building-blocks can be more simple. I think the 'need' for some such way of looking at things is there; and people will see what I am trying to do more and more as further novels come out.
>
> I have already written a bit of a novel concerning the young boy – a modern political setting – establishment politics via his family, Trotskyite politics via his friends. I've got another novel sketched concerning the middle-aged couple being involved in a film being made in Jerusalem. Then I can go back in time to the older people's childhood at the time of the First World War (as in my *Julian Grenfell*) or about youth at the time of the Spanish Civil War (as in the screenplay I've been working on now). Growing out from the nucleus of *Plays* and *Cypher* this structure could develop for as long as I could make it. I think this could be a very interesting way of doing a related series of novels – even more interesting than a series-in-time, because after all what I'm talking about is the way that series-in-time novels have naturally to do with death, whereas the way to write about life is for these to be branching out from a

286

centre in all directions as it were – as if from the nucleus of an atom or a living cell.

The 'screenplay I've been working on now' (the planned film never got off the ground) was a commissioned piece about Esmond Romilly, a young Englishman who had fought in the International Brigade in the Spanish Civil War. Part of it, like my Trotsky script, was to do with the squalid machinations of politicians. This script eventually found its way to Joe Losey, who said that he hated it. He wrote to me – You should keep away from politics! I replied – But I am writing about soldiers, who for the most part despise politicians.

Eventually *Catastrophe Practice* was taken by my old friend Tom Rosenthal, who was then managing director of Secker & Warburg. Tom said that he might not have picked up every nuance, but as a publisher he knew something interesting when he sniffed it. He said he would publish it, and any novels that might follow on from it, on condition that I would sign a contract, now, to write a book one day about my father. I said that I could write nothing about my father until he died. So this was agreed. I thought – Now Dad, live long! till I have finished two or three novels.

There were in fact a few other people at this time popping up in odd corners of the world who were showing an interest in what I was doing: this was an encouragement which counter-balanced the lack of interest in *Catastrophe Practice* at home. There were John Banks, a philosopher in Canada; John O'Brien, an editor and later publisher in America; Richard Murphet, a stage-producer in Australia. By what strange channels – underground or blown over the sea – had such seeds as I had cast out travelled! So there were three or four people ready to write seriously about and to publicise and to display my work: what more could I hope for? and what other pattern was I writing about? One of the *Plays For Not Acting*, *Landfall*, was put on in a fringe theatre in Melbourne; I went to see it. It was a brave attempt: but I wondered – Can actors ever act anything but acting? One or two of these actors however said – This play seems to be altering our lives.

The first novel of the series that I began to write after *Catastrophe*

Practice was called *Imago Bird*: it was about the boy who in the plays had been called various names but here he is just Bert – an eighteen-year-old boy who is in the gap between leaving school and going to a university. His parents are abroad; he is staying with his uncle who is a Member of Parliament and who happens to have become, just before the start of the story, a 'caretaker' Prime Minister. (Some readers said they found it difficult to empathise with the nephew of a Prime Minister: I thought – Good heavens, it would be difficult to be the nephew of a Prime Minister!) The book is written in the first person. Bert opens his story with – Ever since I can remember I have thought the grown-up world to be mad. He finds himself behind the scenes of the central political establishment; he also has a girlfriend who is a member of a Trotskyite revolutionary group. So Bert moves between one set of histrionics and another. At times he has to hide away in alarm from what he sees as absurd; at times he is able to look down on the dramas around him with some illumination.

He is helped to maintain equilibrium by going to a psychoanalyst: he has been sent to this analyst because he has a stammer. This analyst is Dr Eleanor Anders – the old lady from *Cypher* and the *Plays*. I mean a reader can see this if he wishes to watch for connections; what Bert sees is simply – Here is someone, at last, who seems able to understand that one lives with one foot in and one foot out of the maelstrom of worldly dramas. Dr Anders is interested not so much in just curing Bert of his stammer (a cure would be a by-product) as in helping him to look at what might be at the back of it – the fact that if you see clearly other people's histrionics, you are likely yourself to be awkward with words. Bert sees – Words for the most part are not used for the transfer of information; they are used to attack, to justify, to charm, to defend; and indeed perhaps a stammerer wishes to do none of these things. (A therapist had once said to me – Perhaps you do not wish to get rid of your stammer! I had been outraged by this until, years later, I had accepted – You mean, I may need to protect myself from the aggression and special pleading of words?) Eleanor Anders becomes a mentor, a catalyst, to Bert: she is a more fruitful form of protection

– a tree under whose branches for a while he can shelter and from which seeds might fall.

Bert is on his way to becoming some sort of *imago* – the 'final and perfect stage of an insect after it has undergone its metamorphosis'. No human is 'final' nor 'perfect'; but with 'metamorphosis' you are on the move; and 'bird' is an image for the Holy Spirit – so perhaps after all the process might be one to be called perfect.

Bert wants to be a director of films: he has an idea for a new way of filming. The screen would split into separate frames so that two or more separate events of a story could be seen going on side-by-side; an action that one actor does in one part of the screen might bulge out from this part and nudge as it were something that another actor is doing in another; this might be a way of representing how life is to do with the operation of networks and patterns; with what of these might be listened for and looked for; such activity thereby affecting what might be going on round some corner. For the most part in Bert's daily life things seem to occur haphazardly (this is how he sees politics). Then sometimes there are people who pop up in his personal life who seem to be portents, or pointers. Apart from Eleanor there is a girl called Judith with whom he falls in love; by 'love' he feels – This is someone with whom his life will be, is, interwoven in a network. And towards the end of the book, just by having been able perhaps to look down on the crazy world around him from some slightly different level, it is he who is able to give some slight nudge to his oh-so-worldly Uncle Bill and Aunt Mavis – so that even their world might be slightly less crazy. And at the very centre of the story – not all that obviously of course: how could something so vital and vulnerable be obvious? – at the very centre of the story is the child: the child that is gestating in the womb of his sister Lilia (this is set before the story in *Cypher*): the child whose father is probably Jason but might be Max: and so – in this world still so frightened by convention – Lilia has been thinking of getting rid of the child. She goes to a clinic to find out about this – there is a catastrophe knife-edge here – will or will not the child survive? As it happens, while Lilia waits in the clinic, she rings up Dr Anders because she is worred about Bert; in talking to her Dr Anders says – You talk about Bert as if he were your child.

So Lilia, who loves Bert, walks out of the clinic. By one or two coincidences the child survives.

At the centre of all the books in the *Catastrophe Practice* series there is the question of the survival and the birth of the child. By what series of coincidences (but are they coincidences?) does a potential child – a seed on its journey to and within the womb or the mind – survive?

You do not talk about coincidences much, or how would you be watching and listening for them to occur?

In his 'acting' life Bert feels himself in the position of some sort of Hamlet – with all the uproar of a lavish production on stage. Bert's mother has in fact had an affair with his uncle; but, Bert feels – So what? Unless people are insane, they know that at the end of *Hamlet* the litter of dead bodies can get up and take curtain-calls at the front of the stage.

And then there you are, out of the theatre and bumping on your way again through the maze.

What Verity and I had to learn I suppose was that by seeing predicaments in inside or outside worlds one does not get rid of them. We had learned something about right relationships with children; in particular I had learned from Verity that it is by spontaneous demonstrations of emotion rather than by cautious concern about what the emotion should be that children learn that they are loved. What Verity and I had not learned how to deal with, nor indeed to love, were the infants as it were that so often still screamed and yelled inside ourselves. It may be that one never wholly gets rid of these primitive parts of one: they are even ever more visible to us as they come out into the light. One has to learn to look after them? How? I was suggesting – By treating them as if they were characters on a stage? And so in the end one might get so bored with their (one's own) performances that one might indeed get up and leave the theatre (I've seen this play before! Sorry! Let me out!).

– Oedipus Rex meets Hedda Gabler in the marital bed. He says to her – I'm fed up to the eyeballs with your talk! She says to him – I'm sorry, but the gun went off in my hand. And the consequence was ———. And the world said ———. But we did not know the consequence yet. And who cared what the world said.

I wanted to explain – Adam and Eve would have learned nothing if they had stayed in their Garden! We really do know this now. And all right, there are harder things to learn every time round –

– But why should it always be me who has to bring forth in sorrow – (Eve).

– But you and I are also the snake, you see – (Adam).

– You crawl on your belly?

– Yes, yes, I am a yelling fifty-year-old snake still requiring attention, requiring food, requiring love (please note that I am talking of myself): an out-of-control snake, on the loose like Frankenstein's monster into whom someone has put the wrong brain; one that wants to have its love and eat it; one that even when he is offered attention, offered food, offered love, wants to go off and write about it – picking up words and even the fate of children perhaps to throw them like petals into the river – she loves me, she loves me not – and then trundling off bellowing like someone inside the red-hot bull of Phalaris –

– You mean –

– But what an amazing achievement if this is what we have learned!

– You think so?

– Of course we have to trust –

– Trust what? –

– Trust that if one trusts when things go on in the dark, then –

– Yes?

The novel that I began to write after *Imago Bird* was called *Serpent* – the serpent being that which indeed got Adam and Eve out of the Garden of Eden; that enabled them (though of course they did not at first see this) to embark on the journey by which they might become like gods. This is what God himself foresaw? that one day, after hundreds and thousands of years, they might have gone right round the world and come back to the Garden again by the back way –

– The Garden of Gethsemane!

– And of the Tree of Life.

The protagonists of *Serpent* are the married couple, Lilia and Jason, parents of the child. They were represented in the *Plays*, but more specifically as themselves in *Cypher*. In *Serpent* the child is aged three or four, so this story is later in time than both *Imago Bird* and *Cypher*. Jason is a writer working on the script for a film; the film is to be about Josephus – the Jewish leader who in AD 70, in the war of the Jews against the Romans, in a town in which Jews were effectively besieged, managed to get out of a Jewish suicide pact and went over to the Romans – and for this has been execrated by Jews ever since. Jason and the director of the film and two of its potential stars are on a reconnaissance trip to Israel to look for locations; Jason has with him the rough first draft of a script. This script is what he has wanted to write but it is not what he thinks will be acceptable – there is a sense in which he wrote it because he wants to get out of films. He is with the film people travelling first class, also in the plane but in the tourist class are Jason's wife Lilia and their child; Jason and Lilia have quarrelled just before take-off, because Jason has not wanted to get them into the first class compartment because he needs to carry out his battle with the film people on his own. But both he and Lilia know that theirs is a formal quarrel; it is thus that they have to show that they care about not being with one another. And of course they trust!

In the first-class compartment the film people have hatched some plot against Lilia and Jason – the film people are bored and destructive – they know that Lilia and Jason are supposed to have a successful marriage; they plan to break this up. Their plot is to try to get the male film-star's boyfriend, who is also in the third class compartment, by some bizarre and obscene trick to seduce Lilia. To some extent this trick works. But then there is the overriding question – So what?

In the meantime Jason, in first class, has shown the director and the film-stars his script: to them the script seems obviously absurd. How can this self-mocking, self-reflective stuff be acted? It is about people who use acting, tricks, for some quite different ends. The script has taken the traditional story of Josephus and turned it upside down: Josephus now seems to be offering demonstrations about how profitably to get out of murderously self-destructive situations and plots. This may indeed depend on tricks – but tricks to survive the threat of deathly compulsions. Josephus (and thus Jason) seems to be saying – You have to practise to stay alive: there will always be people who out of envy will want to destroy you. And this is what, in the aeroplane, is happening between Jason and Lilia and the film people. Of course the film people can make out very little of what Jason's script is about; or how could they be what they are? There is one woman, however – the secretary of the director – who seems to understand what Jason is saying; and so, to survive, must she too not get out of films? She tells Jason of the plot against himself and Lilia. Oh yes, this is the sort of thing against which he and Lilia hope to have practised: they can defend themselves, surely: but what of the child?

What do you protect, what do you risk, in order for not just yourself but that which you care about to survive?

Serpent contains the story of what happens in the aeroplane, also scenes from Jason's script about life in Judaea and Rome in the AD 60s and 70s. By learning to look at archetypal destructive and self-destructive impulses, situations, and their antidotes, one might learn oneself to survive? What you trust is – that by looking at the age-old scripts you are stuck with in your heads, you may learn the trick of recognising the non-trick that is the fact that the gods within you, the gods outside you, are on your side.

Well, how did Josephus survive?

(– And Queen Berenice, and the Emperor Nero and the Empress Poppaea –)

(– You didn't know they survived?)

(– Of course not, or how would they have survived –)

– And the six children and a woman who miraculously lived through the suicide pact at the siege of Masada? –

(Sh! They were also said to be traitors –)

– And Lilia and Jason and their child, and the red-haired secretary –

And so on. And of course there is the question of who now in the besieged state of Israel will or will not survive.

My novels that follow *Catastrophe Practice* are different from the ones that precede it because the protagonists do not feel themselves to be on their own even when they are watching themselves and involved in tricks like those on one-wheel bicycles; they feel themselves as part of some network – the sort of network that my friend Mary of *The Rainbearers* had written about so long ago – to do with the recognition, indeed the trust, that if you pay attention to what seems true inside you then something is affected on the outside; that what happens to this person here can be linked to what happens to that person there; that there are nudges and also moments of great wonder as one goes through the maze. Again – one cannot talk much about this: agents in hostile territory cannot talk much to one another. But they might recognise one another and wave – Coo-ee! One of the characters in *Imago Bird* says – The only two emotions worth having are ecstasy and despair – ecstasy being when you know there is a network, and despair being when you do not.

In *Serpent* the focus of the network is in relation to the child. What matters, in the end, is what survives. A child is that through which one sort of life or another goes on.

At the end of *Serpent* the child finds in the sand of a beach in Israel an old medallion with on one side of it the image of a bird flying with the twig of a tree in its beak, and on the other the image of a serpent with its tail in its mouth. This medallion is like a coin: there are heads on both sides; the tail has been swallowed.

But what was happening in my own life at this time?

In 1980 my father died. I was sad: I had learned much from him! But now had come the time when I should fulfil my undertaking to my publisher and write some memoir or biography of my father. I had written three books in the *Catastrophe Practice* series.

I had no idea what might have survived of my father's papers.

My father had been involved in some form of self-destruction, but had survived. My mother had not.

I thought – Perhaps I will find here patterns to do with my own self-destruction or survival.

23

I had been on good terms with my father since my second marriage. He got on well with Verity – not because she agreed with his politics, but because they made each other laugh. He would visit us in our London house; we would stay with him and Diana at Orsay. My father had become mellow in his old age; he suffered from Parkinson's disease, and it was as if his very frailty made many of the barriers come down which had prevented him from looking at himself and at his past. Verity and I spent a weekend at Orsay ten days before he died; he would appear in the drawing-room quite early in the morning and open a bottle of pink champagne – it had been his habit almost never to appear socially before lunch – and he would want to talk to me about the past; about my mother, about his infidelities, about the effects of promiscuity on marriage and public life. He said – I sometimes wonder whether, if I had not done so much of that sort of thing when I was young, I might have done better in public life. I said – Dad, it might have been that sort of thing that kept you from doing worse in public life. He laughed.

I told him that I thought a biography of him should be written that would include all sides of his life; that it was the relation between his inner energy and outer events that might explain his life. He had aimed very high, he had gambled, and had failed, all right: but could it not be said of him as of Faust, that the very exaggeratedness of his effort gave some redemption? And in fact there had been no severe horrors in his public life: perhaps he had been saved from these by not achieving power: but then perhaps his devil-may-care attitude had saved him from this. There was in existence the excellent political biography of him by Robert Skidelsky, but for this he had made available none of his private papers. My father listened to me while I went on about all this; and at lunch that day he announced that when he died he wished me to have his papers. That was the last time I saw him.

No one seemed to know what private papers and letters had survived. When he had been imprisoned during the war his belongings had been sifted by security officials; after imprisonment he had moved houses frequently, and the house in Ireland in which he had settled had burned down and many family belongings had been lost. The house at Orsay was small and could not hold much of what had survived, so books and papers had been stored in the cellars of a neighbouring house in Ireland belonging to Diana's brother-in-law. Here they had languished for twenty-five years. Some time after my father's funeral I went to join Diana and my half-brother Alexander at this house to see what papers there might be.

A great number of sacks like those containing potatoes were carried up from the cellars; out of these sacks tumbled – newspapers, pamphlets, magazines; and then an extraordinary number of letters from the time of my father's and mother's life together. Even more extraordinarily there were a great many letters from the time of my mother's childhood; also to do with the childhood of my sister and myself. It seemed that my mother had preserved these and nothing much had been thrown away since the time of my mother's death nearly fifty years ago. It was soon clear that there was indeed material for the sort of book I had thought should be written. Diana and Alexander agreed I should take what papers I liked.

It is difficult to see all the ins and outs behind wanting to write a book about one's father. I thought it would be to his advantage to show him as I felt he truly was: but was this also in order to be able to say – I told you so? To some extent, of course. But with my father there did seem a specific job to be done. Many of his contemporaries had known the complexities of his story and of his character – they had known him as a young Tory radical and a Labour militant before he became a Fascist; they also knew his reputation for charm and intelligence and wit. But there was a generation now that knew none of this, that had an image of him simply as an anti-Semitic thug – even as someone who had been 'on Hitler's side in the war'. This sort of thing my children were now having to contend with: sometimes it seemed that I had had less of this kind of trouble in the days when I had been at school. So I thought at least I could help to lay to rest one or two false spectres here. But if I was to be believed in this area, it would have to be felt that I was telling the truth in others. And about his private life 'telling the truth' would inevitably involve – as well as the charm, the intelligence, the wit – those other manifestations of energy by which people had got hurt.

It did not seem to me that there would be a betrayal here. Had not my father himself been so open about such things: he had known – With energy, is there not, unfortunately, likely to be some hurt?

Rather, what I had found difficult to understand about my father had been – How could someone apparently so sophisticated in private life have let himself go so far down the road of a primitive style of politics – and a style which, after an initial period of euphoria, had seemed increasingly likely to lead to some self-destruction or even what people might imagine as dishonour? But it was just this that I hoped to explain – and thus the judgement on this to change – by an account of his private life. His attitudes in private life had been those of a buccaneer, a one-man band; these seemed to have been his attitudes in politics. He was no sinister Machiavellian schemer. While other Fascist leaders dedicated themselves remorselessly to gigantic schemes of destruction and self-destruction, my father had gone on his way following personal desires and dreams. He had been driven; but in the style of a gambler.

All this I wanted to say. It did not seem that by this I would be doing a disservice to my father.

There remained the question of what, in such a book, I would write about my mother.

In my psychoanalysis it had seemed that my problems with my father were out in the open: but how little I knew of my mother! She was said to have been saintly: but also a victim. Not long after her death I had been told – You know, don't you, that your father by his infidelities was responsible for her death? I had thought both – That is nonsense! – and – She had three children to live for!

Had she really been a helpless victim? In the end are not people – especially saintly people – responsible for themselves?

When I started going through the sackfuls of papers I found many letters from my father to my mother but none, at first, from her to him. His early letters to her were nearly always cheerful, reassuring; they were like those of an ebullient schoolboy boasting of his exploits to his sister or mother. These exploits were political and social. Occasionally it seemed that my mother read between the lines – There might be other exploits here too. But then my father argued so charmingly – Any exploits in a sexual area are so trivial, so silly; how could such flirtations be of any account in a high-flying love such as that between him and my mother?

Perhaps in the end one does not have much chance of getting away with this sort of thing: but to be sure people try.

From the first my stepmother Diana gave me every help in all my enquiries: I went to stay at Orsay; we talked through much of the day and evenings. Over the years we had talked exhaustively about my father's politics; there did not seem all that much more to be said about this now. About his private life – Diana seemed to agree that it would be good for the boisterous personal side of my father to come out, because this would explain, yes, his devil-may-care attitudes in politics. So she patiently supplied me with details of his love-affairs at the time he was married to my mother, about which he had told her. She made up for any omissions in letters to me later. She wrote of his theory, much admired by Randolph Churchill, that a man should 'span' at least fifty years, 'beginning with a woman 20 years older when he was 18, and then 30 years younger when he was 60.' She said he had told her a story which implied he had had an affair with his sister-in-law while my mother was still alive, a story which later I came to believe was untrue.

In his Conservative Party days my father had been enough of a gambler to have risked his political career by running after the wives of influential party members. I thought I understood why Diana was telling me these things – to emphasise my father's insouciance – but later I realised that of course Diana might be telling me all this also in order to emphasise the rickety nature of my mother's and father's marriage so that her own later entrance on to the scene might not seem too catastrophic. (She met my father just over a year before my mother's death.)

There came a day at Orsay when Diana gave me a packet of letters from my mother to my father which she said my father had always kept near his bed. She said she had skimmed through these letters, some of which were very sad, but some of which indeed showed that the sadness had started before she, Diana, had come on to the scene. She said she wanted me to have these letters, and hoped that I would not be sad.

In many of these letters my mother showed an exuberance to match my father's; at first she had been no victim! She adored, cajoled, complained, nagged, teased: she was so young! She was twenty when she met my father and thirty-four when she died. In the early letters there was an anxiety that often seemed to have nothing much to do with what might be going on in the outside world. She seems to be saying – How unfair it is that I do not seem to have as much energy as you! that I do not always keep up with you! I am anxious, yes, about my dependence. But then as time went on it did seem obvious that she had my father's love-affairs to complain about in the outside world. And towards the end of her life the letters did become very sad.

But she and my father had loved. And their story was the stuff of ordinary human tragedy; not a morality play about evil versus good. Or so it seemed to me.

My mother could have left my father if she had chosen; she had a lot of money of her own. Of course there was a sense in which emotionally she could not – but then this precisely is the stuff of tragedy.

Humans can either learn – or refuse to believe that humans are responsible for themselves.

299

My mother's tragedy was that she had so little time to learn. She had died of peritonitis at the age of thirty-four.

But for me at least in her letters something of my mother came alive. She had fought! I was glad that some old ghosts about her helplessness were laid to rest. I saw how sometimes she might have wanted to die; but does not anyone of any sensibility sometimes want to die? It seemed to be the people around her who had made a meal of her dying.

So I wrote my book. It made sense to see the work in two parts, the first dealing with my father's marriage to my mother and his life as a Conservative and then a Labour politician, ending with his founding of the British Union of Fascists in 1932, closely followed by my mother's death. This was one story. Then a second part would deal with Fascism and his second marriage.

But there came a time when I was approaching the end of a readable draft of the first part when it began to strike me – What, after all, might be this strange game (was it a game?) that Diana and I were playing: would she really like what I was writing? I did not think she would mind my account of the conventional politics of the 1920s – many of her views about this and mine would coincide – but what in fact of my father's affairs, and of his tempestuous marriage to my mother? Oh yes Diana herself was giving me information about this – perhaps she wanted to protect herself regarding the role she had played – but there was more to her instinct, I felt, than just this. Very often over the years I had been able to talk with extraordinary openness with Diana about my father; it had seemed that besides her loyalty she herself had a need, and indeed an ability, to see my father clearly; she was able to see his faults, his dangers; she was able to talk of these, sometimes, to me. She was able to do this because after all I, like she, was not outraged by my father; and she knew that in the end he himself could usually laugh about his excesses. Over the years Diana had told me things about my father that she said she had not said to anyone else; and then she had said – Do not say I said that! And I have not. So it seemed to me now, as I approached the end of the first part of my book, that Diana might properly have a need to clear her heart and mind of some of the things she felt about my father – often contradictory things (how could they not be?) – and giving me help to write my book might be one way for her to do this.

But then I remembered the time some twenty years earlier when my half-brother Alexander had been in trouble with my father and I had taken up Alexander's cause and at first Diana had backed me and indeed had been open about the difficulties for anyone involved with my father. But then when Alexander was out of my father's way she had turned and claimed that with regard to my father there had never been much need for anyone to be anything except loyal! – and had blamed me for the part I had played. And I began to feel that there were echoes, and portents, of this old situation here: Diana might be using my writing of the book to sort out and liberate some of the complexities that she felt about my father, but then when this was done she would be able to revert to a more simple form of loyalty.

She would never be able to write herself, I thought, of what she truly knew of my father. In her own autobiography, published some years before, how much she could have written of enormous interest – not only about my father but indeed about Hitler and Goebbels with whom she had been friends – and yet how she had kept hidden almost everything of significance for the sake of so-called loyalty. But still – some part of her must be wanting me to give what she knew an airing.

Just at this time Diana came across, by chance, my biography of Father Raynes; she said she had never heard of it before. She wrote to me to say how much she liked it: 'his goodness shines through'. I thought – Perhaps it is this that has encouraged her to help me so much with the biography of my father.

Then suddenly Diana had to have a serious operation in which a large tumour was removed from her brain. I visited her in the London Hospital: on one side of her bed were some of her old Mitford friends, and on the other some of my father's old East-End followers. I thought – what strange complexities indeed have to be embraced by a life; by a brain!

On my last visit to Orsay there was a cupboard in my father's old room which contained papers that I had not seen before: these were to do with the time after my mother's death, with my father's and

Diana's life together, with the time of Diana's friendships with the Nazis. Diana said that I could take and use what I liked of these papers for the second part of the book. I did not quite know what to do about this. I did take, and later use, such few bits and pieces as seemed proper. But before this my publishers said that they wished to publish the first part that was now nearly complete as a separate first volume.

When I was back in London I wrote to Diana:

Darling Diana,   31 January 1982
    Thank you so much for my time at Orsay. You are so brave. I sometimes get overwhelmed by writing this stuff about Dad; then I feel it is all right. I think you feel as I do that I've got to make the effort to see Dad as he was: to try to make him a safe person I'll only be belittling him. I've got to make him Faustian (in the sense that he would understand this) or I'll lose all sense about him. I suppose you won't always exactly *like* everything I've written, but I'm determined that you shall think it true. And then, in the end, this is what one does like – as you say.
    I don't want anyone to see it until I've got every word as right as I can: feelings so often depend on an almost-chance word. Then, when it's as right as I can get it, I'll show it to you if you like.

Soon after this I got a clean typescript and sent a copy to Diana. While I waited I thought – Perhaps this will be like one of my plays in which there is such-and-such going on on-stage and just the glimpse, hint, of something quite different going on elsewhere. But about the latter – does this not have to be trusted?

A day or two later I got a letter from Diana that I was enormously grateful for: it was warm and encouraging in spite of sadness. With its heartfelt style it was of a kind that I should have liked to quote in full.

She began by saying my book was 'fascinating, beautifully written, excellent, funny, unbearably tragic'. She went on to say that she did not think I had stressed enough my father's incredible optimism and that I made him seem rather 'like a conjuror, and when you look in the hat there is nothing there'. In these respects she felt it was not a fair portrait; and she was afraid that the time was perhaps too soon for such a book, because of the 'Roman holiday' that would be made of stories of his private life by 'stupid newspapers'.

What she felt was unbearably tragic was the story of my mother's unhappiness about which she, Diana, had had no means of knowing; my father had been such a well-known philanderer that she had not worried. If she had known, she said, she might in some ways have acted differently: as it was, she felt she came out of the story as 'a villainess of the deepest dye'. She asked me to believe that it was not only passion that she had clung to, together with a profound faith in my father's ideas and ideals, but 'a feeling so definite as to be knowledge that we were made for each other'.

She asked me to take care to keep a balance in the second volume, but ended by reassuring me that she would continue to help with this – 'All fond love, do come over. I've found so many old letters . . .'

I thought this was a wonderful letter, and telephoned Diana to say so. I said that I was sure that in no way would people think that she, a twenty-two-year-old girl at the time, was a villainess (in this I was right; when the book came out reviewers went out of their way to say so). And with regard to my father – of course in the twenties he had been a bit of a conjuror; his serious commitment to politics would come out in the second volume when he was running his own movement. And about his private life – surely the only people who would think the worse of him about this were those whose hostility to him was so entrenched that they would think the worst of him about anything. (About this I was not so right: I had not realised how immovable many people's hostility to him remained; had not reckoned with the bizarre puritanism of some reviewers who were suddenly savagely censorious of my father's pursuit of women as if none of them had ever run after a woman in his life.)

But this was in the future: for the moment, I was so encouraged by Diana's letter! It was the dignified and heartfelt reaction of someone indeed struggling with love and loyalty on the one hand, and on the other the courage to face much of what she recognised as true. She made one request which was that I should remove the name of her first husband from my script, which I did; and she appended eight hand-written pages of suggested amendments and corrections of detail, all of which I paid attention to. Then four days later came another letter.

Just as it is difficult to paraphrase the quality of Diana's first letter, so is it difficult to convey the opposite quality of hostility of the second.

It began by saying that she had dashed off her first letter to try to save her first husband from pain. Now she would give me a more considered opinion, which was that my book was a bitter attack on my father, on his politics and on his whole being, such as no enemy but only an insider could have written. By publishing the intimate letters between him and my mother I had given the press the chance to attack him in an area in which he had hitherto been unassailable. She had never read the letters she had given me, and had trusted me to make proper use of them. Instead I had painted the portrait of 'a brute and a fool'. There was nothing to be done about this because it was the bitter tone throughout the book that was so painful. The book was brilliantly done, so that it would be read for its excellence as well as for its scandal and tragedy. She asked – Had I felt no love; no admiration for 'his nobility, his courage, his endurance'? She ended: 'Oh Nicky, I started this letter "darling" and to me you have been a darling, but my poor wonderful real darling – you have kicked him below the belt over and over again.'

I thought – Oh damn, here we go again.

It is not just that someone has got at her?

(Of course the name of her first husband could always easily be removed!)

– So what is it that she really minds: not the love-affairs? Is it the baby-talk in the letters between my father and my mother –

– Baby-talk being the language of love? Is it the realisation that my father and my mother had a true sort of marriage?

But surely this makes her, Diana's, later successful marriage to my father more remarkable, rather than less!

It is my way of telling of the dark things as well as of the light that seems disloyal?

– But in simple eulogy there is no sense of truth: it was this sort of atmosphere around my father that was always so damaging to him!

It seemed that there might be something irreconcilable here – between people who think that loyalty is expressed by protection from reality, and those who do not –

– And for the former, who need to keep the heroic image of my father intact, there might always be the need of a scapegoat.

But Diana had said that there was nothing of substance to be changed. And she had not in fact said that what I had written was untrue.

24

Because Diana had only asked for minor alterations and had not said that she would try to stop the book, it seemed to me that, as I had imagined, part of her might almost sense that it would be good for the book to come out, and that it would just be necessary for her, with another part of her, to make a public protest about this. And so it seemed, as before, that the best I might do was simply to sit things out. But then it appeared there was a danger that with the backing of other members of the family who were showing strikingly hostile reactions, there might be a concerted effort to get it stopped, and Diana might change her mind; and if I was to prevent this, I had to fight. For years my father and Diana and others of their family had shown a withering contempt for any 'turning of the other cheek': they claimed that this was only asking for both cheeks to be given a slap. Because of this, and because there was a part of me that was irked at accusations of lack of love and loyalty, I wrote to Diana a letter that contained its own brand of exaggerations:

Darling Diana,   20 March 1982
   On what level do I try to answer your letter?
   1. For the last fifty years or so of his life Dad cocooned himself with admirers and sycophants who told him how wonderful he was and gave him no criticism except that which he could laugh at or treat with contempt. I think it was these (and his appetite for them) that prevented him being taken seriously in the post-war world.

Yes I was fond of him, and I did love him, but for the last thirty years he did ward off any criticism I gave him, mocked it even with all that anti-Christian stuff, and I did rage from time to time against his acceptance of the people who kept him protected and, as I saw it, thus politically doomed. You yourself seemed to play an amazing role in all this; because although in some sense you kept him more protected than anyone, you also, it seemed to me, appeared to see what you were doing – this after all was your proper role – and you also seemed to see pretty well everything that I saw, in fact at moments you precisely formed what I saw. There is very little of the attitudes I express in this book that you have not expressed to me over the years, especially over the last year; how else have I got so many of the details of my story? Your *tone* of expression might be different: but with your tone you could hardly write anything of the truth of what you knew at all – this is what I did not like about your autobiography, that with all your knowledge you seemed to say almost nothing. My tone, I believe, is not one of hostility: it is one, often, of irony, yes; because I think this is the proper (almost only) tone in which to write of the things I have to write about. But other readers have felt my irony to be affectionate and kindly. It is only other members of our family (it seems to me) who have this crazy idea that by protecting Dad from any idea of adult self-responsibility they will somehow make him seem adult and responsible.

2. When I was coming to the end of the book the idea did begin to form in my mind that what would happen would be just what has happened – I would finish the book, you would read it, you would say how excellent, funny and fascinating it was, you would say that there was almost nothing untrue about it, but that of course it was incomplete (Vol. II to come): but then, after a week or so, the whole self-justifying we-have-no-responsibility it's-all-the-fault-of-someone-else mechanism would start turning and I would be cast in the role of the wicked demon who has kicked in the teeth the immaculate victim . . . It's all a repetition of that time twenty years ago when you asked me to help rescue Alexander from Dad which I proceeded to try to do (by no means all that nobly or well) but then when Al was to some (though dangerous) extent free, you turned on me with letters saying how wicked and irresponsible I had been, and I was fed with stories about Dad's jeers at do-gooders. And then a month ago you were saying that of course about that time I was right and Dad was wrong. (This doesn't make me think that I was right: I was playing with the sort of fire that I haven't done again.) But the point is you KNOW and always have done as

much as I do the ways in which Dad was crazy: what you have chosen is also much of the time NOT to know it: and *I* don't blame *you* for this: this is what I think life has often to be like. I don't know how much I mind your pouring all this blame upon me now: I think I mind quite a lot – expecting that something will happen doesn't make it any more palatable.

3. You told me you had read my mother's letters (some or much of them); we discussed the very sad letters; you told me of the letter about my father's affair with —— which you said made you feel better about yourself. I am sorry if the way I have told the story has affected you in a way in which you have not been affected before: I do NOT think other people will feel the story in the way that you feel it now: I do not think they will see you as a villainess (in fact no one who has read the book does except yourself). I think the people who from it will think I see Dad as a villain are those who have thought of him as a god. But for a few people around him to have thought of Dad as a god has made him for forty years almost worthless to people further afield: what I had hoped is that by my book he may be liberated from these terrible and crippling swaddling bands of adoration or hatred and what he stood for may at last be able to grow up. The only way in which a writer in 1981 can make the Fascist movement of the 20s and 30s seem reasonable or even heroic is by portraying the late 20s and early 30s as a period of such farce that it was brave and logical for a politician to try for something different – but he would have had to have felt something of the farce *in himself* or the whole effort would be suspect from the beginning – he would simply be suffering from paranoia. The sort of book that you would, I imagine, have wanted me to write would have resulted for the thousandth time in people just feeling that Dad was something out of a fairy story – and thus continuing to give him no serious thought whatsoever.

There was indeed some special pleading here: did I really think that in my next volume I was going to make Fascism seem reasonable and heroic? Oh well, 'heroic' in some self-destructive sense perhaps. And my criticisms had not had much in them of 'irony'. But my letter was my own effort to be heartfelt and it did seem to serve its purpose: in fact after it Diana and I corresponded fairly amicably for a time. She asked me to make one or two more omissions, which I did – one of them about my father's practical jokes. She made it clear that it was the letters between my father and my mother that she thought were 'by far the worst part . . . if only you would take them out!' But she did not seem seriously to be pressing this; and if what she disliked about these letters was that they showed the closeness of my mother's and father's relationship, I did not see why I should take this out. I wrote to say that I hoped by the end of the second volume 'what will be seen of Dad will be as serious as it can be got, by me at least'; also – 'I am desperately sorry that you are so hurt, I do not know what to do about this, you have been very good to me recently and over the years.' Diana wrote – 'Darling Nicky, thank you for a much less horrid letter.' Then there was nothing much more to be done until the book came out.

When this happened the book got a lot of coverage and there were several reviews that said I had obviously wanted to do as well as I could by my father ('his dedicated search for the truth about this remarkable man is clearly a labour of love': Anthony Storr in the *Sunday Times*); but there were other reviews that indeed pounced with glee on the details of my father's and mother's private life, and thus at least by implication questioned my purpose and sense in thus exposing him. I had (though 'perhaps unwittingly') 'emptied a bucket of mud over his head' (*The Times*); others commented that from my story my father emerged as 'cruelly ruthless' 'savage', 'hypocritical', 'vain and breathtakingly arrogant'. It was true that I had not expected the violence of this sort of thing; what these people were talking about was my father's propensity for going to bed with women! He had hurt my mother, yes; but it is not unusual for married couples thus to hurt one another. All this was being used as a stick to beat my father.

So in this respect Diana had been more right than I had expected: still, she was treating so respectfuly the opinions of people whom she would previously have treated with contempt: and indeed what political leader is not at times 'ruthless' and 'breathtakingly arrogant'? But Diana could now use these reviews as a stick with which to attack me. She wrote letters to the press, gave interviews, referred to my book as 'sad little tittle-tattle . . . second-rate psychology like a cheap novel, nauseating and monstrous . . . the degraded work of a very little man'. About myself she went on in interviews and letters to the press:

It is all very well to have an Oedipus complex at 19, a second-rate son hating a brilliant father, but it's rather odd at 60 . . . Nicholas wants to get his own back on his father for having had more fun than he's had . . . It's appalling to have published those letters and it's appalling to try to take away the whole of his incredible cleverness and genius and make him into a frivolous playboy . . . If his father were alive he would doubtless laugh at such a classical example of filial jealousy . . . but in this case there is also nauseating hypocrisy. Nicholas Mosley said in an interview that he loved his father, which even for a Hampstead Thinker is going too far.

My half-brother Max had a dossier printed in which there were quotes from reviews that might seem most damaging to my father, together with copies of letters I had written to Max before publication saying that I was sure that in the end my book would not seem damaging to my father. Max circulated this dossier to members of Diana's and my family together with a copy of a letter from him to me. Max's quotations from the reviews were indeed damaging – to me as well as well to my father. His point in his letter was that I must have known that such reviews would occur, and so I had set out deliberately to destroy my father. In so doing I had hurt the whole family – the prospects for the younger generation to lead a normal life – and I had done this from the privileged position of having a private income. I had done a hatchet-job on my father because I had resented him laughing at me and my work, and telling stories that showed me as 'a confused hypocrite'. My worst sin was my present 'ghastly, drivelling, hypocritical pose' that I was doing this to try to restore my father's image. Max's peroration was on the lines of – When I died no one would be interested in my dismal love-affairs or unread novels. Max's letter indeed showed the passion of resentment against me: but was this not a mark of the family's own reluctance to look at any truth about my father?

Almost any biography that concerns people still living is liable to cause some upset, but the emotions aroused here seemed peculiarly violent. On the surface what seemed still to be the focus of family outrage (and what provided reviewers with poison for their barbs) was the matter of publishing my mother's and father's letters – those passionate, rending, crying-out-and-reassuring baby-talk letters in which my father was like a fencer and my mother was like someone wearing her heart upon her sleeve. Was it this that people reacted to – that emotions usually hidden were here so open! There seemed to be awakened here in readers personal rages and resentments and hurts. There was also the continuing impression with regard to the family at least that my book was a diversion and protection from any emotional reassessments they might have had to make.

In the meantime there was the pressing question of my second volume, which by now was almost ready to go to the publishers. This was the volume by which I hoped, even with regard to those most hostile, to restore my father's image. But this time Diana was making it clear that she would try to prevent or to cripple publication. My publisher's lawyers received a letter from her lawyers in which she expressly forbade both myself and my publisher to use 'any letters or papers of which she owns the copyright as Sir Oswald's universal legatee in any book he may write or you publish'. This was a serious move, because Diana held the copyright of much of the material on which my second volume depended. But I told my editor at Secker & Warburg, Barley Alison, that I did not think that this threat was to be as much feared as it might seem; this was for reasons that were difficult to explain but were to do with the fact that Diana had not tried to prevent the first volume being published, and my impression that with some by now doubtless almost unconscious part of her she had not wanted to prevent it, but only to feel free to abuse it afterwards. In a remarkable act of faith Barley agreed that Seckers would go ahead with plans for publishing the second volume as I had written it; and we would see what would happen.

The pattern of the second volume had seemed to fall into place as that of the first had done: I was able to show my father's passionate commitment to his own brand of politics – there was no more playboy image. I could also show, which had seemed to me important, that his fight for peace in the run-up to the 1939 war was in no conceivable way involved with treachery. And I hoped that if I was felt to have been truthful about other things, then I might be felt to be truthful about this.

In the first volume I had tried to balance some so-called 'objective' view of my father with my own memories and impressions of him when I was a child; I had hoped that this dimension would give immediacy and liveliness to the story. Towards the end of this second volume I brought myself into the story even more; the years when my father had been in prison and I had been in the army were the years in which in some ways I had been closest to him; I had spent days visiting him in prison: we had written each other long letters about life, literature, philosophy. I brought these letters into the book to show the knowledgeable and speculative and humorous side of my father. I also told the story of my wartime career in the army; I wanted to show the ways in which I both had been and yet had not been influenced by my father; about how one of the gifts he had passed on had perhaps been the ability to break away.

It was towards the end of the book that there was first the problem – In so far as it had seemed proper to tell 'bad' things as well as 'good' about my father, would I not thus have to tell the same about myself? There was, for instance, a letter which I had written to my father when he was in jail and I had gone from school to Oxford for a scholarship exam; I wrote to him that Balliol appeared to be 'stiff with Jews'. I was of course ashamed of this now; but I thought I should put it in; it was part of the pattern at that time of my relationship with my father.

Towards the end of this second volume I described the incident that was the first and perhaps crucial turning-point in my life: the one which, looking back, seems to have been the beginning of some liberation from what might have been crippling from my past. I had been ambivalent about the war (the ambivalence depicted in *Spaces of the Dark*); with part of me I accepted the rightness of the war; with part of me I felt with my father – What was the point of a war which in real terms Great Britain could only lose? During the last day I spent with my father in Holloway Prison before I went abroad, he had talked of some weird scheme about how he might get a message through to me if I were taken prisoner: that is, if I were in a German prison camp and he were – what? – in some position in England to get a message through to me? We agreed on some sort of code-word that we might use. All this was perhaps a bit of a joke. But this was the time when I was myself apt to talk (not quite a joke?) as if the most desirable thing to happen to one in this war might indeed be to be taken prisoner quickly and then I would in a sense have done my duty but I would be out of the war. However – Would this not be carrying out some destiny according to a pattern set up by my father? But then there was the incident mentioned briefly before in this book in which on the very first day I saw any action in Italy I was in fact for a few minutes taken prisoner: we were in the mountains in deep snow and a German raiding-party came down on myself and the men I had only a day or two ago been put in charge of and we were so frozen that we hardly fired a shot: but I was so angry, or ashamed, that I felt it imperative to get away: it seemed that I could not live with the knowledge of my previous attitude unless I got away; and so I did in the continuing confusion. And in so doing I was preserved from being shot by the man pursuing me by himself being shot by my friend Mervyn Davies at some vast amazing range. This story is told in the second volume about my father. The moral of the story seems to be – If there is to be a change in what might be the patterned destiny of one's life there has to be choice and risk, and also luck.

When the second volume was in typescript Barley Alison sent a copy to Diana's lawyers with a request to let the publishers know of anything she objected to. Although my father had given me his papers, it was possible that Diana might claim that she still held the copyright. But her lawyers, after a bit of prompting, said that she had in fact no legal objection to anything except the publication of the intimate letters that had passed between her and my father when they had been in separate prisons during the war. Barley wrote to say that of course her dictate would be respected; but in her, Barley's, view, this was a great shame, because the chapter in which these letters appeared showed my father in the best possible light – loving and gentle – and this was a side of him that in any other way was unlikely to be seen so clearly. So after a time Diana agreed that even these letters should be published. The book thus came out as I had written it – with just a statement inserted at the end at Diana's request saying that 'she is not associated in any way with these memoirs, and that she strongly disapproves of many of the interpretations and of the publication of private letters'.

The reviews this time said almost without exception that the book was a notable defence of my father. John Vincent wrote in the *Sunday Times* – 'Lucky the father who has such a son to plead his cause.' Peregrine Worsthorne wrote a review for the *Listener* which began:

> A few days before his death in 1980, Sir Oswald Mosley agreed to make over all his papers to his eldest son Nicholas, with a view to allowing the truth to be told as fully as possible. This decision on the part of the father, taken after much agonising, and wholly against the wishes of his second wife, was the purest act, and the bravest, which he ever made and the result – this book – is a work of literature which does something to redeem, and even lend posthumous dignity to, an otherwise squalid and even pathetic life. Mosley *père* knew full well that his son passionately disapproved of his political views since the two, after quarrelling bitterly about them, had not been on speaking terms for many years. So he cannot have been in any doubt that he was entrusting his papers to an idealogically hostile hand. But a gambler to the last, he took the risk and, for once, hit the jackpot. Other Fascist leaders may have achieved more while still alive. But none has been memorialised with such loving intelligence.

and he ended:

> The attempt at authenticity is on such a noble scale as to invest the whole subject, incredible as this may seem, with an aura of holiness.

This review came out in a week when the *Listener*'s printers were on strike, so it appeared in a makeshift edition which was seen by hardly anyone – which seemed a pity. But it was perhaps not the kind of review after all to have mollified Diana. In any case neither she nor other members of my family took any notice of reviews or opinions which said how well I had done by my father. But for myself there remained the question – In what sense was it true to say that my father's life had been 'squalid' and 'pathetic'?

It was with reference to my father's private life and love-affairs that reviewers had previously used such words as 'squalid'. And for some time it had been being brought home to me that in this respect there might be resonances between my father's life and my own. And from facing these I should not be looking for a diversion.

It had seemed to me that such attacks on my father had been to do with envy: my father had had such an ability to get away with things! But then – each of my own wives had been apt to say, at moments, that I was behaving towards them in such a way as my father had behaved to my mother; and I did not believe there was much of envy here.

At the time of my involvement with Natalie, Rosemary had written – 'I am "cast off" as your mother was cast off for a younger woman who wanted to share your father ... most of your positiveness seems now to boil down to enjoying yourself at all costs on holidays.' And now Verity was writing – 'Did you think I would not mind when I read your mother's letters?'

What might I say – But don't you see that my father was some sort of greedy baby screaming at the edge of a bed? Or – All right, this can be called squalid if you like; but it is the managing not to be miserable and guilty that makes people so angry.

But this did not seem to be a justification.

Rosemary had fought. And, unlike my mother, she had felt free to fight – I had not entangled her with cajoling letters like those of my father. There is in existence a copy of a letter of mine to her in which I say – 'All marriage is some sort of collusion, unless you believe that women are somehow inferior to men, which I don't ... There's a sense in which girls perhaps choose shits for husbands because they (the girls) can thus evade some responsibilities in themselves – as well as the fact that the shits may have something – some insight or dash – that the decent man lacks.' Well, at least Rosemary had known what she had to fight! And it often seemed that what she fought for was freedom. She had written – 'I don't want to cheat, or go mad, or die, or do too many wrong things. But I do still want to live – and also, and this is the good thing, for everyone else to live as well.'

All this had happened what seemed a long time ago. But now here was Verity writing as if something of the kind was happening again. What Verity had had to complain about was my writing – 'the mistresses in my head'. I had been reminded of this when I had read my mother's early letters to my father in which she seemed to be anxious and even accusatory towards him on account of his being away from her in the course of his work. Later, of course, she had had more sensible cause for hurt and anger; but by this time what, in a sense, had my father to lose? If he was felt to be unfaithful anyway, then why not . . . and so on. I began to notice increasingly how like my mother's letters to my father were some of Verity's letters to me: I was by this time spending much of my time in another one-room flat down the hill where I could spread out my father's voluminous papers and concentrate on work. This did not, indeed, make things easier for Verity and me. But how does a husband and father concentrate on work? And then Verity, at the time of the trouble concerning the publication of my first volume, feeling herself in some position like that of my mother, joined the ranks of people who felt that my mother's letters should not be printed. This was a difficult time, with obscure and ambivalent battles being fought all around. Within myself I had to ask – In trying to explain my father was I trying to justify myself? Instead of thinking my father was not too much of a shit, should I be taking more note of myself in this light? I could not analyse this too much if I was to get the work done; I had a sense of urgency, as writers do, about how the work should be done. But then – had my father not felt like this about his work? And so had he not, indeed, after a while, taken encouragement where he could. The mistresses in his head, that is, had never been far from mistresses on the ground. I had not wanted mistresses on the ground! But now here was Verity fighting battles that I did not think should be battles; and after the publication of the first volume I was feeling hard-pressed all round; so indeed there were temptations at least to get encouragement where one could. But Verity was fighting in a way which even Rosemary had never fought. She was fighting for possession or dispossession; for victory or defeat. And in some odd way there was liveliness in this all round.

I suppose in the books I had been writing I wanted to say to my dead father, my dead mother – to all those who had been around them at the time, to all those who were around me now, certainly to myself – Look! this love business, this commitment to work business, this sex business, this struggle for reassurance like pariah dogs scrabbling on the ground for bones – all this is a universal predicament! For the predicament itself people are not to blame: for a vindictive reaction to it, yes, for that people can be blamed – for casting the first stone, for not recognising that they themselves are human. Some catastrophes are more terrible than others: people die young instead of turning into husks. But from any catastrophe or potential catastrophe if people live to look at it they can learn.

To Verity, particularly, I think I wanted to say – Look, we loved very much and married because we thought we knew about such things. They are difficult, yes, but this is part of what we know. Either we trust, and things may turn out all right; or we do not and they will not.

This is a matter of choice? of luck?

Have we not seen that there are connections between the two?

25

It is in the coming up towards the present that there are things that
are difficult to say: perhaps partly because there is a proper and
decent need for one or two smokescreens; but also because words
themselves seem likely to light up false trails in a continuing journey
that has to be trusted largely in the dark – if there is to be any
hope, that is, of anything coming out right.

How can one know what to say, how can there be anything to
be said, about a pattern still being worked out?

One can, perhaps take note of resonances: say – By looking at
that pattern there, by suggesting a universal predicament here, one
might shed light on a particular present –

By this there might even be a chance of influencing a future?

Verity and I were having a difficult time on our journey. There
were similarities and differences between our journey and that of
my father and mother. My father had argued – Look, marriage
must not be a trap: or what is the point of being human? But my
mother had not been able to go her own way.

My father's energy had demanded a series of sexual conquests:
my own proclivity had been more that of a reluctance to run away
from what turned up. Also now I was so much older than my father
at the time of his marriage to my mother; but there were still some
forms of friendship from which I did not want to turn away.

Verity and I knew that marriage had to be some bearing of
tendencies that pull in opposite directions; of dealing with the seven

devils that come in the place of one. This is some ordeal, yes, rather than a solution.

According to convention, my father's behaviour was that of a shit. It was held to be the duty of those with over-exuberant energy to limit themselves in order to protect those with less, and thus to guard the relationship they have got. But the result of this has been the acceptance of a system of traps and lies – a system in which a person becomes the character that is required of him or her by someone else; or pretends to be such a character and succeeds only by further manipulation. Occasionally, or for a while, the being what another requires is freely given; this is the luck of love, and often does not last.

The system of traps and lies is what Nietzsche (and indeed my father) called 'ressentiment': the pattern formed by – 'You must not do that because if you do I will be hurt' and 'I will resent you either if I obey you, or if I lie to you because I do not want you to be hurt.' With such attitudes one stops looking at what is happening and plays games; one does not notice the man-hole, or man-trap, opening under one's feet.

On the other hand – there has to be observed some system of caring if there is to be trust.

It had seemed to me that a way of carrying on with energy might be through the recognition that in pattern there is always darkness as well as light: humans should not accept being trapped, but should recognise that as they strode along they were indeed apt to fall down a coal-hole – into the darkness of their own nature as well as of the hurt of those upon whom they fall. But by the recognition of this – the fall into the coal-hole or just the chance of it – there would be a chance of being redeemable (and indeed possibly preventable) whatever it was that occurred or might occur. It is difficult for humans rationally to accept this idea; for what is reasonable about a cheerful and wide-awake journey into the dark in which there will be at least the risk of hurt? Acceptance of this depends on trust in a system in which there can be a use for darkness – a trust that if this is trusted then it can turn, after due journeys, into light.

My father, when he wished to make things better with my mother, would write of their joint involvement 'in great enterprise and high adventure . . . in dark and terrible things'. But this was to do with rhetoric rather than with recognition; he did not see dark things much in relation to himself. The idea of involvement with darkness as well as with light – the idea that one can be involved with the formation of light only as part of a pattern – all this is to do with the belief that the function of life is not to achieve serenity or integration (let alone power) but to recognise oneself as part of processes of evolution. It is for this that there is inevitably some involvement with turmoil and suffering; if this is not denied, then it can be turned to good effect. All this of course is Christian – a person who would save his life must also lose it, and so on. In the image of the hags in the temple there is the demand that in order to become one of the serene people walking on the beach one has to see oneself as also the hags and the child.

My father and mother, in their social context, could not have spent much time meditating on things like this.

And so what of Verity and myself – myself now feeling I had to get away to work (how can one work dedicatedly in the middle of the demanding to-and-fro of even quite normal family life?), but as a result of this it seeming that I had one leg again on the point of going down a coal-hole. It was to Verity that I wanted to say (as in my car-crash) – Do see if you can get my leg out together with the rest of me at the same time! But Verity said that she was feeling like my mother.

Often enough, even like this, we seemed close to the beautiful people walking on the beach:

> My darling love. Oh dear I do miss you. I have a terrible ache and dread and feel quite near to tears much of the time. Never mind, it truly doesn't matter if you are managing to do some good work and feel happier. It was awful that you felt so ill and sad; perhaps the quiet beauty of Majorca is helping to heal it all. And of course if you can work that will help too enormously.
>
> I miss you terribly, it is quite odd. I could never live without you; so please try to get better so we can be happy again. I'll try to be more what you need. I do miss you so much.
>
> Poor M. misses you. He wrinkles up his nose when he goes to bed and says Daddy Daddy in such a sad puzzled way. But he's a

very lucky chap to have such a good Dad. And he must have you in his heart by now. Won't it be lovely for him to see you again.

You are such a wonderful person. I think sometimes you take on too much and try to change things too hard.

So how lucky I was! Yes. But if I could just finish off this bit of work (oh yes, I know this may make me a bit of a shit –)

– Then back to the beautiful people walking on the beach?

Or might this indeed not rather involve a return to the temple with the hags – I mean myself performing in the role of the hags – with each person in oh-so-ordinary family life being or liking to see himself or herself in the role of the child –

– Your father killed your mother and now you will kill me –

– By saying this you show that it is you who want to kill me –

And so on. With such savagery, so fruitlessly repeated, dissolving into chaos –

– Into a black hole, a cosmic coal-hole, that is indeed like the death of a sun. And then suddenly there it was –

Dear Sir,
Our client tells us that you left her in September last year and that you have lived apart from her ever since. She takes the view, regrettably, that the marriage has broken down irretrievably and that there is no prospect of reconciliation. In due course she will wish to obtain a divorce . . .

I thought – But at least Verity is fighting! Nothing happened to my father and mother like this!

– Verity who has shown herself to be someone who can stand on her own –

– And is it I who might be jealous?

But is it not the characteristic of a black hole that within it one does not in fact know what is going on.

– Perhaps we will have to sit things out through a long winter –

– What were those games, all right, one used to play to pass the time? Hoopla? Upsadaisy? –

– One-wheel bicycles in the dark?

Or you mean – Old ground is being broken up; from this same ground something new may grow.

I replied –

Dear Sir,
I did not leave my wife in September last year, we had been having damaging quarrels in front of the children and it was mutually agreed that it would be best for a time if I stayed in the room that I was already using as an office and my wife stayed in the family home . . .

And so on.

But what on earth was it I was trying to write at this time, in the light of which such terrible ructions might not seem too deathly; in the context perhaps even forming (God help us) patterns?

The novel that I had begun to write even before my father had died, and which I now went on with as I waited for whatever would happen both in family life and in the business of the second volume about my father coming out, was called *Judith*. I had originally chosen this name for a character in my *Catastrophe Practice* books because I had been haunted by the story of Judith in the Apocrypha – the beautiful Jewish woman who, when her home town was being besieged by the Assyrians, got herself taken into the Assyrian camp and then, because of her beauty, into the tent of their captain Holofernes; and when Holofernes wanted to make love to her but got drunk instead, took down his sword and cut his head off. And then she went home with his head in her bag, so that when this head was displayed on the town walls, the Assyrians fled in panic.

I had thought – Perhaps I like this story because I hope that women may have an instinct that good may come out of what is conventionally called evil.

In my series of novels Judith is the girl glimpsed by Bert and with whom he falls in love in *Imago Bird*; in *Cypher* she seems to be carrying on with both Bert and Jason and even Max. In *Judith* she first appears before these other times as an aspiring young actress who wants to make her way in the London artistic-and-media world; she feels that men can be used – she knows the story of Judith in the Apocrypha. She gets some distance up the social rat-race ladder;

but always there is some part of her that seems aware of the worth-lessness of what she is doing. With this part of herself she sees she may in truth be going downhill: but with the whole of her she wonders what there is to do except watch and see what will happen. She comes across Max, the elderly protagonist from *Cypher* and the *Plays*; he becomes her mentor – just as Eleanor has been to Bert in *Imago Bird*. Max tells her – You will, I suppose, go on for a time playing your games with yourself and with other people; no one changes much until they hit some sort of rock bottom. Judith becomes involved increasingly in promiscuity and drugs; one of her entourage dies; she does reach some rock bottom. She is rescued by Max, who sets her on her way to a healing ashram in India.

I had got as far as a draft of this when my father died. I set *Judith* aside to write the biographies. I had myself visited an ashram in India just before this time; Verity and I had been on a package tour, and I had travelled further on my own. I had wondered – You mean, Verity and I may have to approach some rock bottom?

In the ashram in the book Judith learns – Of course terrible things occur! people die, people hit bottom; sometimes they bounce like rubber balls; sometimes they do not. But anyway – none of this really matters. What matters is that there is a part of one that can become detached and observe all this as it were from another level; and see – well, if not always exactly a pattern, at least the wonder of being able to look.

Jason, Lilia's husband, comes to visit Judith in the ashram; he has heard of her through Bert, Lilia's brother. Jason has been on one of his scriptwriting assignments – but this is just before the time when Lilia's child is due to be born, so what is Jason doing taking time to visit Judith? Judith has already herself had a finger in the business of Lilia not having got rid of the child: now, in the ashram, Jason and Judith want to make love. In England the baby begins to be born. It has a huge head; the doctors say – It may be a question of the mother or the child. If Jason had been present he might have had to have made the choice – and then, whatever he had chosen, how would Lilia have forgiven him? But Jason is in the ashram dallying with Judith. So in his absence Bert, Lilia's brother, has called in – Max and Eleanor. And Eleanor – not only having trained

as a doctor but also being something of a witchdoctor as it were –
saves both the mother and the child. So you see – Upsadaisy! If
Jason and Judith had not been dallying, then – but what can one
say about this sort of thing? Everyone must see (still not quite say?)
what they like.

Jason comes home. Judith gets better in the ashram; then comes
home.

The last third of the book takes place some seven years later
when each of the six characters of these stories – Eleanor and Max,
Jason and Lilia, Judith and Bert – have been getting on with his or
her own life – in the hope, knowledge even, that if one keeps one's
head then something that is required, even if it is not known
precisely what, will be going on off-stage. Four of them come
together at the scene of an anti-nuclear demonstration at an American airbase in England. The human race may be on the way to
blowing itself up; and then what will have been learned? Judith
joins up with Bert who is making a film about the demonstration;
later she meets Lilia, who has found out that during these seven
years Judith has occasionally been carrying on with her husband
Jason. So Lilia, with part of her that is like the vengeful Medea,
wants to kill Judith; but here they are outside a nuclear airbase and
Lilia's child has become lost. So there are more important things
to be done, are there not, than the acting of dramas in the style of
Medea wanting to get even with Jason. And in fact, did not Medea
self-destruct to such an extent that she killed her own children?
And have not these protagonists known over the years that they are
all in their different ways involved with the survival of the child?
So Lilia and Judith get their jealousy scene over quickly; and then
they go off to look for the child.

The child has gone into some no-man's land where, literally,
humans do not come. This is a battle-area, not far from the airbase,
which has been set aside as a training-ground for soldiers. On a
perimeter fence there are notices – Keep Out! Danger of Unex-
ploded Bombs! – as if indeed these were angels with flaming swords.
The child has gone into this area to look for a two-headed sheep
that he, the child, had come across earlier in the year and had
befriended; this sheep is a mutant that is likely soon to die. Into

this area come the other protagonists of these stories who are looking for the child: the landscape is dotted with sheep and trees precisely as if in a painting. There is a model village in which there are houses like toys; these are the props, off-stage, for the games of war which men play. Here, together with the sheep, the protagonists find the child. Some bomb does in fact go off near the American airbase: not the big Bomb, but something possibly radioactive set off by the demonstrators to show the dangers of Bombs: might or might not this be a proper game for humans to play for the sake of peace or war? The protagonists of the stories are out of danger from this bomb because they have been looking for the child; they are in a landscape which is like some Garden of Eden; or like some Noah's Ark.

The two-headed sheep seems to be an image of a sort of humanity that may die. The child calls the sheep Hopeful Monster – a hopeful monster being a mutant that, according to context, may live or may die. But it is the child, putting his arms round the sheep, who in this context is the true hopeful monster – one who sees that by looking for things, looking after things, one might affirm rather than suffer what may live and what may die.

It is the women, and the young man Bert, who see this.

The man called Jason is not there: he is away writing his plays, his stories.

The man called Max is not there: he is ill, he may be dying.

I did not know how my own particular story would continue at this time.

In some Noah's Ark? I was joking!

More likely I was the poor old two-headed sheep! in a bed-sitting-room, dreaming (as my father used to do, but in more elegant surroundings of course) of altering the world; of altering at least the way in which people look at the world –

Whereas in fact more probably was happening –

– Roll up! Tonight at seven-thirty! Jason and Medea, the destroyers of their children!

– The Beast from Forty Thousand Fathoms: The Creature from the Black Lagoon!

Indeed why should I not myself, along with most of the rest of humanity, be wiped out?

Oh but here (after indeed a longish time of winter) is the child with its arms round the two-headed sheep! the hopeful child that might survive, grow up. I had a letter from Verity:

Dearest Nicholas,

It seems to me that we are a very odd couple indeed. None of the 'normal' ideas of marriage or relationship apply. You do know this but when it suits you, you go into outrage. 'Normal' people do not cope with the rows and the drinking and the bashings and the absences, but it seems that we do because we have some very deep tie. I am very sad at the moment and I am sure you are too. Your determination to hang on to what I did wrong is very hard to bear though.

We've had terribly tough times but we are still here. Do we have to spend so much time punishing and being punished? Saying – how could you do that! – as if we were some perfect imaginary couple who had never had a cross word. Suddenly you talk as if we were this 'normal' couple and sadly we are not.

I feel so lonely but thank God I'm managing these days. However sad it seems I do thank God for being able more or less to cope and not to fall apart when you go away. That was terrible, terrible; falling, falling apart. You say I should know I am not the only one who suffers. Of course I know that, but I wouldn't expect sympathy from those whose suffering I am increasing. Is it too difficult to accept that all that went on increased my suffering even if it didn't cause it? The reason I go on about this is truly not to blame but to try to help you accept that what went on – goes on – is all right – part of life – part of the burden of being a human being. We are not expected to be perfect. Until we can bear to accept that, we are left with such horror – indeed such suffering.

Oh please God – that bird coming back with a root-and-branch of a tree in its mouth?

And I thought I was in a coal-hole, not an Ark!

Oh yes there had been all that flood coming down; the dark and golden rain on my head; those old hags, myself, clucking and plucking at the child, myself – and others. And there had also been those terrible animals, my books, in the hold, in my head – the smell down there, honestly! – but I had tried to look after them; I had tried to look after them –

Verity said – You think I have not tried to look after them too?

I said – If I had not been on my own, how could I have put my arms around them?

– But you did not put your arms around me!

– I know.

And so on.

Indeed my father and mother were not like this!

Nor was Rosemary, nor Natalie.

Bold Verity.

– Look! Isn't that the top of a tree? –

– The Tree of Life do you think? –

(Oh I know one shouldn't talk like this!)

Where's that rainbow!

So there we were, Verity and I, venturing out two-by-two once more on to dry land –

God, what a mess! All those plastic bottles –

(Noah still sometimes got drunk, didn't he?)

(And his children saw him naked –)

You think that's what you're writing?

Catastrophe practice.

26

The book that I began to write after *Judith* was called *Hopeful Monsters* and was the last of the *Catastrophe Practice* series. I had come to almost the last scene of the overall narrative in *Judith*, when the protagonists find themselves in a so-called 'forbidden zone' in which new life either will or will not survive. But there was still a story to be written about the origins of the attitudes and way of thinking of these people: how much was application; how much was 'chance'. *Hopeful Monsters* is the story of Max and Eleanor when they were young; who were later gurus and mentors to the other characters in the stories. What influences formed them: what chances did they accept.

'Hopeful monsters' was a term used by biologists in the 1940s to describe mutations that were on the edge of going one way or the other – either to extinction or, if some change in the environment that suited them happened to coincide, to the establishing of a new strand of life. Obviously in the enormous majority of cases mutants die; what is suited to the environment is naturally the existing strain. But very occasionally there happens to be a change in the environment coincidental with a mutation that the latter can use to its advantage; and then there is the chance that the mutant and its progeny may live, and the old strain will die.

In my *Catastrophe Practice* books all my protagonists are hopeful monsters – they have developed a slightly out-of-the-normal way of seeing the world; they recognise this in each other; they are at odds with the society around them. Their way of seeing things is to do with the faculty of being able with part of themselves to stand back and see the forces and dramas by which other parts of themselves are driven; and by this faculty perhaps to alter the forces and dramas themselves. This had been the point of the *Plays*: here were actors stuck with their scripts but in so far as they knew they were actors in this sense they were not stuck; they knew there was some 'reality' going on off-stage. And thus the style of the dramas changed. In the novels what was hopeful and perhaps sometimes monstrous about the characters was a style of mind in which they could be ironic about themselves as characters but by this be in contact perhaps with whatever it was that was beyond 'character' – be aware of some patterning, that is, in which human dramas, however terrible or absurd, were yet bumps and threads through a maze. This faculty of mind might be seen as some mutation. It is likely that a new mutation would be to do with mind – consciousness and self-consciousness having been the last big jumps in evolution. So what about a next jump being that of consciousness becoming at home in being conscious of itself? and thus being perhaps what is required. This question is more than that of whether by chance the human race will survive; it is perhaps – How can humans now use for life what have hitherto been their murderous and self-destructive patterns –

– Some things indeed having to die: some possibly to survive –

– A hopeful monster being perhaps anyway less a person than a faculty of vision or of mind.

In the book *Hopeful Monsters* Eleanor and Max tell the story of themselves when they are young. Looking back from a distance they see patterns; of course these patterns are what they have made as well as discovered; on their journey through the maze they have found their own ways in the dark. They watch, listen: learn how to move in response to what turns up. The darkness is shot through with lightning flashes and echoes.

Eleanor and Max grow up in the 1920s and 1930s at the time when old orders in Europe indeed seem to be cracking up – old systems of society, of science, of states of mind. Human beings had found themselves trapped in a world war; it was difficult to see that parts of themselves seemed intent on cracking up. In the 1930s there were the huge experiments to try to deal socially with the danger and the débâcle: Communism and Fascism were efforts to reconstitute societies by ideology and efforts of will. But in fact these seemed only to make the processes of destruction and self-destruction more organised and virulent; human nature does not change by effort of will. What a person can do (this is what Eleanor and Max learned and believed and said) is to stand back and see what the situation is to which they are largely attached but from which part of them might become detached; to see if by this there might be liberated some natural process of change.

Eleanor and Max are both children of parents working at the frontiers of efforts to understand what is going on in the world. Eleanor's father is a philosopher of science trying to look at what might be implied by the physics of Einstein and Bohr; Eleanor's mother is a socialist politician trying to see whether socialism will reverse tendencies to self-destruction or will just organise them. Max's mother is a student of psychoanalysis, the practice of which is just catching on in England; Max's father is a Cambridge professor working in the field of genetics. In genetics there has been a recent theory that evolution need not wait as it were for the chance of coincidence: there are enough potential mutations in what is called a species' 'gene-pool' to make evolutionary change not dependent on random chance, but rather on some 'recognition' of what in the outside world might be necessary for survival.

In all these areas there is information about something new going on – even about the fact that this has to be perhaps largely in the dark; understanding having to come as part of a process. What is required is perhaps an understanding of what it is to understand! That is – What are the mechanisms between and around ourselves and the world by which we are able to learn how it and ourselves work. This style of enquiry indeed seems to be moving on to a different level. It can be accepted that humans are responsible for themselves: the question is – In what way might they be responsible for the outside world?

Eleanor and Max are brought up in separate countries – she in Germany, he in England. They meet at a students' congress in the

Black Forest. Each recognises in the other a style of consciousness that they have, or hope to have, in themselves. Each knows that the other will be a life-long love. But what each recognises in themselves and in the other is that they each have some task to do; they have their personal journeys through the maze. So after they have met, for a time they move apart. But from now on each has the knowledge that they are in some way connected – like those sub-atomic particles which (so they think they have understood!) however far apart they move, once they have been together always have a life together in some reality that might be called off-stage.

Max becomes a physicist at Cambridge; Eleanor fights to survive as a Jewess in the inferno of Nazi Berlin. Max comes to rescue Eleanor: they manage to spend a longer time together. But then – perhaps just because they have been so lucky! lucky even to see there is so much to do! – off they go again on their ways through the maze.

Max goes to Russia. Eleanor goes to Africa. Sometimes they feel – Indeed we are mad! some sort of monsters.

The mark of this sort of hopeful monster is that you watch, and listen, and choose to move this way or that, and trust to luck: in this way life appears to have meaning. You cannot talk about this much because if you do the luck may go – you are not listening. But if you trust, then there do seem to be kindly pointers, oddities, waving and nodding as you bump round corners. Luck seems to come your way – Sh!

Dare you even say – The maze is beautiful!

From different directions Eleanor and Max come to the Spanish Civil War. They are not on any 'side': they seem to have come there as part of each of their journeys; as a putting of things to the test. (Indeed, is this not an experience of war?) Max, having been involved in a skirmish on the Republicans' side, journeys on to the other side and once there is likely to be shot as a spy. Eleanor, finding herself amongst the Nationalists in the role of Judith in the camp of the Assyrians, learns that there may be more important tasks than that of cutting off the head of some Holofernes – for one, rescuing Max. This can occur because of – oh call it chance, call it what you like. And Eleanor needs a passport. So of course they must also now marry. One learns – The processes of chance.

Max and Eleanor settle down for a long time now. They are very happy. But then there is the Bomb.

Max is working in this area in physics: he has learned – How enormously self-destructive is human nature! but how closely connected are potentialities for destruction and creation. So – Might not the one thing potentially destructive enough to save humanity from its own self-destructiveness be – a Bomb?

Not if the Nazis get it first! And so on. Max goes to work on the Bomb. And Eleanor listens to promptings – It need not be left just to chance whether or not the Nazis get the Bomb!

She is a hopeful monster after all, trusting in connections between worlds.

So off she goes – to see what an individual might do about this or that possible catastrophe. And after this she and Max are sometimes together, sometimes they go their not-quite-separate ways. But always they seem joined through some central point which is their (and that of those they have influenced) understanding of the maze.

At the very end of *Hopeful Monsters* there is a jump forwards to a time just after the end of *Judith* (and in the meantime there have been *Catastrophe Practice* and *Imago Bird* and *Serpent*). Max is an old man and is supposed to be dying of cancer; all the protagonists of the stories gather round his death-bed. There is with them Lilia's child; also a new baby girl that has been born to Judith. They are waiting for Eleanor to arrive – Eleanor having continued often to go, even when old, on something of her own way. Eleanor does arrive: Max feels that now he might give up and die. After a time he says – I can't die! Eleanor says – Why not? Max says – Because I'm too happy! Eleanor climbs up on to the bed beside him and they hold each other. She says – I think it is the cancer that is dying.

When I had finished *Hopeful Monsters* it was an enormous book – the sort of book that sends publishers' hearts into their boots. But how otherwise could the novel itself be a hopeful monster? It seemed for a time that it might get lost down a coal-hole. Then suddenly – oh yes there were coincidences all right! a copy flipping here and there and landing on this or that desk –

– And there it was, winging its way like some great whale over rooftops.

And I was thinking – Perhaps after all it will have some small walk-on part in what Nietzsche called (this is quoted in the book) 'the great hundred-act play reserved for the next two centuries in Europe: the most terrible, the most questionable, the most hopeful of all plays' –

– a struggle between, on the one hand, the vast armies who see survival as a matter of being one up on everyone else and by this are likely to ensure self-destruction; who are comfortable in this role because at least they do not feel different from anyone else. And on another level the comparative few who see this pattern and know they are part of it but hope also to be guardians of what might grow in secret. So even though armies do seem to be hurling themselves over cliffs –

– I am still talking about what goes on in the mind, of course –

– So in books at least, which is the area in which I operate, there will be some battle between those that continue to depict just the terrible quaintness of human character, the terrible hopelessness of human characters, because by this writers and readers can feel unchallenged and undisturbed; and books (a few) about the effort to look down on this and say – Persons may remain, God help us, in whatever pattern they like: but for anyone who wishes – Coo-ee! – there is this other level. And there, by watching and listening, by making the best of what turns up – even disaster – persons may find they are not helpless even in that the world works for them.

An incident occurred when I was half-way through *Hopeful Monsters* which was uncannily relevant to what I was trying to say, and indeed encouraged me to have faith in this. I had done a first rough draft of the book and was half-way through a second; I had come to the place where Eleanor finds herself on the edge of the Spanish Civil War; she has travelled in a small boat from North Africa and goes up the river to Seville. I realised I could not remember enough of Seville (I had been there some thirty years before) to know where a small boat might moor, what could be seen from the quayside, and so on: I was also feeling that my first draft about the Civil War was much too glib, too frivolous; I was saying something about the senselessness of war, but this had been a time of great passion when Europe had been once more girding itself up for self-destruction; and I knew enough about war not to want to make it seem trivial. So I got in my car (this was a time when I was again very much on my own in a small London flat) and caught a boat to Santander and drove through Spain taking with me the only copy of the hundred-and-fifty pages of the draft I was working on (this was the only copy perhaps because I knew I was not satisfied with it?) and in Seville I drove straight to the river and was so excited to see what I would find there that I left my car locked with my luggage in it for five minutes on the road while I looked over the parapet; then went down a few steps towards the quayside; then when I turned back I found that the door of my car had been wrenched open and the case with my hundred-and-fifty pages in it had gone. I became so demented by this – it made no difference that I had not been satisfied with my draft, I needed it to work from – that having gone to the police and the British Consul I put an advertisement in the local paper offering a reward for the return of the typescript, saying keep the travellers' cheques and the rest and no questions asked – and while waiting for a reply absurdly poked about in street refuse-tips where I imagined my pages might have been discarded. I also set about reconstructing what I remembered of my first draft – but in such misery and rage and self-reproach that I was indeed now closer to what must have been the mood of my heroine Eleanor on the edge of the Civil War. And then when I had given up waiting and was driving back through Spain – I had originally planned a meeting with my ten-year-old son on the coast but my despair was such that I had cancelled this – I found myself on a route that in other circumstances I would not have been on; and when I was near the Pyrenees I read in my guidebook of a strange monastery built half underneath and half on top of a vast rock; and this sounded intriguing; and I thought I should spend the night there. And then indeed I found it was a place of such haunting and resonant beauty that I realised – Of course, this is the place where Eleanor and Max come together decisively on their intricate journeys through the maze! by chance and yet not by chance: here they decide to marry and settle down to what seem to be their tasks in the world. In the original draft I had never found a pretext or a location for their meeting that was anything but trivial: now I saw a climax to my story that not only made practical sense but was also mythical. And all because the door of my car had been wrenched open by the river in Seville! And I had been in despair but not quite in despair – and so had gone on a different route from the one that I had planned. And I had known some trace of the emotions that my characters had been feeling; and so – had found a suitable centrepiece to their story.

Hopeful Monsters became one of the most approachable of my novels, perhaps because of a sense of my involvement with my characters, also because it was written somewhat more in the style of my biographies. People used to tell me – Your biographies are comparatively easy: why can't you write your novels like that? I would say – Biographies deal with the past: a biographer's job is to clarify what is there: in novels I try to portray experience of the present, in which it is so often an open question what is, or what might be, there. In *Hopeful Monsters*, however, I was for much of the time looking at the past – at the history and the politics that I had been trying to understand in the volumes about my father. And for years in an amateur way I had been trying to get a grasp of the science of this period too; and there had been enough written about it both by popularisers and experts for the diligent enquirer to imagine at least that he could see what was there. So perhaps because of this it was natural for me to write *Hopeful Monsters* somewhat more in the style of my biographies; and because of this it had a success wider than that of my previous novels.

On the coat-tails of *Hopeful Monsters* I was asked to be a judge for the 1990 Booker Prize and in this role I found myself caught up in what I had seen as the battle between different kinds of novel. Most of the hundred-or-so novels I had to read indeed seemed to me to depict just 'the terrible quaintness of human character, the terrible helplessness of human characters'; very few portrayed humans as beings with a chance to look down on what might be their fate and by attending to it perhaps affect it. My four fellow judges each chose for their short-list six books which seemed to me to epitomise what I had felt so desperate about novels; none of them cared for the six I chose. There were five judges and six books to go on the short-list, so I imagined that I would get on just one of my choices; but the voting system was such that for the final round I found myself represented by none. So I resigned, because this seemed to me sensible; also it would give me a chance to say publicly something of what I thought about novels.

In the meantime I had begun to write this present book.

And in this I would have a chance to look at my own particular battles –

– To see their pattern; to form this even –

– And by this affect the future?

***

I do not want to write much more of what might be going on in the real world now: I do not want to push my luck. It is enough to say – Yes, we seem to be lucky.

About the strains and patterns that seem to have been completed in the past –

She whom I called Mary in *The Rainbearers* has died. I did not know of this at the time. I felt I should have known! But my pattern with Mary, so redolent of life and death, had always gone its own way: it was to do with learning; the strange activities of grace.

Hugo Charteris has died. His best book, *The Tide Is Right*, which had been prevented from being published years ago because of threats of libel, has just now been published for the first time.

Natalie has returned to this country after years abroad. When I told her I was writing this book, and asked her if she would mind if she were in it, she said – I would mind if I were not!

Rosemary has died. I have tried to write of this. People say – You must have been affected by Rosemary's death. I say – Yes, I sometimes wonder about my own death.

Sorrows and regrets are mostly not for what has been done but for what has not been done – the lack of caring; the old days of uselessness and waste.

One of the most bitter things that has happened in the year since I finished this book is that after we, the children and I, had arranged and held a memorial exhibition of Rosemary's paintings in London, and had then sent a selection of the best of them for an exhibition in the Isle of Man, this lot were destroyed there in a warehouse fire. There are some blows of fate through which it is indeed difficult to see patterns.

Regarding the troubles with my stepmother Diana: she continued to show her anxiety over the years – in her book of reminiscences *Loved Ones*, in an interview with Naim Attallah in which she said I had not shown her scripts of my books about my father until it had been too late to make any alterations. She continued to quote the reviewer of the first volume who had said I had 'emptied a bucket of mud' over my father's head, and continued to ignore any reviews of the finished book such as the one which had said 'lucky the father who has such a son to plead his cause'. For the purposes of this present book I sent her copies of her letters from which I hoped to quote; I hoped also that when such evidence was in front of her there might be some renewal of understanding between us if not exactly reconciliation. We corresponded; and for a time Diana chose to stick to whatever guns have seemed necessary for her. She wrote that she had never read my second volume about my father, and had asked my publishers not to send her any reviews. But then at the last moment as it were – just before the proofs of this book had to be completed – I had a letter from her saying that she was sorry if in the past she had been unfair: I wrote back to say how grateful I was for this, and as for fairness or unfairness we had all been fighting for what we believed; and then I had a card from her saying yes, perhaps we both loved my father in our mysterious ways. And then there was a letter from Max wishing the book well, and I had already had a visit from Alexander – so perhaps in the end this book was having a hand in effecting the idea that is set out in it: that if one trusts, then things may indeed work out in proper, if mysterious, ways.

Regarding my life with Verity – Verity has fought her way bravely through whatever have been the fogs and fears of her maze: she watches over my extended family; she came to be trusted by Rosemary. She has used her travails to learn and to train and to be a practising psychotherapist: she is one of the people who point a way at the corners of the maze.

Verity and I live in a big new house. We are still occasional performers in the odd melodrama that goes on in the evenings – Nightmare on Whatever-it-is Street; Babes in the Wood. But the children seem increasingly able to say – A bit overdone, last night, don't you think? And it is more fun for them to watch television.

From Verity I have learned that it is not all dreams that I have trusted: there is still a part of me (and indeed of her!) that can be like The Creature From The Black Lagoon; but so what? Some pain, of course; but from pain one can learn – I'm so sorry – also – How else can there be such wonder at the outcome of trust? With Verity I have discovered the reality of what can go on off-stage; and what greater gift is there than this? In my dedication of *Catastrophe Practice* to Verity I quoted from Nietzsche:

> Supposing truth to be a woman, what? Is the suspicion not well founded that philosophers, when they have been dogmatists, have had little understanding of women?

and:

> What meaning would our whole being possess if it were not this – that in us the will to truth becomes conscious of itself as a problem?

So this was a prophecy as well as, it seems to me, one of the best things one can say about a marriage.

I do not know how to write more about this. There is no end to a story until the protagonists are dead. And even then what matters is what is passed on to children – and to their children and their children's children. It sometimes seems to me (I am writing this on my sixty-eighth birthday; revising it on my sixty-ninth; doing the proofs soon after my seventieth) that it is just this about what is passed on that has been so painstakingly learned – and then one can die. And what I have learned from my son Marius and my stepson Jonathan is that children can survive human monstrosities so long as those that love them do not make out that monstrosities are other than they are: and then how wise children may become! And when this has been passed on, then one can die.

There is perhaps one more story I might write. This would be about children – as it were my children – walking through a wood. They come across an old man sitting collapsed against a tree. They say – I know, Old Godadaddy, you have been eating again of that tree!

And he says – But this isn't the Tree of Knowledge of Good and Evil, this is the Tree of Life.

And they say – But you would call anything life!

And he says – I've been right round the world, and you know what I found when I got back here?

They say – What?

He says – Call it death, call it life, children.

Index

341

Mosley, Marius (son) 275, 279, 284, 320, 338
Mosley, Max (half-brother) 126, 147, 156, 309
Mosley, Michael (brother) 146
Mosley, Nicholas: marriage and honeymoon 7–8, 9; first novel 8–10, 11–12, 13, 17; army service 10, 11, 43; attitude to war 10–11, 12–13, 15, 314–15; Grand Tour 15–17; and Christianity 16–17; 30, 31–6, 37–41, 47, 61–2, 75, 77, 132, 141, 142, 170; farming in North Wales 17, 19–20, 21, 28, 29, 30, 37; second novel 18–19, 23, 24–6, 43 (later writings listed at end of this entry); London circle 20, 36; depression and projection of fear 23–4, 28, 30, 33; difficulties in marriage 29, 30, 46, 60, 63–4, 247–52, 268; friendship with novice monk 30–31, 33, 37–41, 44, 47, 61, 134; move to Sussex 36–7, 44, 46; and 'free' marriage 42–3, 46; romanticism about girls 43; first meeting with 'Mary' 46–7; continuing relationship 47–58, 59, 62–5, 67–71, 134, 157–60, 199; plans for Anglican magazine 61–2, 75; increased parental concern 66–7, 72–3, 75–6, 147–9; country-house and London life 73–4, 76, 114; difficulty of combining family life and writing 76, 285; literary style 79–82, 163; journey through West Africa 90–98; edits Prism 98, 99, 107–12, 114–17, 132–3; trip to Berlin 99, 100, 101, 155; and CND 99–100; criticism of Church 108–12, 119, 137; and local parish affairs 112–14, 172, 179; relationship with father 115, 118–22, 124–9, 156–9, 261–3, 295–6, 307, 310, 312; and integrity 115–17, 124; and Union Movement violence 123–6; responsibility for half-brother Alexander 126–30, 146–7, 155; in South Africa 132, 134–41; malaria 133, 134; reading of Bible 133–4, 171, 178; and Community of Resurrection 134–5, 137, 143–5, and Afrikaners 137–9; on racialism 140–1, 146; on writing of 'good' novel 150–51, 188; increasing alienation

from Rosemary 155, 191, 214, 226; on contemporary fiction 168–70; signing-off from organised religion 173–80; and African refugees 178; in America 179–81; and father's libel actions 182–4; first meeting with 'Natalie' 193; filming 203–4, 228–47; inherits Ravensdale title 210–12; and family lawsuit 212–14; Hampstead house 214, 223, 239, 266, 274, 284, 285; erratic family life 223–5; in car crash 225–7, 228, 229; break-up of marriage 247–52; death of Rosemary 256, 257; psychoanalysis 260–4, 266, 268, 269–70, 273, 288; marriage to Verity 275; biography of father 295–305, 306–17, 323; relations with Diana 299–311, 313–19, 337; marriage difficulties and their resolution 318, 320–2, 326–7
WRITINGS:
Accident (novel) 161–7, 172, 179, 187, 194, 203–4
Aerodrome (later Landfall) (play) 250, 252, 273
African Switchback (travel book) 98
Assassination of Trotsky, The (filmscript and book) 228–39, 244–5, 246
Assassins (novel) 190–1, 211
Beyond the Pale (memoirs) 7, 11, 124
Catastrophe Practice (novel and novel series) 282–3, 284, 286, 287, 288–94, 322–5, 328–32, 333, 335, 338
Cell (play) 275–8
Corruption (novel) 77–9, 81–2, 83, 90
Cypher (short novel) 279–81, 286, 288, 322, 323
Experience and Religion (theology) 172–81, 179, 187
Fool's Game, The (play) 26–7
Garden of Trees, A (novel) 18–19, 23, 24–6, 27, 28, 29, 34–6, 37, 43, 44, 46, 64, 65
Good Samaritans, The (play) 122, 143, 250
Hopeful Monsters (novel) 328–32, 333, 335
Imago Bird (novel) 288–90, 291, 293, 294, 322, 323, 332
Impossible Object (novel and filmscript) 195–8, 201–2, 204–10, 216, 217, 218, 220, 221, 225, 228, 229, 232,

343